Contents

Acknowledgements

In the course of completing this book over the past 3 years, many people have lent help, guidance and support. First and foremost, though, I want to thank Laura Marcus, whose rigorous judgement was fundamental to refining the initial scope and critical sensibility of this study from its inception. Her companionship, wisdom and intellectual generosity remain personally and professionally inspirational.

I am indebted to Philip Tew for many candid discussions about the diversifying priorities of contemporary fiction studies, and he has alleviated my anxieties at important stages of this project – not least over that always-tricky task of selecting who and what to include. Roger Luckhurst and Julian Wolfreys likewise reassured me of the need to propose an alternative vocabulary for addressing literary cityscapes. At the University of Nottingham, Peter Howarth comforted me as a colleague who, fresh through the door, was tackling new and challenging responsibilities while trying not to forget the small pleasures that motivate us to write about literature in the first place. Also at Nottingham, Dominic Head, Julie Sanders, Mark Robson and Sean Matthews remain superb mentors. On various occasions, they have all reminded me never to feel cautious about starting with the texture of what we read over and above subsidiary concerns, and to have the conviction to write about contemporary fiction rather than about contemporary theory. Always putting these principles to work, Andrzej Gasiorek remains for me a most powerful and exemplary scholar of postwar British writing, one who demonstrates that we can't divorce contemporary novelists from their modernist predecessors. This book bears the mark of his invaluable friendship and advice, and I share his determination to show how history and aesthetics can intimately inform one another in the course of doing justice to literary form.

To my dear mum I give a last (and eternally inadequate) word of thanks for supporting my academic pursuits through times when intellectual ambitions seemed irrelevant. If it weren't for my dad I would never have appreciated firsthand the fascinatingly complex rhythms of the countryside. I thank my two brothers for not being academics, and I honour the way they never allow me to take myself too seriously. Finally, this book is for María del Pilar Blanco, whose patience I have shamelessly and repeatedly plundered while re-reading, worry-

Contemporary British Fiction and the Artistry of Space

Continuum Literary Studies Series

Also available in the series:

Contemporary British Fiction and the Artistry of Space

Style, Landscape, Perception

David James

continuum

Continuum International Publishing Group

The Tower Building   80 Maiden Lane, Suite 704
11 York Road   New York
London SE1 7NX   NY 10038

www.continuumbooks.com

British Library Cataloguing-in-Publication Data
A catalogue record for this book is available from the British Library.

ISBN: 978-1-4411-3192-8 (paperback)

Library of Congress Cataloging-in-Publication Data
A catalog record for this book is available from the Library of Congress.

Typeset by Newgen Imaging Systems Pvt Ltd, Chennai, India
Printed and bound in Great Britain by Biddles Ltd, King's Lynn, Norfolk

ing and rewriting – instead of saying what I intuitively wanted to say first time around. I will forever thank her for giving a purpose to it all. Into the emerging life of a book about fictional space she arrived to make the world seem such a very small place.

A previous version of Chapter 2 appeared in *JNT: Journal of Narrative Theory* 36, no. 3 (2006): 424–45, and material from Chapter 4 informs a forthcoming essay in *Critique: Studies in Contemporary Fiction*. I thank Eastern Michigan University and Heldref publications, respectively, for granting me permission here to incorporate material partly disseminated in article form. Sections from Chapter 3 build upon a more focused essay which originally appeared in *City Visions: The Work of Iain Sinclair* (2007), and sections from this are republished with the permission of Cambridge Scholars Publishing. I especially want to thank that volume's editors, Jenny Bavidge and Robert Bond, for the stimulating conference and conversations which confirmed my commitment to working on landscape and the novel.

I would like to thank the Continuum editorial board as well as all staff involved in the book's production for all their diligence and enthusiasm in seeing this book through to press.

Introduction

The Spatial Imaginary of Contemporary British Fiction

Every novel has to be set somewhere. All fictional worlds surely depend upon some indication of locality, named or anonymous. Moreover, characters' decisions and their pivotal consequences are often intensified by the demands and opportunities of where they take place. Beginning a novel, we might indeed expect the writer initially to assume the role of a tour guide, acquainting us with the quintessence of his or her chosen locale. For how can novelists hope to secure our sympathy without first setting the scene? Such are the assumptions that this study seeks to explore, assumptions that seem at once self-evident and yet all too unrefined for understanding how writers transport us to geographies other than our own. Conspicuous or unnamed, fictional settings are never rudimentary and rarely inconsequential. Instead, they raise a series of pressing questions that are less obvious than they sound: Do landscapes themselves have a determining effect on our emotional engagement with the novel as a form? If so, to what extent do places in fiction mediate our response to the very texture of narrative prose by functioning not simply as background sceneries but as vibrant figures in their own right? If literary landscapes draw attention to the interplay of description and embellishment, documentary images and rhetorical flair, might the formal and figurative aspects of fictional space give us an insight into the way novelists today are experimenting with style? That we readily entertain, if not take for granted, the plausibility of novelistic settings, and that the language of topographical description plays such a pivotal role in securing our absorption in the page, implies that the poetics of place calls attention the reading process itself. And as Graham Swift makes clear, our immersion in the verbal craft of landscape description puts us imaginatively in touch not only with environmental sounds, colour and scale, but also with a place's intimate rhythms and modes of inhabitation. Novelists succeed in connecting us emotionally with the domains they describe precisely because literary settings convey something more than 'just physical place, it's the sense of people having their territory'.[1]

Swift sets a standard here that unites the aspirations of the very different novelists considered in this book. Though formally diverse, they compel us to reconsider the relationship between topography and textuality, spatial depiction and our own sensuous engagement with fictional craft. Precisely *how* novelists convey a sense of geographical scale or ambience is far from patently obvious, however effortless its execution. Yet scenic description in all its variety and vitality may go unanalysed in the writers we most admire. More than any element perhaps in the construction of fictional worlds, place draws attention to our movement between enthralment and detachment, absorption and disbelief. Our visceral reaction to the depiction of place is too easily taken for granted, so long as the devices by which spaces are relayed pass unexplored. For the journey into a novel's landscape can be so absorbing as to divert us from the analytical task of retracing one's steps. And the fascinating irony is that the more we become immersed in envisioning habitats through the words on the page, the less inclined we are to analyse the linguistic and cognitive processes that underpin that envisioning process. Nevertheless, the need for a narratologically informed *and* aesthetically attentive account of narrative space remains. A renewed alertness of this kind to technique might be especially pertinent for addressing the contemporary scene, where writers today are exploring novel geographies as an occasion for expanding the frontiers of aesthetic form.

Close reading after the 'spatial turn'

Offering a wide-ranging but by no means comprehensive inquiry into the formal role that landscapes play in contemporary British fiction, the following chapters attempt to do justice to the distinctive properties and implications of this spatial poetics, selecting exemplary texts from a broad spectrum of geographical contexts. Lending primacy to spatial tropes and techniques in this way is hardly a new venture. Since the pervasive 'spatial turn' in conceptual thinking across the humanities and social sciences, it has become common to hear of a range of artistic phenomena being discussed with the aid of cartographical abstractions. Yet at the same time, the compelling metaphoricity of *space* – when appropriated as both a framing topic and an analytical tool – has attracted the scrutiny of cultural geographers and literary historians alike, who echo Henri Lefebvre's salient warning that spatial practices are forever prone to conceptual aestheticization. In his pioneering analyses of modern urban existence, Lefebvre offers a lesson for discussing literary landscapes by indicating that the conceptualization of space must take as its starting point the lived experience of place. Spatial representations, for Lefebvre, always entail practical consequences for the ways in which people interact with their changing environments.[2] And his concern with the ramifications of spatial representation not only highlights the implicitly mediated nature of everyday experience; it reminds us too that geographical discourses are themselves far from transparent as they inform our perception of the social spheres we collectively occupy. Continuing in this vein, Caren Kaplan offers a refreshingly sceptical account of the privileging of *displacement* and its tropological variants, remarking that cultural critics have often valorized the language of migrancy by overestimating the emancipatory potential of travel. Kaplan argues that 'terms such as "borders", "maps", "location", "space", and "place", do not necessarily liberate critical practices from the very conundrum of aestheticization and universalization that spurred a search for alternative metaphors and methods in the first place'.[3] Caveats of this kind are frequently sparked by post-structuralism's susceptibility to neglect the contingencies of environmental change, and by its susceptibility to apply ahistorical frameworks to landscapes and communities which are not entirely amenable to postmodern paradigms. In recent years some of our most provocative materialist thinkers have attempted to provide answers to these concerns. Working among the legacies of Fredric Jameson's iconic 'cognitive mapping' of the late-capitalist age, Edward Soja and David Harvey have re-examined the brute effects of metropolitan expansionism to test and extend the conceptual insights of postmodern geography, even as they speculate in a more utopian vein on the city's shared liberation. For these theorists, our most intimate, quotidian engagements with communal routines are culturally conditioned: they symptomatically reflect the institutional proscriptions and commercial imperatives that govern our experience of urban space.[4] And their reassessment of geography's postmodern inflections and preoccupations responds to the ongoing need for a combative revision of spatial terminology as it travels across disciplines.

The justification, then, for invoking these theoretical vocabularies for considering the poetics of place in the novel is far from unproblematic.[5] Bringing cultural geography to bear on a stylistic analysis of fiction raises the issue of how we might at once attend to the specificity of narrative form while evaluating the responsiveness of new writing to empirical conditions and transformations in the built environment. 'Since the early 1990s', as Andrew Thacker notes,

> questions of space and geography have become recognised as legitimate and important topics in many areas of literary and cultural studies, and setting out the sphere of literature, if not life, by some form of map a more familiar hermeneutic strategy.[6]

And yet, where our understanding of the relationship between literary form and the spatial imagination is concerned, spatial metaphors may limit the rigour and precision of our aesthetic insights. While *space* has become an umbrella-term for a suggestive cluster of recyclable tropes, it may equally obscure the specificities of novelistic craft. Indeed, Thacker is right to qualify his own advocacy of spatiality as an interpretive resource. He offers a cautionary aside, suggesting that critical geography has yet to contribute as fully as it might do to contemporary fiction studies. When trying to correlate literary settings and material environments, 'it is important', notes Thacker, 'not only to discuss space and geography thematically, but also to address them as questions with a profound impact upon how literary and cultural texts are formally assembled' (63). These complex methodological debates are open-ended in a productive sense, and they look ahead to an ongoing consideration of how landscapes today continue to play a vital role in the choices writers make about formal innovation.

With its commitment to engaging with issues of form, then, this book offers an aesthetically attentive introduction to reading issues of space and place *through* the very texture of literary craft. Taken together, the chapters below are by no means exhaustive in the locations they survey; rather, they chart different topographical 'sites' in recent fiction where the interface of landscape and stylistic experimentation also mediates the way we apprehend the formal and ideological imperatives of writers today. In each case, my focus on the artistry of spatial representation highlights the implications of incorporating the wider insights of cultural geography into analyses of narrative perspective, language and register. Over a decade on, Edward Said's assertion seems altogether pertinent, when he insists that '[a]fter Lukács and Proust, we have become so accustomed to thinking of the novel's plot and structure as constituted mainly by temporality that we have overlooked the function of space, geography and location'.[7] And as I contend in Chapter 1, in order to correct what Said saw as that curious neglect of literature's spatial features and their formal and ideological implications, our concerns must hinge in two directions: navigating between form and feeling, between representation and absorption. David Lodge has grandly declared that 'The novel is arguably man's most successful effort to describe the experience of individual human beings moving through space and time'.[8] Yet the widespread application of paradigmatic thinkers like Gérard Genette and Paul Ricoeur again testifies to a fascination with narrative temporality that has rather served to eclipse *time*'s counterparts – *space*, *place*, and their role in how we, as readers, react to novelistic setting as a highly *experiential* medium.[9] While it may not be critically practical, or indeed desirable, to rehearse William Empson's imperative that our 'sensibility needs to act ahead of theory',[10] it is surely reductive to assume, as Richard Cavell does, that the 'spatiality of literary texts is a relatively uncomplicated notion'.[11] Cavell may be right to remind us 'that spacing is the basis of linguistic signification'; but to cite this as a justification for ceasing to explore how space affects the language of fiction – its register, diction or grammatical construction – belies a tacit subversion of the literary-aesthetic in the interests of broader theoretical conjecture. Post-structuralism may well have 'turned to the category of space as its prime arena of critique', as Cavell asserts (95). But this is hardly sufficient ground for withdrawing from the specificity of literary space.

The insinuation here is that a close appreciation of technique might contribute only peripherally to our appreciation of novelists who explore spatial experiences and environmental conflicts. This relegation of fiction's capacity for argument and persuasion neatly forgets Gaston Bachelard's famous maxim, by which he characterizes the phenomenologist of interior space as an observer for whom greatness tends to lie in the miniature.[12] Scrutinizing the 'function of space', as Said emphasized, not only means scrutinizing how writers actualize landscapes through specific textual devices, but also how those devices inform the reader's emotional interaction with narrative textuality. Cognitive and affective pleasures mutually inform and recalibrate one another in the course of responding to a novel's aesthetic form. And as this study aims to show by crossing a variety of geographical representations, the task of defining space's formal and rhetorical contribution to contemporary fiction redefines our assumptions about the very nature of interpretation itself.

Novelists aren't geographers, of course, and representing place is more than a mimetic exercise. Yet one wonders why Eudora Welty felt the need to concede that place is 'one of the lesser angels that watch over the racing hand of fiction', and that ultimately it is 'feeling' instead – along with characterization and thematic events – which in her 'eyes carries the crown, soars highest of them all and rightly relegates place into the shade'.[13] It seems contrived to assume that our sensory intuitions as readers are somehow extricable from a novel's setting – feelings that are surely intrinsic to what makes the depiction of place work so arrestingly upon us. Curious as they are, though, Welty's prevarications are instructive. Only by suspending such preconceptions of what place can *do* for the novel can one respond to the sensuous spectrum of contemporary fiction's spatial imaginary: its agility, its inventiveness, its demands upon our underlying methodological values. To address Said's concerns, then, is hardly an excuse to neglect the politics of place, but it does mean paying closer attention to aesthetic form in a manner more heuristic than sociological criticism might allow. This study will be tracing the ideological implications attending the work of novelists who express metaphors of place through the spatial textures of narrative discourse. Yet I also try to register how the emergence of a certain place-oriented fascination in such writers has initiated new methods for representing perceptual experience – methods that radically alter the way readers themselves engage with figurative language in fiction, as it evokes the impact of social environments on human selfhood and belonging.

Particularizing novelistic space

Myriad 'species of spaces' have thrived in contemporary British fiction.[14] Capturing the complexity with which this spatial discourse has manifested itself at the level of form, this book offers a point of departure. In order to answer that often-neglected question of why it is that readers find certain settings more deeply affecting than others, we need to entertain a more nuanced approach to the techniques that distinguish such novelistic geographies. Nearly a decade on, Lorna Sage's remarks are no less instructive, when she highlights the disciplinary uncertainties faced by contemporary writing within the academy. It's not that contemporary writers have suffered neglect from literary scholars so much as there is a lack of consensus about *how* their work should be read in post-structuralism's wake. Sage notes that academic criticism has scarcely begun to do justice to the singularity of individual practitioners. For one, an allegiance to tangential theoretical discourses has hindered the task of understanding novelists through the idiosyncrasies of their craft, since the 'deconstructive doctrines aimed at demystifying the great (past) figures of the canon leave no real room for contemporary writers who are trying to make themselves a character and space. In other words, the present is already accounted for'. Sage proposes that critics should refine their objectives, and calls for a more contextually sensitive account of aesthetic practice that empha-sizes the *particularity* of respective innovators:

> Writing on 'the postmodern' softens and disguises and carnivalizes this state of affairs, so that it looks as though there's a great deal of celebration of contemporary fiction – its use of parody, pastiche, reflexive jokes of all kinds, and its recyclings of others' texts, and rewritings of the past. A lot of contemporary texts and names get mentioned in passing. However, this style of critical writing is still a long way from offering particularizing accounts of individual writers and works, and indeed doesn't aim to. Reading contemporaneity in this spirit you tend to locate particu-lar novels in a story of fragmentation and reflexivity (the postmodern condition) and you abstract diversity into a condition of all texts.[15]

The present study follows Sage's salutary lead, attending to the ways in which geographical concerns have catalyzed new advances in recent 'fiction-making', as she puts it, while seeking to particularize the strategies that writers employ to achieve such states of 'real "newness"' (269). By no means have I aimed to provide a complete survey. Such an approach would demand little more than an inclusive overview: rapidly shifting between authors to offer summary discussions that scarcely afford the opportunity for exploring aes-thetic form. By the same stroke, while emphasizing the primacy of technique, neither do I offer a systematic narratological investigation. Instead, this book brings into dialogue a rich ensemble of British novelists, each representative of the influence that space has had upon the very properties and priorities of stylistic experiment.

By advancing this author-centred approach to different spatial sites and socio-geographical relations, this study uses the poetics of place as a lens through which to view a range of connections between apparently distinct writers. Each discussion in turn aims to communicate something of the vivacity of narrative space as an *event for reading* itself, by which settings become scenes of process and reciprocity, rather than as an aspect of fiction to be described in inert, topographical terms. In fact, we will encounter many instances where 'the act of reading', in Robert Macfarlane's phrase, 'emerge[s] as a vital force for brokering dignified and durable relationships between people and places'.[16] The forces of urban expansion, capital distribution and the preservation of local attachments deeply inform the responsibility that writers evince towards the places they depict, especially when they navigate between specified landscapes and visionary territories left all but obscure. Indeed, *obscurity* soon becomes a needlessly pejorative term when cataloguing literary settings and determining their ontological currency. Susan Sontag rightly asserts that 'there is no such thing as empty space. As long as the human eye is looking, there is always something to see'.[17] Richly figurative spaces, where imagined and material zones coexist, are scrutinized throughout this book. The tension between metaphor and actuality is directly addressed in Chapter 3, where I position the work of Iain Sinclair and J. G. Ballard on the crest of a recent wave of writers committed to banishing received images of London. Such practitioners challenge our terms for evaluating spatial writings that blur between materiality and abstraction. But they also invite a more nuanced account of how fictional settings often coerce us to participate in the way spaces are perceived.

Historicizing the poetics of perception

Getting in touch with the spatial features of fiction today not only promises to enrich our attention to composition itself. By looking closely at the craft of landscape description we can also appreciate how contemporary writers are extending long-standing traditions that point back to late-Victorian and early-twentieth-century fiction, where the relationship between physical place and narrative poetics evolves with comparable intensity, for instance, for Hardy, Conrad and Lawrence. One of the most prominent lines of inheritance emerges in the prioritization of narrative perception as a device for constructing fictional sceneries. Conventions of perspective continue to inform the relationship between vision and voice for novelists today, as they elaborate settings through their characters' felt experiences. And it's the work of perceptual space which reveals an unceasing dialogue between influence and innovation in contemporary fiction, a dialogue that can be heard in the recent work of two writers at the height of their powers.

Our first stop is Rose Tremain's impressionistic exploration of mid-nineteenth-century New Zealand. A deserted gold-prospector's wife returns to survey the sun-baked remains of the plot where the couple 'had tried to begin their married life', the house they built as English emigrants now reduced by storms to a 'wild assembly of objects':

> Harriet dismounted and walked slowly towards the peculiar scene.
>
> In the still air, almost nothing moved, not even the calico, which was here and there stretched taut, attached to nails or snagged on thorns.
>
> Staring at this, it came to Harriet Blackstone that what she was looking at was a painting of life, a torn canvas which, at the moment of cutting, instead of holding its colours flat and fast to its surface, had spilled out what it had once depicted into three-dimensional space.
>
> In escaping the confines of the painting that had held them together, objects had forgotten what purpose they were supposed to have. One of the iron beds stood on its end, as though offering itself as a perch for eagles. Pillows, lying here and there in the tussock, had the appearance of mushrooms. Broken shards of plates and cups decorated the ground like flowers.
>
> Harriet remained a little way off. Dorothy Orchard had once said to her that men and women were destined always to make 'a small world in the midst of a big one' and she remembered this now and saw it was exactly what she and Joseph had tried to do.[18]

Moving between figurative and mimetic responses to the landscape, Tremain draws our attention to the duration over with spatial features are observed and understood. This description thus highlights the sense of temporal delay that often characterizes narrative perception, the delay between immediate observations of space and their subsequent intellectual dissemination. Yet these descriptive dynamics also disclose something of the aesthetic heritage upon which Tremain implicitly draws. By picturing this haunting and 'peculiar scene' as 'a torn canvass', she reveals how indebted *The Colour* (2003) is to the Victorian novel's visually panoramic approach to landscape depiction. She certainly extends Thomas Hardy's ambition to engage phenomenologically with places rather than reduce them to topographical labelling. 'I don't want to see landscapes', cautioned Hardy in 1887, either as purely 'scenic paintings', or as 'original realities', but rather as 'the expression of what are sometimes called abstract imaginings'.[19] This commitment to perceptual experience as a catalyst for style itself is so evident in Hardy's later work from *The Return of the Native* (1878) to *Tess of the D'Urbervilles* (1891), where he disposes his register to the counter-pointing of sensation and intellection, realism and impressionism, often dispensing with visual reportage to transmute rural terrains in metaphorical terms. Similarly, as Tremain telescopes towards the framed tableaux of ruins, moving in tempo with Harriet's slow approach, her diversion away from specific objects to ambient details, details intensified by 'the still air', recalls Tess's feeling of remaining 'akin to the landscape' even as it becomes unknown.[20] Over the ensuing paragraphs, Tremain pays homage to that same interplay in

Hardy's work between perceptual levels, between immediacy and abstraction. This alternation is again exemplified by Hardy when his heroine perceived how a 'change in the quality of the air from heavy to light, or the sense of being amid new scenes where there were no invidious eyes upon her, sent up her spirits wonderfully' (*Tess*, 119).

Tremain's own focalized way of describing place complements this intersection of feeling and thought – formally as well as dramatically. In the passage above, her startling analogue for the scene as a onetime painting now rupturing forth all that it once enframed matches, at the very level of style, the interplay between direct perception and abstract contemplation that Harriet is experiencing as an observer. For just as Tremain modulates from the sensuousness of pictorial analogy to that unsentimental catalogue of strewn objects, so her heroine is compelled to confront memories etched into the present surroundings, as though this derelict site itself compels Harriet to accept what 'she and Joseph had tried to do'. Register, place and perception thus operate symbiotically in this scene, as Harriet surveys the remnants of belonging in ways that modify the very narrative mode in which this landscape is conveyed.

Our second port of call again leads into a rural landscape, closer to the historic present this time, but no less focalized in the way the visible landscape is sensed, pictured and disseminated. (I'll leave the episode anonymous, for now, so as to give primacy the poetics of place over authorial persona.) Unlike Tremain's static portraiture, though, we have here an instance in which the visualization space is altogether more mobile. It's a scene whose atmosphere is governed by anticipation rather than by the paralysis of remembrance or regret. As we speed through Suffolk 'along a deserted minor road',[21] the sense of temporal progression, of onrushing tarmac, inflects the very manner in which spatial dimensions are relayed. Travelling alters the rhetoric of place, as the journey makes 'wide curves through miles of conifer plantation' (93). Scenic snapshots overtake static portraiture, with the passing terrain so intimately harmonizing pace and observation as to confirm Elizabeth Bowen's advice from the mid-1940s that the 'locale of the happening always colours the happening, and often, to a degree, shapes it'.[22] We might think that a novelist's proleptic hints run the risk of pre-empting the reader's response; but here, as we draw up to the rear of a truck, that predictive gesture in fact enhances our sense of expectation. And this oblique forewarning affects our experience of the way setting is perceived:

In what followed, the rapidity of events was accommodated by the slowing of time. He was preparing to overtake when something happened – he did not quite see what – in the region of the lorry's wheels, a hiatus, a cloud of dust, and then something black and long snaked through a hundred feet towards him. It slapped the windscreen, clung there for a moment and was whisked away before he had time to understand what it was. And then – or did this happen in the same moment? – the rear of the lorry made a complicated set of movements, a bouncing and swaying, and slewed in a wide spray of sparks, bright even in the sunshine. Something curved and metallic flew off to one side. So far Stephen had had time to move his foot towards the break, time to notice a padlock swaying on a loose flange, and 'Wash me please' scrawled in grime. (93–4)

Unfolding 'time' here is not simply an organizing principle for describing a scene in motion, or for measuring the seconds over which 'something happened'. Rather than offering Ian McEwan – for McEwan it is – a device for countering the multitude of impressions conferred by 'the rapidity of events', our sense of narrative duration is itself coordinated with the intensely focalized reception of distances and proximities, moment to moment. Throughout *The Child in Time* (1987), McEwan emphasizes these perspectival restrictions, conveying spectacular events by accreting successive details rather than intervening as a narrator. Indeed, the episode quoted above is all the more memorable for the way it compromises McEwan's narratorial authority, a compromise felt in his use of diction and phraseology. Impressions overtake firm declarations, and the repeated indeterminate pronoun *something* reflects Stephen's struggle to comprehend a flurry of events that seemed to 'happen in the same moment'.

McEwan reveals his fascination in this episode with how we can distinguish between our perceptions of time in relation to the places we move through. As he confirmed for Zadie Smith: 'I don't have any conscious design on time', to the extent that 'if there's anything going on about time in my novels it's really a spinoff of some other concern. Something to do with the fine print of consciousness itself', with 'how to represent, obviously in a very stylized way, what it's like to be thinking'.[23] And McEwan shows us how space in the novel can rarely be dissociated from the artistry of narrative perception. In turn, the perspectival organization of spatial descriptions seems to mediate our emotional response to fictional landscapes, especially in respect to their magnitude, atmosphere and scale. For instance, in that episode from *The Child in Time*, McEwan chooses to accumulate details on a partial rather than panoramic plane, a syntactic choice that renders the whole scene more pressing, more suspenseful at least, than Tremain's magisterial *tableaux vivant*:

Now, in this slowing of time, there was a sense of a fresh beginning. He had entered a much later period in which all the terms and conditions had changed. So these were the new rules, and he experienced something like awe, as though he were walking alone into a great city on a newly discovered planet. There was space too for a little touch of regret, genuine nostalgia for the old days of spectacle, back then when a lorry used to catapult so impressively before the impassive witness. Now was a more demanding time of effort and concentration. (94)

Whereas Tremain dismembers a redundant dwelling-place in pictorial terms, McEwan analogizes here the protraction of time itself as a journey into uncharted landscape. In so doing, he dramatizes the temporary separation of spatial experience from the demands of time, questioning our assumptions about the way we construct a sense of place.

Taking McEwan and Tremain as case studies here, we can appreciate the extent to which fictional settings can scarcely be considered as neutral back-drops, and should instead be analysed for the way they dynamically influence narrative perception. By the same stroke, it appears that the spatial qualities of narrative form cannot be divorced from the time-frame over which events are perceived. More recently McEwan has confirmed this mutual interpenetration of time, space and chronology in *On Chesil Beach* (2007), where Edward's 'desire for Florence was inseparable from the setting' in which they met, with 'the scented blossoms of North Oxford' serving as an olfactory correlative for their passionate engagement.[24] Likewise, *The Child in Time* demonstrates that land-scape depictions often shift between memory and immediacy, abstraction and 'concentration' in ways that have distinctive consequences for register and structure alike. McEwan often reflects on the formal aspects of spatial represen-tation through his characters' phenomenological reactions to location, duration and scale. Following his near-miss with the overturned truck, and caught in mild delirium 'before the shock', Stephen imagines how his wife 'Julie would have appreciated what had happened to time, how duration shaped itself round the intensity of the event' (95). In the following chapters, and for quite different writers, we will re-encounter this same interrelationship of temporality and 'intensity', as it becomes a sensuous part of reading literary landscapes. Durational devices are always shaping themselves around the location of events, highlighting the palpable intersection of space and perception in fiction today. For as we shall see, space facilitates a conference between setting and cognition, style and immersion, in which the reader is rarely an 'impassive witness', but an active participant in the way places are conveyed.

Hardy himself knew how dynamically our sensation of ambient space informs our understanding of physical place – a connection between perception and intellection that Tremain and McEwan exploit at the level of style. For Tess herself also recognizes that momentary reactions can hold deeper cognitive insights, when it became 'impossible that any event should have left upon her an impression that was not at least capable of transmutation' (*Tess*, 119). Hardy seems emblematic as a precedent for such writers today, who incorporate the heritage of Victorian realism in the course of experimenting with new modes of landscape description. McEwan and Tremain show how crucial it is that we relinquish the view of fictional settings as static, unreflective and therefore peripheral to assessing technique, lending implicit advice for exploring relations between space and novelistic form.

Landscapes in fiction thus compel us to develop an aesthetically focused account of devices that we readily take for granted. An account of this kind, of course, highlights our own preconceptions about the way spatial relations affect literary style and structure. Zadie Smith echoes Sage's call to particularize the strategies of contemporary writers when she considers that fiction-reading, as a potentially immersive yet self-reflective activity, should be thought of as a 'commitment' to '*recognise* one's own beliefs'.[25] Evidently, Smith took away from her 2005 interview with McEwan himself something of his fascination with 'how perception is distorted by will', along with his 'sense of how interestingly flawed we are in the ways in which we represent ourselves and "what we know" to each other' (Interview by Smith, 50). Criticism today, in Smith's view, should incorporate this level of self-awareness, remaining watchful of preconceived models or evaluative criteria that do more to distort than facilitate our affective contact with fiction as a craft. As an activity which at best declares its own prior compulsions, for Smith novel-reading should be 'intimate, painstaking, with nothing at all to do with Hegelian system-building or theoretical schools, and everything to do with out ethical reality as subjects' ('Read Better', 21). In a global age in which novelists are concerned with doing justice to representing intercultural encounters, Smith implies that the ethics of interpretation are inescapable when comparing literary landscapes. In turn, only by dispensing with the notion that place and spatialization are simply generic features or structural operations necessary to all narrative texts, can we tackle the distinctiveness of writers under comparative scrutiny. It's then that we can begin to treat literary geographies with the degree of specificity they demand. Through their experiments with language and design, novelists today solicit us to engage aesthetically with the question of how we sense, and make sense of, literary space. That our wider understanding of environmental issues can be transformed by our experience of reading landscapes in fiction invites a profound revaluation of our affective encounters with form.

Modes of narration, means of emplacement

Separate narrative modes, of course, illuminate different relationships between place and perception. Novels unfolding entirely in the first-person offer pristine exhibitions of interiority. And as Chapter 4 reveals in turning to questions of landscape and memory, writers as distinctive as A. L. Kennedy, Trezza Azzopardi and Graham Swift have shown how vital the voice of the singular pronoun can become when remembering and memorializing environmental change. In these parables of belonging, the narrators' immediate responses to social space are often overwhelmed by agonistic retrospection – arguably to the point of introversion. Other recent practitioners might disagree. Asked whether he felt he had adequately distanced his autobiographical self from the first-person speaker in *Afternoon Raag* (1993), Amit Chaudhuri asserted that his 'narrator, the "I" in the novel, was not uppermost in my mind'.[26] Instead, Chaudhuri allowed his chosen setting to dictate the stylization of voice, rather than the other way around. Space preceded and directed his sensibility as an innovator. Indeed, it is with a relatively conventional use of the solitary speaker, pivoting between memory and immediate cityscape, that *Afternoon Raag* develops its parable of acclimatization. Everyday Oxford is the novel's unlikely environment for tracing the expectations and disenchantments of a Calcuttan newcomer. Through the eyes of this thinly veiled version of Chaudhuri's former self as a student overseas from Bombay, Chaudhuri defamiliarizes Oxford's workaday rhythms at once 'harmonious and self-dispersing', utilizing the oscillations of his first-person narrative between introspection and external reportage to convey 'the unreality of the scene and one's relationship with its unreality'.[27] He seems preoccupied with the way visible 'absences between one lane and another, untenanted, unexplainable spaces' cause those 'places one has walked through or passed daily to loose their known features' (73). Although contrasting Oxford with Calcutta, Chaudhuri's use of highly cerebral perceptions evokes for both cities a sense of spirituality burgeoning amid the flurry of workday life. In *Afternoon Raag* Chaudhuri retrieves from imperial sentimentality what he has recently called the 'romantic creation of a spiritual India'. For him, this 'new domain of the spiritual' is a space which 'has been crucial to secular Indian moderns, to their paradoxical, poetic sense of rootedness in, and exile from, the country they belong to'.[28] And with this kind of revisionist trajectory running throughout, *Afternoon Raag* exemplifies how a writer's historical sensibility affects the degree to which he or she innovates with style: 'What was uppermost when I was writing it was examining the strangeness of India and Oxford and how each meet the other'. In accomplishing this examination, though, the relaying of immediate, street-level experiences of those two distinct cityscapes presided for Chaudhuri over the temptation to showcase his own style. Chaudhuri employed some restraint when renavigating such suggestive locations in memoirist prose. While stirring up what Chaudhuri calls 'something of the cultural strangeness, of the strangeness of perception' ('On Belonging and Not Belonging', 47), *Afternoon Raag* is a novel more concerned with how delicately those two ancient cities are conveyed than with using their topographical idiosyncrasies to justify artful depictions.

Writers like Chaudhuri who commit to first-person narration exemplify just how dependent landscape descriptions can appear upon the modes that vocalize and embellish them. In this sense, free indirect style might seem an altogether more agile way of evoking perceptions of place. In contrast to a novel unfolding in first-person recollections, third-person focalization disrupts our sense of a stable narratorial idiom or provenance, allowing writers to shift between the inner thoughts of characters separated in space and time. Both modes, though, compel us to mark Jonathan Crary's insistence that *perception* is not only to do with vision. When attending to technique, this study certainly heeds Crary's advice that 'the problematic term "perception" is primarily a way of indicating a subject definable in terms of more than the single-sense modality of sight, in terms also of hearing and touch and, most importantly, of irreducibly *mixed* modalities'.[29] Moreover, by bringing this idea of perception as a sensory complex into our understanding of narrative fiction, we move beyond the unending debate over whether *focalization* offers a preferable alternative to its predecessor-term, *point of view*. The examination of how, and with what formal and ideological ramifications, a text's described world is focalized and by whom, has been prominent among narratologists in the North American academy at least since the 1970s. What this preoccupation with observation subverts, however, is the question of *voice*. Since the concept of focalization concentrates on the visual devices by which the world of a literary text is received and relayed, it has become more suited to the discussion of narrative perspective. Yet voice in fiction lends such a vitally important dimension to the illustration of place. Where landscape descriptions are concerned, narrative voice ruptures the undifferentiated perceptual mode of observation that one often associates with highly scenic projections.

What McEwan, Tremain and Chaudhuri demonstrate, despite their thematic and stylistic differences, is that in the course of reading physical settings we incorporate into our visualization of space an acknowledgement of how partial the transmission of scenic details can be. The recording of places and atmospherics in these fictions depends so intensively on the behaviour, responses and preoccupations of perceiving characters as to involve us in the cognitive work of perception itself. Such is the circulation between noticing and reflecting, between a character's vision of immediate space and their recollection of places now past, which continually alters and adjudicates our capacity to engage with imagined situations and terrains. Landscapes in fiction thus require a kind of *transactional* reading that moves between character, action and style: an interactive approach that's alert to perceptual dilemmas or personal decisions taking place in different settings across a given plot, but one that also substantiates our notion of space as a dynamic and affecting property of aesthetic form.

Navigating the contemporary scene

As much of this introduction so far might imply, the relationship between physical space and narrative style could be approached from a range of directions, exemplified by a wide array of contemporary writers in Britain. Structuralist theories of 'spatial form' don't altogether help us solve this dilemma of selection. Loosely defined, formal space could encompass a variety of rhetorical, grammatical and architectural ways of describing novelistic discourse. These considerations have informed this book's exploration of the role that landscapes play in our aesthetic and stylistic engagement with novelistic technique. Although my motivations are 'particularizing', in Lorna Sage's sense, rather than comparative, I have brought together novelists with contrasting ambitions by grouping them in chapters based on affiliations between their adopted settings, representational practices or environmental concerns. Bringing dissimilar novelists together in this way allows us to reconsider familiar links between certain genres and geographies. And the following chapters synthesize phenomenological and topographical modes of analysing place to relate different landforms and spatial experiences to recent developments in narrative craft. As we have seen, Chaudhuri intimates that contemporary novelists are developing ever more innovative ways of figuring the 'cultural strangeness' of well-known places, provoking new generations of readers to respond to landscapes, both familiar and imaginary. Chapter 3 explores this strategy of geographical defamiliarization in the work of Ballard and Sinclair, who have each exploited the allure and historical density of famous place-names, while disclosing a literary heritage peculiar to London that stretches from Dickens through to later modernists such as Elizabeth Bowen. With this inheritance, London's contemporary chroniclers reveal the curious sense that '[p]lace names', as J. Hillis Miller suggests, 'make a site already the product of a virtual writing, a topography, or, since the names are often figures, a "topotropography"'.[30] My assessment of this intersection of topography and tropology in recent London fiction evaluates the various oppositional stances assumed by writers who are seeking an alternative urban order, where signs of spiritual and social restoration are obscured by everyday life. Their phantasmagoric portraits of a world-famous cityscape call into question the mode with which such novelists critique that city's economic privation. Milan Kundera has recently pointed out that 'when the novel's magic came to lie in the visual and auditory evocation of scenes, *plausibility became the supreme rule*'.[31] For these authors' aesthetic impulses incite ethical contentions: questions arise as to how far London visionaries like Ballard and Sinclair operate self-reflexively with the implication that '[r]epresentations', as Rob Shields has warned, 'are also metonymic in their tendency to *displace* the city completely so that one ends by not dealing with the physical level of direct social exchange and brute arrangements of objects but with a surrogate level of signs'.[32]

Chapter 2 will also be considering how far this tendency to substitute the realities of urban experience with rhetorical embellishment might also apply to a specifically rural context. Various spatial 'signs' have been co-opted as guiding metaphors by postmodernist analyses concentrating on the modern metropolis, to the exclusion of a more capacious account of regional novelists today. Such a reassessment of provincial fiction seems vital given the kinds of discriminatory commercial pressures under which regional writing is often published. Provincial novelists from Scotland, Ireland and Wales, have been united by the 'dilemma', as Richard Todd describes it, of deciding 'whether to support local small presses or surrender to the London publishers' marketing muscle in order to reach a potentially global audience'.[33] Writers like Adam Thorpe and Pat Barker dramatize the concerns of distinctly local populations, presenting new landforms through the interface of social realism and spatial politics, while challenging assumptions of the kind voiced by Jeremy Seabrook, that '[t]here are no longer any provinces in the bland topography of globalism'.[34] We cannot rely on the city as a setting in exploring the range of literary techniques for evoking space. Simply by focusing on the metropolis, and beyond that, solely on landscapes indigenous to the British Isles, utterly homogenizes the contexts out of which writers from several generations have complicated the geopolitical sovereignty of former imperial powers. As Chapter 5 explores, postcolonial writers have long been speaking to that 'global audience', evoking a spectrum of historical perspectives on Britain's nation-space through experiences of encountering it from abroad.

Such are the ways in which this book combines culturally oriented thinking about the politics of place and environmental change with a more attentive concern with the local details of language and style. It is this kind of dual-focus that seems crucial for reading the aesthetics of spatial representation in historically responsible ways. What Doris Lessing has described as 'a certain passivity in reading' chimes with such interpretative responsibilities. This may sound a rather misleading phrase for our present concerns, especially since I have emphasized the importance of developing a transactional approach to narrative space, one that remains alert to the sense in which literary geographies elicit affective responses. But Lessing's model of hermeneutic sensitivity is in harmony with the aims of this book. What she implies is that interpretive passivity doesn't condone inactivity; rather, it is about learning to relate to fiction in the knowledge that our theoretical predeterminations can detract from its uniqueness and presence. For Lessing, conceding the mediating force of our own conceptual premeditations is where the act of critical response should begin. And it commences by

> taking what the author is offering, and not what the reader thinks he should be offering, not imposing himself (herself) between the author and what should be emanating from the author. That is to say, not reading the book through a screen of theories, ideas, political correctness, and so forth. This kind of reading is indeed difficult, but one can learn this sort of passive reading, and then the real essence and pith of the author is open to you. I am sure everyone has had the experience of reading a book and finding it vibrating with aliveness, with colour and immediacy. And then, perhaps some weeks later, reading it again and finding it flat and empty. Well, the book hasn't changed: you have.[35]

Just as readers change, so do the literary landscapes they encounter across an evolving and vibrant era for new British writing. If, in the afterlife of first reading a novel, we are subject to intellectual changes that rapidly reform our previous opinions of that text, then it holds that with every new published work the map of the contemporary scene is potentially redrawn.

Mapping style

The complex and ultimately open-ended speculation as to what constitutes a uniquely 'spatial' novel matches the difficulty of selecting which writers to assess and why. Avoiding a mere survey, this book has created what might appear to be a disparate corpus of recent novelists in Britain, but with the intention of evoking the wealth of techniques in contemporary prose. Conventions of selection are no less contentious where the present book is concerned. In recent decades, writers' geographic ambitions have enhanced the generic hybridity of the novel itself. Novelists today have complemented that 'heterogeneity' which Peter Ackroyd has found 'at the centre of the English sensibility',[36] refracting it formally when experimenting with new paradigms of time and space. To present a catalogue of examples of spatial stories and their accompanying devices is thus not the ambition of this book; and it is desirable that as I move from critical reflection in Chapters 1 and 2 on to specific authors, strategies and environments, it will invite readers to pursue further an array of unexplored avenues for reading the geographies of contemporary British fiction.

Today, the stock assumption merely that all fiction must be set somewhere is inadequate for understanding the stylistic functions that novelistic settings performs. As I've already suggested, fictional spaces incite complex forms of readerly engagement, calling to account current mechanisms of response. By compelling us to shift between vocabularies in alternate episodes of absorption and estrangement, reading place lights up our pathway to involvement with literary texts. It is our oscillation between immersive and analytical reading postures which points to a reconsideration of spatial form as an emotive as well as technical focus of analysis. By developing an approach to quite different novelistic settings that scrutinizes the particularity of their aesthetic and political implications, one begins to discover just how far the dynamism of place informs both our intellectual engagement with and affective purchase on the textures of contemporary fiction.

Seductive at the level of description, self-reflexive in composition, absorbing as an interface for the reader – the impact of conceiving novelistic space as such is likely to have repercussions for our understanding of the correspondence between impressionistic and historically specific approaches to depicting landscape. This distils indeed one of the key objectives of this book. By refusing to consign the conjunction of space and style to a solely pragmatic exercise, the following chapters demonstrate that one *can* retain something of narratology's conceptual rigour when closely attending to the wider considerations of novelists' dialogues with actual geographies. My contention throughout will be that a novel's aesthetic composition, its synthesis of texture and topography, style and setting, is inseparable from the political concerns to which it deliberately or implicitly gives voice. Often what makes the novelists here so distinctive is their capacity to unite technique and content in this manner: coordinating polemical and philosophical aims to represent landscapes through alternative perspectives, perspectives that in turn lend new understandings of human belonging and emplacement. Michel Foucault's often-quoted appeal is still pertinent for our purposes of addressing the contemporary novel, insofar as a 'whole history remains to be written of *spaces,* from the great strategies of geo-politics to the little tactics of the habitat'.[37] At least one chapter of that incomplete history would trace the internationalized frontiers of British fiction today. Nigerian novelist Ben Okri recalls the figure of the frontier when positing new horizons for technical ambition, obliging contemporary writers to extend the possibilities of language in fiction, to infringe existing thresholds of style and form. 'In storytelling', asserts Okri, 'there is always transgression'; and without this formal imperative, 'without the red boundary, there is no danger, no risk, no *frisson,* no experiment, no discovery, and no creativity'.[38] It's certainly an accretive list, chiselled out with a paratactic insistence as resolute as the act of artistic infringement it prescribes: with those percussive negatives, Okri is steeling his typology against dispute. His catalogue appears to insist on the idea that the relationship between thematic 'transgression' and formal 'experiment' is mutually enhancing.

Not all novelists addressed in this study, though, are explicitly experimental. A side-effect of Okri's infectious enthusiasm is that it gives the impression that avant-garde commitments are an inherently good thing to nurture, as though the faculty for pyrotechnic invention is something all writers should relentlessly strive for and perfect. As I have been suggesting, spatial formations raise many implications for responding to and classifying formal innovation. And if novelistic settings constitute more than impassive backdrops unmediated by what occurs within them, then our scrutiny of aesthetic categories with which we value fiction's communication with place today becomes of paramount importance. As Robert Macfarlane bemoans, what seems to have 'vanished is writing that might help us to reacquire, even temporarily, the sense of inhabitation and attunement out of which modernity has hustled us'.[39] Yet given the plurality of their stylistic priorities, novelists in this study seem unanchored to any single campaign. Instead their fictions allow us to envision new ways of being and belonging in urban and rural environments. Rather than prescribing ecological cures, contemporary novelists have set new precedents for becoming 'free to choose to try to alter', as Raymond Williams had hoped, 'that which is really pressuring you, in your whole social formation, in your understanding of the possibilities of writing'.[40] And Williams's own interrogation of the personal and social implications of representing physical landscapes resounds again in my closing chapter, as we turn to writers whose diasporic imaginations reach beyond the nation. For postcolonial novelists like Caryl Phillips and Andrea Levy, the relationship between geography and depiction, scenery and its imaginative dissemination, emphasizes the part that readers play in the perception of the natural world, through the roles they assume as witnesses to places held in the shadow of empire.

This kind of participatory involvement with narrative space is considered throughout this book as it moves between specific writers and territories. As the opening chapter contends, by surveying the afterlife of structuralist ideas about 'spatial form' we are prompted to rethink our assumptions concerning the treatment of place and perception in fiction. And although this book is organized thematically to encompass the capacious geographic reach of recent British novelists, it retains throughout a certain metacritical objective, too, by remaining as concerned with methods of reading as with manners of style. In this respect, I have sought to offer a broader contribution to contemporary fiction studies by insisting on the importance of exploring the aesthetic properties of narrative discourse, thereby reasserting the critical currency of pleasure and affect for analysing form while reflecting upon the guiding procedures of that analysis. The politics of literary settings and the spatial characteristics of their stylistic evocation can reform the criteria through which we assess their interrelationship. Evading typification or programmatic inspection, writers are increasingly posing the opportunity for testing a more interactive approach. That is, novelists are inviting us to detect *how* spatial representations can hold us in thrall while scrutinizing the ethics of our enthralment. Compelling us to engage with the craft of literary geographies, writers today spotlight Iain Sinclair's conviction that space is far 'more than a metaphor'.[41]

Chapter 1

Landscape and Narrative Aesthetics

As the complexity of their distinctions suggests, space and place operate in contemporary fiction in ways that require us to rethink some of our most cherished critical assumptions. Labels like *location, genius loci, setting* or *mise-en-scène* appear to mean so many things for novelists in practice; but such *figural* terms can detract from understanding the various roles that spaces play within the very texture of novelistic *form*. Topographical references might familiarize us with empirical settings, allowing us to recognize by name. Yet place-names are hardly the sole ingredients for writers who use landscapes to experiment with style. Moreover, it now seems commonplace to think of our physical environment as all but saturated in mediatory systems of representation. Of all the ways in which landscapes are manipulated by publicity, tourism offers some of the most sanctioned cases of spatial mythologization. The commercial appropriation of territories to the point of idealization is yet another 'indication', in Edward Said's words, 'of how geography can be manipulated, invented, characterized quite apart from a site's merely physical reality'.[1] Similarly, the idealization of rural spaces as unadulterated spheres of benevolence and restoration has led Simon Schama to caution that '[e]ven the landscapes that we suppose to be the most free of our culture may turn out, on closer inspection, to be its product'.[2] But to believe that all places are ideologically mediated to the same extent can spawn generalizations, not least when trying to arrive at a precise understanding of that relationship between setting and formal innovation for novelists today. For if landscapes in actuality should be subjected to 'closer inspection', as Schama suggests, so must the landscapes of contemporary fiction, in ways that illuminate the aesthetic strategies by which novelists invite us to experience their narratives of place.

Sensing narrative space

There is always a temptation to recruit literary fiction as emblematic of socio-geographical issues and forces, or as an adjunctive resource for assessing the way place has been turned into a cultural 'product'. How landscapes influence communal prosperity as well as the affect of industrial progress upon the welfare of the land has certainly become a dialectical point of interest at the forefront of ecocritical thought. Environmental criticism has done much to reassert the importance of place-relations for studying the novel form.[3] Yet equally, the over-arching imperatives of socioecological critique can detract from fiction's own aesthetic distinction, enlisting novelists tangentially in correspondence with activist affairs. As Andrew Thacker has rather tersely put it, '[t]o investigate a novel as a spatial text must amount to more than simply considering how that text represents an interesting location' ('The Idea of a Critical Literary Geography', 63). A more focused account is therefore required of space, place and their implications for the *experience* of reading. No less for contemporary fiction, we need to have the conviction to take the texture of what we read as our point of departure, over and above the precepts of cultural theory. As I attempt to demonstrate throughout this book, a formalist approach to literary space need not exclude a wider awareness of contemporary fiction's parabolic implications or polemical force. In this respect, Richard Strier shrewdly indicates that 'formal features of a text, matters of style, can be indices to large intellectual and cultural matters'.[4] Strier draws a distinction between 'indexical' or allegorizing approaches to linking cultural history and literary technique, from our ongoing aesthetic response to a work's formal textures and affective appeal. This distinction seems to me vital for considering how we can alternately respond to a literary setting at the level of immediate content – when reacting to a location's dramatic implications – while fully aware of, and emo-tionally consumed by, the style in which that setting is embellished and conveyed. This distinction alerts us to ways of synthesizing thematic and formalist readings of landscape description in contemporary prose, by connecting a novel's most discrete syntactical, tropological or structural patterns to broader issues of identity and displacement. Correspondences between narrative form and depictions of social space are nowhere more apparent than in writers who absorb us in their settings while evoking the intimate demands of habitation and belonging. When reading novels of this kind, we're invited to connect our involvement in the very texture of what we read with the physical places being described, showing the extent to '[t]he level of style and syntax', in Strier's phrase, 'is the level of "lived" experience' (212).

The task of addressing landscape and style in fiction today thus attests to the critical complexities we face in trying to cultivate an aesthetic sensitivity to spatial representation alongside an evaluation of how writers express personal and social histories of place. Moreover, on a formal level alone, the sheer range of devices that novelists utilize to represent space in material and metaphorical terms surely necessitates, in Edward Soja's words, something of an 'appropriate interpretive balance'. By way of this concession, Soja calls for a more creative vocabulary for grasping 'space, time, and social being or what may now more explicitly be termed the creation of human geographies'.[5] Yet this appeal to a more sensory manner of addressing and analysing spatial experience only persuades us to appraise the novel's distinction as an affective medium for putting us in touch with built and natural environments. And precisely how we relate critically *and* emotionally to the artistry of spatial description is a question that motivates this book, a question that my formalist attention to detail has tried to answer as each chapter negotiates different novelistic registers and geographical conditions.

Famously for Georg Lukács, spatial relations were an integral part of the *shape* of narrative discourse. There is something implicit, he notes, about the way novelists lead their readers between spaces of encounter and conflict, en route to the denouement, leading us towards the thresholds of recognition. In this sense, the locations through which a plot takes us serve to pinpoint the progressive stages of reading as an experiential process:

> Every written work is constructed round a question and progresses in such a way that it can suddenly stop at the edge of an abyss – suddenly, unexpectedly, yet with compelling force. And even if it leads us past luxuriant palm groves or fields of glowing white lilies, it will always lead to the edge of the great abyss, and can never stop anywhere else before it reaches the edge. This is the most profound meaning of form: to lead to a great moment of silence, to mould the directionless, precipitous, many-coloured stream of life as though all its haste were only for the sake of such moments.[6]

Evocative yet insistent, cascading forth in a peal of declarative assertions, Lukács is resolute about the kind of frontier to which the novel inevitably leads. He might have looked to *The Wings of the Dove* (1902) for a prototype, where James's impulsive Milly relishes every new opportunity to 'move in a labyrinth'.[7] Not only is she incredulous towards the idea that 'there are not abysses' (174) awaiting even the most settled family units; she actively goes in search of the secrets they harbour, since 'abysses were what she wanted' (175). But by addressing 'Every written work', it may sound as though Lukács is venting a wild set of generalizations, reducing the poetics of place to a single narratological and philosophical purpose. However, his exertive language is merely a distraction here from the level of detail to which he aspires. Those totalizing determiners – 'every', 'always', 'never', 'most', 'only', 'any' – chime with his ardent search for greater specificity when categorizing narrative space. Not nearly as unmitigated as his parataxis might imply, then, Lukács is campaigning for precision when describing how writers relate topography and textuality. Sentence by sentence, he insists on the particularity of 'form' while accruing and discarding its abstract associations:

> Written works differ from each other for no other reason than that the abysses can be reached by many paths, and that our questions always arise out of a new astonishment. Forms are natural necessities for no other reason than

that there is only one path leading to the abyss from any one place. ('The Moment and Form', 114)

Shrewd, impassioned, acquisitive – Lukács's surprising essay embodies an impulse readers regularly identify in literary fiction, one exemplified by many writers considered later in this study: that impulse of the *quest*. His appetitive commentary rhetorically complements the rhythm of those quest-conventions he describes, so that adventures in theme provoke inventions in form. Thus the very grammar of Lukács's forum oratory, with its building tempo, evokes precisely the sense of imperative with which novelists involve readers in voyages 'to the edge of the abyss'. Yet the critical implications of this are broader still than he makes them sound. Lukács is actually expanding our view of the possible territories into which the novel can draw us, rather than offering an all-encompassing map of the metaphysical destination to which every narrative is supposedly destined. He proceeds in the knowledge that with every broader view of the horizons open to literary form, with every new depicted landscape opening 'many paths' before the novelistic imaginary, the necessity of defining how 'works differ' from one another becomes all the more crucial. The sense of imperative Lukács assigned to fiction as a journey thus offers a timely analogue for exploring space in contemporary fiction. Given the diversity of their formal techniques, British novelists today cross a variety of modes for transporting us to the 'abysses' of human inquiry. They have followed the example of 'old storytellers', as Ben Okri has called them, who 'were the first real explorers and frontierspeople of the abyss. They brought the world within our souls' (*A Way of Being Free*, 39). In an age in which temporal and spatial dislocations punctuate our everyday lives, 'with certainties collapsing about us', Okri warns that literature needs disciples of 'those fictional old bards and fearless storytellers' (39) – disciples whose myriad strategies request and reward our careful inspection. For to acknowledge that, ultimately, 'there is only one path leading to the abyss from any one place', as Lukács described it, is to highlight the necessity of specifying the forms that writers adopt to follow that path and by doing so make it their own.

Voyages of reading

This emphasis upon specificity is no means exclusive to literary criticism, of course. But what we can usefully take from cultural geography is a commitment to retaining the materiality of place, especially when comparing different landscape descriptions at the level of style. Even as Maria Balshaw and Liam Kennedy observe that cityscapes can 'take on contours of identity and location through representation',[8] they also admit that while 'language plays an important part in shaping our comprehension of the city, representation also involves material, visual and psychic forms and practices that cannot be reduced to textuality' (4). It might seem obvious to state the difference between how we experience landscapes in literature and our visceral encounter with physical places in ordinary life. Yet there is always a temptation to evaluate spaces in fiction as historical, documentary reflections of environmental conditions. To avoid this kind of instrumentalism, we would do better to follow the lessons of Edward Said by tracing how 'different kinds of novels derive some of their aesthetic rationale from changes taking place in the geography and landscape as the result of social contest'.[9] Mindful as I am of the tendency for writers of place to be extrapolated as social or environmental allegorists – their novels praised because they appear to 'symbolise a nation', as Zadie Smith worries, or 'speak for a community' – the present study nonetheless argues that narrative space can yield local and universal implications ('Read Better', 21). Each of the following chapters, despite their thematic differences, explores why it is that 'some novels transcend their geographical and temporal settings', as Ken Warpole observes, 'and become resonant with wider allegorical or symbolic meanings and others stay resolutely earthbound and short-lived'.[10] In unpacking this distinction, this book looks beyond scenery and emplotment to the ways in which narrative stylization informs, and is informed by, fiction's engagement with landscape. It explores how writers build upon the interface of place and prose to examine new relations between spatial description and the aesthetics of readerly engagement.

This is not simply an expository exercise, however, or a promotion of formalist readings over the insights of cultural geography. As Lukács might remind us, not every novel leads off on the same journey. Using *travel* as a critical metaphor eviscerated of history carries its own risks, of course. But one can refuse to aestheticize mobility while still retaining, as Andrew Gibson has done, what is conceptually fruitful about the idea of reading as exploration. Every 'path' into each episode, writes Gibson, 'modifies the narrative situations accordingly. There is thus no fixed or single narrative space in this adventure. There is only a set of potentials which can be activated in different ways, and where each activation is an event'.[11] Much is productive about entertaining narrative fiction as though it were an arena for chance encounters, whose effect upon us cannot be predicted in advance of their arrival. Improvising with space as a model for comprehension, Minrose Gwin similarly emphasizes the idea of reading as perpetual motion. 'As readers', she suggests, 'we may often find ourselves visitors in a different land, perhaps a strange land; we learn its dimensions as we travel through, not by any maps we have constructed prior to reading'.[12] Accelerating with the unfolding text, entailing a whole series of relocations in critical posture and approach – each new literary quest will spell readjustments in our exegetic terms of inquest.

How we conceptualize novelistic locations, then, seems inextricable from how we conceive reading itself as a *voyage* punctuated by discovery and qualification. Environmental descriptions foster these interpretive conditions,

conditions of affective reflection and ethical response that materialist geography often elides when turning to novelists as chroniclers of land use and reform. Defining place in fiction is a task that can't be divorced from the way different literary settings spell moments of empathy and estrangement, contrasting moments of immersion and recoil. Given that space, when socially occupied, becomes '*practiced place*',[13] as Michel de Certeau famously declared, so in a novel our visceral relationship with its aesthetic form from one scene to the next can generate new critical practices. A reader's path to absorption with every turning page affirms that '[e]very story is a travel story – a spatial practice' (*The Practice of Everyday Life*, 116). Yet the trouble with de Certeau's assertion here is that he reduces geography to metaphorical generality, conflating the very distinction between *space* and *place* that he typically avoids so assiduously. Indeed, so much is fluid and subjective about the definition of literary space that the task of addressing its formal properties must dispense with the notion that every novel is simply 'a travel story'. That contemporary British writers have engaged so variously with place-relations, is all the more reason *not* to invoke ungrounded notions of 'spatial practice' when analysing their respective techniques. For although de Certeau's model of spatial practices may appear highly conducive to describing our engagement with landscape description, it runs the risk of consigning space to a level of philosophical abstraction in which spatiality loses all shape and distinction. This is what provokes Paul Smethurst's concern, that what often hampers the study of narrative space is critical theory's own affinity with the science of topology. A conceptual plethora of 'spatial indicators', as Smethurst describes them, can result in the 'mathematization' of literary form; while on a thematic level, too, space slides into inaccuracy, viewed solely as an experiential phenomena distinguished in terms of a 'knowable *inside*, and a vast and undifferentiated outside'.[14] Such analyses of novelistic setting, warns Smethurst, are reduced to conversations about 'straight lines and geometric shapes', leaving literary spaces 'devoid of the detritus of history, and the bustle and chaos of everyday life' (374). Paradoxically, then, the more we conceptualize place and spatial practice in strict, quantifiable terms, the more vulnerable are literary landscapes to generalizing forms of critique, whereby the metaphoricity of topographic descriptions presides at the expense of their social and ecological currency.

It is not difficult to see, then, how numerous aesthetic categories and theoretical paradigms might be combined when mapping the formal geography of contemporary fiction. But a disparity of approaches does not always entail their mutual enrichment; and not every approach facilitates our engagement with novelistic technique. Where the close reading of fictional space is concerned, that temptation to invoke topography as a critical tropology reaffirms the importance of invoking *space* and its many derivatives with conceptual and grammatical precision. Jeanette Winterson's reminder seems apposite here, that 'the language of literature is not an approximate language', since those 'spaces it allows are not formless vistas of subjectivity, they are new territories of imagination'.[15] For Winterson also insinuates that imaginative literature has increasingly served as critical theory's subsidiary resource. Observing her caution, this book considers in adjacency novelists who push at the borders of form, while refusing to adopt their writings as accessories for demonstrating certain narratological terms. Practitioners as diverse as Trezza Azzopardi, Iain Sinclair, Pat Barker and Caryl Phillips have often adopted relatively confined settings to evoke the personal ramifications of wider social and racial tensions. Such writers tread new paths through apparently localized situations while challenging received ideas of nationhood, class identity and belonging. Moving between such established and emerging novelists, *Contemporary British Fiction and the Artistry of Space* highlights the way our reading of landscape description can create distinctive and surprising affinities between modes, revealing the way space has remained a stylistic catalyst for some of the most innovative writers in Britain today.

Genealogies of 'Spatial Form'

Location can mean many things for narration. And although it might be attractive to think of *space* as an inherent property of literary form, the complementary relation between structure and metaphor is far from inevitable for even the most scenic passages of description. As Mieke Bal has pointed out, 'few concepts deriving from the theory of narrative texts are as self-evident and have yet remained so vague as the concept of space'.[16] In this her second edition of a landmark study of narratology's key tenets, it is significant that she leaves unaltered her rather sombre reflection over 10 years on. Yet Bal is right, nonetheless, to offer this caution about defining narrative space – counselling us against the pre-emptive categorization of something that remains so ephemeral. For just because a novel may devote a substantial amount of chronological space to describing the place in which it is set doesn't necessarily mean its structure will epitomize the traits of 'spatial form'. When Joseph Frank originally coined this term over 50 years ago he could neither have predicted its subsequent impact on structuralist thinking in the 1970s, nor the debate that ensued for decades to come over its literary-critical application.[17] In stating its own case for space in literary art, narratology's opacity alone can frequently sound unyielding. One might think it advisable to look elsewhere for a frame for literary space, to seek an approach less enclosed within its own insular debates. In fact, such is the methodological rigidity of those early theories concerned with spatial form that our historical understanding of the relation between place and technique can fall prey to the inanities of metacritical self-inquiry. Though certainly a committed formal innovator as her dazzling *Textermination* (1991) affirms, Christine Brooke-Rose wittily recalls how 'the study of narratological phenomena, as happens so often, turned into an endless discussion about how to speak of them. The story of narratology became as self-reflexive as a "postmodern" novel. But after all every age has the rhetoric it deserves'.[18] What Brooke-Rose is deriding is not the admirable task of building a more specific language for talking about literary fiction, but rather the level of prescription and systematization to which narratological inquiry is often prone. Nevertheless, if spatial form theories did induce something of a hiatus in hermeneutical thought in the 1970s, their influence in shaping new principles of narrative discourse repays our attention, and their afterlife in the 1980s and beyond is worth retracing.

For what made the conceptual revisiting of 'Spatial Form' so conspicuous was the attempt by structuralists to engage in an arena of conflicting priorities which the interpretation of literary space itself illuminates. In effect, the theorization of narrative spatiality spurred an active reconsideration of narratology's objectives. Nothing more incisively than textual space, it seems, drew attention to this disciplinary space of contrary commitments.[19] It was as if the tendency for theories of spatial form to evade systematic rules were rehearsed within the very language used to clarify it. In effect, the elusiveness of narrative space was mirrored by the way it was discussed – its equivocal status dramatized by the way the original terms of 'Spatial Form' were persistently redefined but without consensus. The idea of allowing spatial concepts to reform certain core principles in narratology as a discipline thus emerged from a cluster of discussions about whether or not it was fruitful to promote debates of this kind when key terminological conflicts were being left so unresolved.

Seemingly resistant, then, to methodological prescription, the poetics of space remained in flux throughout this transitional moment in narrative theory. On the cusp of Deconstruction's succession, Anglo-American commentators pursued a variety of working definitions of literary space, both as a textual trope and as a critical tool for talking about narrative design. The question was how to allow formal analysis to take centre stage without separating ideas of spatial form from space as it functions semantically at the level of content. Hence, in their preface to a collection in honour of Joseph Frank's founding model, Jeffrey R. Smitten and Ann Daghistany justly maintain that '"spatial form" includes not only objective features of narrative but also subjective processes of aesthetic perception' (*Spatial Form in Narrative*, 13). And it's this correspondence between structural, stylistic and sensuous aspects of literary space which I return to throughout this book. For novelists today request that we stay in tune with emotional vitality of spatial description, even when seeking a more precise vocabulary for classifying spatial form.

This is one of an array of fine distinctions between the stylization of space and our sensory response to spatial symbolism. And it's a distinction that W. J. T. Mitchell deemed worthy of maintaining in the wake of Frank's original scheme. While reminding us of the internal eccentricity of narrative literature in an effort to liberate textual space from its 'binary oppositions as literal and figurative',[20] Mitchell suggests that readers construct a novel's presented world via a series of signifying 'levels'. Not altogether dissimilar from Deleuzean lines of force, Mitchell's architectonic model is one in which meanings emanate from the page out of a 'complex field of internal relationships, the most common of which is the phenomenon of stratification' ('Spatial Form in Literature', 549–50). Might this be too rigid, though? Is not the thought of *stratification* amenable to systematic rather than sensuous or heuristic ways of reading narrative space? In fact, by making the very taxonomical gesture he would seek to avoid, Mitchell outlines a network of textual effects resistant to the degree of typological classification that stratification implies. Such a potentially programmatic conception of literary space stymies the serendipitous idea of moving across a text's various levels of association and implication. To see Mitchell's account of narrative space as entirely diagrammatic is misleading, though. Indeed, he remains as generous in retracing, as he is insistent upon refining, the value of space as an exegetical tool. And by suggesting that 'spatial form is a crucial aspect of the experience and interpretation of literature in all ages and cultures' (541), Mitchell opens the way for thinking in a more capacious sense about how novelists immerse us in their depicted landscapes *through* the very style of spatial description.

Not that Joseph Frank had ignored these cognitive and affective implications when defending his own founding proposals. He certainly anticipated the emerging 'cognitive turn' in English studies today, using literary space to speculate about the importance of reader-oriented criticism while appealing to a more informed psychology of reception.[21] Frank suggested that formal space is better understood as simultaneously textual and extratextual: it is applicable not only to describing the way narrative form is constituted by the action we witness, but also to the new kinds of interpretative pathways that our witnessing procedures themselves open up. This twofold model encourages us to imagine criticism as an *event*, as something which happens *for* the words on the page. Jeannette Winterson has called it 'the paradox of active surrender': an acknowledgement that 'I have to work for art if I want art to work on me' (*Art Objects*, 6). And Frank's model of spatial form amply complements this sense of readerly interaction. Indeed, in the wake of those initial caveats played out across the pages of *Critical Inquiry*, Lynda D. McNeil offered a defence of 'Spatial Form' theory by remedying what she saw as a fundamental misconception of Frank's theoretical stance by reappraising his critical style. Many charges levied at his original manifesto deemed that Frank's priorities were haunted by New Criticism, and that this latent formalism sidelined political issues in those European modernists to whom he turned as exemplars of spatial techniques. Yet as Frank reflects, 'my preoccupation was never abstract or theoretical' ('Foreword', *Spatial Form in Narrative*, 7). Likewise, if his position seems ascetic, his impersonality is deliberate, if not necessary to envisioning the kind of reader that he does. As McNeil points out, 'Frank casts his reader of works using spatial form in the distanced and disparate role of *reconstructor*, the mason who builds houses no one will occupy'.[22] Although he himself, then, never deployed the term in an entirely decontextualized sense, Frank nevertheless incited a dispute over how far 'Spatial Form' might shed its affiliation with New Criticism and be employed in more historical discussions of literary technique. By sounding as discursively 'distanced' as the readerly 'role' he prescribed, Frank's methodological speculations thus ended up detracting from their future relevancy. And as the debate concerning its value for analysing aesthetic design entered a key structuralist phase, the dividing opinions over *space* as a tool appeared to spring as directly from the reception of Frank's interpretative style – 'returning text-ward', as McNeil describes it, 'to an abstraction about "the temporality of language" rather than outward to experience' (358) – as they did from any genuine conceptual *impasse*. Occasionally arcane, frequently insular, these debates may seem a far cry from the concerns of contemporary British novelists; but their self-consciousness is pertinent today because of the assumptions it exposes. For what spatial form theory still brings to light is the extent to which *space* is one of many literary-critical terms liable to congeal and stagnate by so rarely receiving qualification – terms of the kind used freely so long as they don't need to be defined.

The ambivalent and elusive symbiosis between style and spatial description continues to compel our attention. Susan Sontag's point about the way we perceive zones of absence, confinement, or incalculable expanse is again useful here. To distinguish between such environments in a visual artwork 'is still to be looking, still to be seeing something' (*Styles of Radical Will*, 10). So it is for the novel; only that *looking* is replaced by *listening*, since the reader attains a visual conception of place only by hearing of the experience of its terrain either from characters perceiving it at firsthand, or from a shadowing narrator who beholds the effect of their observations. This rhetorical integration of vision and voice, sight and insight, is especially penetrating for writers in this study who have exploited the dexterity of *free indirect discourse*: that is, when they forfeit the detachedness of authorial commentary, articulating instead observations of space focalized by their characters' immediate responses or spells of recollection. 'Style' itself, as Martin Amis has declared, 'is not something grappled on to regular prose; it is intrinsic to perception'.[23] Amis points to the contention made throughout this book, that the technical diversity of British writers today persuades us to reflect on how we respond terminologically and emotionally to the represented perception of space. As we have seen, there are limitations and advantages of reviving methodologies from the past. And if Spatial Form – at least as it was originally conceived – seems less fruitful as a systematic model to be emulated and applied, than as a constellation of critical metaphors for describing a given writer's decisions about form, what I hope to demonstrate here is a more integrative approach to reading landscapes in fiction. It's time that aesthetically committed approaches to fiction responded to the dominance of cultural geography in criticism on literary space, enabling us to pose more intimate questions about our engagement with novelistic settings. While underestimating Frank's own endorsement of a highly self-reflective approach to correlating space and style, Ronald Faust nevertheless maintained that '[w]hat criticism has not stressed is that spatial form is primarily a theory of perception that focuses on the reading process [. . .] calling for empathic participation while admitting the possibility of actual coextensiveness between reader and text'.[24] Faust's preoccupation, however, is with how 'the reading process' alone might be reconceived in terms equivalent to spatial perception. Envisioning in the mind a novel's dramatic scenery, implies Faust, is a logical counterpart to surveying a landscape in actuality. Curiously, though, Faust neglects the significance of places as they appear physically at the level of content, offering little insight into how reading is altered by novels richly focused on material environments. Nor does Faust address the way writers search different landscapes to find different ways of 'calling for empathic participation'. By the same stroke, although Peter Middleton and Tim Woods reiterate the importance of 'the spatial dimensions of narrative' for criticism of the novel, rather than 'focus[ing] instead on an unlocated psychology of the characters or atopic themes and plots',[25] what they neglect in turn is that question of readerly involvement and response. This may sound as though I am advocating an exhaustive approach to the relation between literary settings and their spatial impact upon fictional prose. But in many ways, this book is step towards developing a more expansive view of narrative space, one that takes into account a range of structural, grammatical and phonetic features which contribute to the pleasure of reading literary landscapes.

'Every novel represents a new problem to be solved', admits Michèle Roberts, 'and therefore you have to find and invent a new form'.[26] Yet the conceptualization of narrative form in spatial terms is hardly the only way of thinking about the wider philosophical, polemical or emotive functions of landscape in contemporary fiction. What the structuralist idea of Spatial Form precludes is precisely an evaluation of *where* a novel is set, in addition to how that setting can affect the internal arrangement and chronology of events. Margaret Anne Doody goes as far as to remark that criticism 'might be better off not speaking of "formal" elements at all', since the novel throughout history has called into question 'the distinction between General and Particular, between Form and Matter'. If we want to speak about the significance of form, warns Doody, 'we must do so under the proviso that in using the metaphor of spatial shape we know that it is here a rather unimportant metaphor and must yield to others'.[27] Having stated this, Doody pursues her preferred framework by focusing on the rhetorical (rather than formal) constitution of the novel in terms of successive *tropes*. And yet, notice the symbolism threading her argument: taking 'spatial shape' to task for being somewhat nebulous, thus analytically 'unimportant',

Doody's commentary nevertheless invokes spatial dimensions by analogy. Space as a tool returns with a persistence that suggests she cannot altogether dispense with its expressive appeal: 'If we say that the tropes are "moments" (considering them temporally) they can also be imagined spatially, as "points", like places on the stations of the Cross, or special places sought out in the journey of a pilgrim, like the major sites of Mecca' (305). While suggesting that we think about the novel as a ritualistic performance of these intensified 'tropic moments', Doody's best effort to ward-off the usefulness of Spatial Form actually ends up reaffirming its efficacy. She rehearses that dry, impersonal notion of narrative as a semiotic *architecture*, but reinflects it with a series of startling metaphors when applying it to the history of the novel.

It's hard to let go of space as a critical metaphor. And what is more, Doody's own observations are no less rigorous or conceptually acute for unfolding in a vocabulary that is so spatially suggestive. She emphasizes the way narrative events can be 'sought out', 'imagined spatially' and be distinguished by the reader who can appreciate the singularity of certain events by virtue of where they take place. Stage by stage, with every turning page, Doody insists that readers remain as committed as 'a pilgrim' might be to valuing the impact of *what happens* on a novel's 'journey' regardless of its destination. Again, as Lukács did when asserting that every novelist in some sense leads her reader to the brink of an 'abyss', Doody's opulent use of territorial similes offers here a portrait of the novel as an experiential *voyage*. This isn't just another hermeneutical template either, one stencilling out the activity of reading novels as an extended 'journey' of equivocation punctuated by many 'special places'. More than that, it reminds us of the vitality with which those places themselves shape that sense of contingent, uneven progress so compelling across fictional plots. A shift in location, however slight, has consequences for interpretation as well as characterization, factoring in a whole new range of demands and opportunities for critic and narrator alike. And indeed these spatial shifts reveal just how far the importance of individual events over their cumulative outcome is often brought to our attention only in retrospect, after we have shifted perceptual frames, moving on to the next episode, the next site of encounter, with all the sense of expectation a new setting entails.

*Re*reading, of course, rekindles in altered form the affect of these relationships between unfurling landscape and unfolding events. It turns the narrative world of Doody's fictional 'journey' into somewhere in perpetual motion in the reader's mind. Responding to a plot a second time around can be highly performative: not only an acknowledgment of, but an active re-engagement in, new and unexpected interpretations. Landscapes in the longest narrative texts can have an affective afterlife, leaving a residual presence in the mind when reading ends. And though Joseph Frank may have hindered the wider application of his propositions in 1945 by focusing on the role of space in avant-garde poetics, the notion that settings persist emotionally after we leave a fictional world, with the locations we have envisioned there lingering on in the mind's eye, offers one way of reappraising Frank's sense of textual space as a spring-board for readerly participation. Rereading is a case in point, insofar as it occasions our voluntary immersion in descriptions we've already enjoyed. Mediated by an inevitable sense of familiarity, re-recognizing places in fiction can of course blemish what once surprised us. But on this return voyage, re-readings can be as evanescent as initial readings are. The pleasure of reading literary settings entirely for their own sake attests to this possibility, to the value of revisiting writers whose landscape descriptions we cherish primarily, if not especially, for their style.

Location and periodization

Between the symbolic and the material landscapes, between literary space as part of the reading experience and social places as challenging zones of encoun-ter – for a book of this kind, all these distinctions and negotiations highlight that ever-contentious issue of selection. London-based novelist Maggie Gee has found a correlative in the visual arts to the dilemmas of literary-critical selectiv-ity and elimination. What curators face in 'group exhibitions', so the present study faces in the contemporary writing. Collective displays, writes Gee, 'pose a political problem of sorts which too often diverts attention from the individual works of art: who is in, who is out, and why?'[28] By periodizing the evolution of certain formal concerns from 1970 to the present day, I realize that this is a vola-tile terrain now spanning at least two distinct generations of writers. But on that question of selecting representative novelists from the past 30 years, I agree with Bruce King, who for his own study faced a far more challenging task than mine. Covering an exceptional range of established and emerging figures in order to survey the overlapping contexts of English literature's 'internationali-zation', King arrives at something of a practical concession about who and what to choose. Within his acquiescence, though, resounds a fruitful assertion about what it actually means to select from the amorphousness of the contemporary scene: 'While divisions by decade are arbitrary, they are a way to observe histori-cal trends while organizing material'.[29] To King, any process of selection must be practicable for the exegetical directives and limitations in hand. Therein lies the selector's consolation: an admission of who cannot, yet who could have, been included and why. Moreover, King's own insistence upon charting 'trends' through strategically grouped 'material' complements my caveat earlier that questions of technique in contemporary fiction have been inadequately addressed by postmodernism's metacritical preoccupations. Overlapping gen-erations of novelists have woven a diverse series of stylistic and thematic textures into the fabric of Britain's literary landscape; and they are weaving them still, rendering any map of the geography of contemporary fiction ceaselessly yet productively incomplete.

The sheer range of landscapes figured as settings in the contemporary novel is formidably unmappable. To confront that spectrum in its entirety would demand a limitless survey, covering terrains both concrete and phenomenal, natural and built environments. Any landform with which writers potentially come into contact would fall under this remit: waterside communities like the riparian topography of Russell Ceylan Jones's *Ten Seconds to the Sun* (2005); such real and imagined coastlines as those mapped by Iain Sinclair in *Dining on Stones* (2004); or by Maggie Gee herself in her recent apocalyptic fable, *The Flood* (2004). Likewise, the city itself presents a more familiar but no less complex scenery upon which to focus a survey of space in contemporary fiction. Inevitably, then, my inquiry below is subject to discriminations as it examines the way novelists have experimented with that ancient device of setting-the-scene. By restricting the choice of places, it may appear as though I privilege certain landforms over others, providing a partial rather than panoramic view of the British novel's expanding horizons. But given its susceptibility to philosophical abstraction, polemical allegorization,[30] or mimetic readings that compare literary metaphors against actual landmarks, an account of the aesthetics of fictional space needs this inelegant process of selection to focus its priorities. This study sustains an author-led account of novelistic space by approaching novelists as broadly representative rather definitive of different geographical contexts and concerns. I have restricted the number of key exponents so as to explicate in detail the spatial features of their distinguishing techniques, as well as the stylistic legacies and affinities borne out by those techniques. Each chapter considers writers quite distinct from one another in mode and subject-matter: from Sinclair's metropolitan travelogues and Graham Swift's suburban narratives of remembrance, to regional counterparts such as Pat Barker and Adam Thorpe who rework earlier realist aesthetics to re-envision provincial landscapes. Posing as a cultural commentator who crosses national boundaries in his criticism and fiction alike, Amit Chaudhuri has noted how novelists have become fascinated with the movement across space as a metaphor for the displacement of 'British fiction' as a ethnically stable categorization. It's this dissonance between national identities prescribed or self-assumed and the need for asylum and settlement which has been frequently dramatized by postcolonial writers like Caryl Phillips and Andrea Levy addressed in Chapter 5. While neither valorizing displacement, nor reclaiming a sense of authentic belonging, such novelists have 'realised what a strange place this is', in Chaudhuri's phrase. Dissatisfied with the way Britain has figured in literary fiction, such writers have sought to envision nation-space as 'a local culture rather than some place called England' – envisaging an island-realm continually 'transformed by movement, by permutations, by migrations' ('On Belonging and Not Belonging', 46).

It is precisely these global forces, of course, which continue to propagate disharmony between states, forces detrimental to the health of intercultural

communication, exchange and accountability. That the brutalities of involuntary emigration frequently contradict the ideals of cosmopolitan migrancy has
compelled novelists to interrogate the constitution of 'native' public spaces.
Phillips himself has pointed out that over the last three decades of the
twentieth century, the impact of the British Empire's legacy on the novel's
formal development cannot be underestimated. For the early 1980s offered a
heated climate in which writers reassessed their aesthetic aims. To Phillips, 1979
thus hailed a significant watershed, when the Thatcher government hatched a
basilisk of regressive nationalism. Pointing to the post-consensus period
from which this book derives its corpus, Phillips describes an epochal shift in
novelists' priorities, as they sought 'to respond to the radical changes wrought
in the heart and soul of this nation by a political revolution, the full magnitude
of which many of us have still not grasped'.[31] Amid the shock waves emanating
from the 'magnitude' of Tory rule, novelists writing at the new Millennium have
registered the afterlives of that demise in social consensus while mapping
new formal and thematic frontiers for literary fiction. As Philips implies, the
pioneering subject-matter and technical diversity of novelists of a younger
generation from the 1980s requires that we now rethink the borderlines of an
already-provisional contemporary literary canon.

To another established figure, though, the emerging novelistic response to
those socio-political 'changes' – which in Phillips's view had such a 'radical' and
detrimental impact upon the constitution of Britain's public sphere – was
altogether disappointing. For Salman Rushdie, the upheavals of nation-space
in the 1980s were preoccupying a burgeoning generation of writers to the
detriment of formal innovation. Reflecting in 1993 on his nomination that year
to *Granta*'s board of selectors for the 'Best of Young British Novelists', Rushdie
bemoaned the fact that 'it was easy to see, all over the landscape of contemporary British fiction, the devastating effect of the Thatcher years. So many of
these writers wrote without hope. They had lost all ambition, all desire to
wrestle with the world'. And Rushdie continues with this metaphorical deploy-
ment of space, drawing a qualitative chart of areas of literary experiment where
younger writers had yet to venture with any ambition. Rushdie transposes this
generation of novelists onto a map of alternative aesthetic zones, some splen-
did, others dire: 'Very few writers had the courage or even the energy to bite off
a big chunk of the universe and chew it over. Very few showed any linguistic or
formal innovation. Many were dulled, and therefore dull.'[32] With this evaluative
artillery, Rushdie mixes his metaphors between space and soma, theme and
form: between the borders of a human 'universe' in need of critique, and the
borders of what is possible when experimenting with technique. By eliding
together the magnitude of political change and the scarcity of writers able to
'chew . . . over' that change, Rushdie offers an atlas of the contemporary scene
in which so 'few writers' seem able to devolve narrative conventions when
offering social commentary. He appears to prescribe a daunting path towards
creative success by prescribing writers a level of technical expertise, hard to

accomplish, and attainable only by the most ardent in any given writing community.

With this peculiar vocabulary of spatial tropes, Rushdie attempts to chart the status of formal invention as a 'landscape' solely for the brave. Just as Britain's mining communities were weakened by the rise of free-market entrepreneurship, so in Rushdie's view the landscape of British fiction has also suffered neglect. What he implies is that novelists caught up in the critique of capitalist avarice were left stumbling for over a decade across the rocky territory of Tory government policy. Yet in assuming the needs of the social present are antithetical with those of stylistic innovation, Rushdie's literary mapping reveals much about the uneasy alliance of context and assertion, and about the danger in deferring to political history as a background for making artistic value-judgements. Albeit inadvertently, what his survey highlights is how the very act of framing a period from which to select novelists most *representative* of aesthetic innovations can be as problematic as defining the parameters of what qualifies as an original style. It's an apt caution for the task of building a historically substantiated consideration of spatial poetics in contemporary fiction. For we need to take into account how the heuristic process of reading narrative space relates to the very meaning of literary experiment itself as it has been valued and advanced by contemporary British writers.[33]

Each of the following chapters heeds this imperative, by navigating quite different formal terrains, but without compromising the respective differences between the authors discussed. In each case, I trace a series of thematic contours in an effort to reveal the interpenetration of material locations, their aesthetic representation and wider symbolic implication. Surely D. J. Taylor is understating the diversity of place-related preoccupations as they have expanded the novel form, by stating that now is 'a time when one significant strand of the English novel is busy reinventing itself around the ideas of settlement and rootedness'.[34] Hardly representative of this single vein, various British novelists have developed new modes of expressing notions of settlement. And for some it's a biographical impulse more than an opportunity for formal experimenta-tion, an impulse that remains all the more urgent for novelists for whom displacement is as much a personal reality as it is an aesthetic compulsion. Caryl Phillips reiterates this when prefacing his edited collection of writers who have tackled that 'vexing question of belonging', so radically informed by contrasting expatriate and exilic experiences of postcolonial migration. The fact is, Phillips writes, in life and literature alike, 'Britain has been forged in the crucible of fusion'; and yet the nation's self-definition too frequently appeals to the ideality of Britishness as a stable and authentic cultural condi-tion.[35] In my final chapter, recent historical novels from Andrea Levy can be seen as extending Phillips conviction here, that even contemporary writers 'seeking to understand how they "belong" to Britain' must do so in the knowledge that 'the mythology of homogeneity not only exists but endures' (*Extravagant Strangers*, xiv).

Writers considered across this study, then, together represent more than simply 'one significant strand of the English novel', as Taylor describes it. Fictions of immigration and ethnic self-identification from V. S. Naipaul and Hanif Kureishi, for instance, deal frankly with the brute challenges of moving to alternative communities. Yet their concerns have also been directed at the status and sovereignty of literary genre itself. Inheriting Alisdair Gray's impetus in *Lanark* (1981) and *1982 Janine* (1984) to synchronize stylistic experiment and radical social critique, A. L. Kennedy's spare narratives have invoked the most everyday landscapes to dispel any impression of Scottish fiction as bereft of innovation. And yet she also addresses highly intimate issues concerning post-devolution identities, in order to express something of the personal ramifications of nationhood under rapid change. Kennedy's exacting and often quirky attention to evoking the sensation of urban space holds associations with early twentieth-century Scottish provincial fiction, and its equally intensive emphasis on registering spatial perceptions and their associations. Although Cairns Craig places Kennedy along with Muriel Spark and Alan Massie in a group of novelists resistant to prose forever 'rooted in the vitality of the local',[36] Kennedy's work still recuperates something of the focus and density of what Craig earlier describes as Walter Scott's 'psychological regionalism' (244). In her latest experiments, as I suggest in Chapter 4, she fuses memory and perspective to redeem everyday spaces as intimate sites for personal renewal. As in the title story of Kennedy's *Now That You're Back* (1994), we find that one's 'perception of the meaning of a landscape requires "seeing" the past in it', in Craig's words, while 'adducing from the remnants of the past the customs and manners of the human beings who were shaped by their environment' (245). As someone convinced that although 'His memory wasn't the best thing about him [. . .] he was sure he had never seen a place like this' (*Now That You're Back*, 227), the narrator of Kennedy's slim tale is emblematic of her longer fictions of dwelling. Ordinary locales, like the church ruins in that story, frequent her work. Populated by those exiled by family or religion, such landscapes are replete with mnemonics for stimulating unsettling recollections. Yet equally, Kennedy complements Trezza Azzopardi's objectives in showing that fictions of belonging are far from interiorized, as they dramatize the interpersonal nature of dwelling. The agility of such writers to operate on social and psychic levels allows them to negotiate universal and local repercussions. Kennedy alone surpasses narrow national allegiances. For despite the extent to which '[m]any Scottish writers feel torn', as Richard Todd observes, 'between loyalty to their own national roots and the desire for wider recognition' (*Consuming Fictions*, 132), Kennedy is an ambassador for that generation including Janice Galloway and Ali Smith, whose short-fiction techniques evidence their singularity as stylists. Together they exhibit a crystalline attentiveness to quotidian environments, a quality Chapter 4 detects in Graham Swift, whose recent work has reclaimed suburban space as an opportunity for enriching the affective textures of the novel form. Alongside Kennedy and Azzopardi, Swift's deceptively simple prose exemplifies how everyday environments can stimulate mnemonic sequences that in turn fuel structural and linguistic innovations. By exploring the very material consequences of navigating everyday life as a landscape of associative recollections, such writers chronicle the fusion of memory and perception, involuntary retrospection and voluntary journeys in public space, evoking the hidden anxieties of dwelling in ordinary built environments.

As the technical diversity of contemporary fiction increases, then, it seems necessary to refine our critical vocabularies for defining space's relation to narrative form itself, alongside our awareness that the evolving social constitution of *place* has realigned the political targets of key British novelists. Chapter 5, for instance, argues that postcolonial writers have engaged with the historical novel implicitly to refuse their media image as national spokespersons for postwar immigration. Instead, their work has renewed the prescience of Benedict Anderson's landmark account of post-imperial mythology, sensing England's nationalistic resonance as an island for successive generations in the nineteenth and twentieth centuries.[37] With a rarefied label, constantly in flux, the purity of the 'English Novel' today is fundamentally under duress. In and of itself, this denomination is at best provisional and at worst a parochial misnomer. For this category has long seemed tenuous when attributed to the cosmopolitan reach of recent British fiction, all the more insubstantial for novelists who experiment with style to remap the sovereignty of home.

Migrancy and the nourishment of rootlessness

When Hilary Mantel asserted that '[i]n our minds each one of us draws a line between homeland and exile', she was careful to follow it up with the qualification that, equally, '[i]t is very hard for one writer to speak for other writers'.[38] Intimations of not-belonging, of being unable to inhabit a national identity as one's own, of rarely viewing a single country as *home*, have served as points of departure for postcolonial novelists descending from first- and second-generation immigrants to Britain. As Chapter 5 reveals in relation to Caryl Phillips, such writers have become uncomfortable with the personal and historical positions they occupy in the eyes of the media as cultural broadcasters. Likewise, the formal diversity with which they have addressed the legacies of empire requires us to particularize that *ownership* of space, of which Mantel speaks, as a struggle continuing into the present.

As if heeding Mantel's caution, Salman Rushdie refused to equate himself with exilic writers when charting his own expatriation. He draws a careful distinction between intentional migrancy and paths of emigration that so many diasporic populations have scarcely chosen for themselves. Reflecting on his self-identity as an Indian Muslim, Rushdie complements Saleem's fantastic journey across national frontiers in *Midnight's Children* (1981). To Rushdie, like his fabulating narrator, liberation comes with being uprooted from one's originary country. It's a path from displacement to reacclimatization, in Rushdie's view, free from the self-deception of clinging to a single homeland as essentially and fixedly one's own. *Home* is an illusory target here, increasingly less important for the postcolonial subject than reconciling the apparent disparity between migrancy and belonging. This raises a question concerned less with the issue of whether homelands are irretrievable or forever impermanent, than with the differentiation of migration itself as a voluntary act or one that's brutally enforced:

> It may be that writers in my position, exiles or emigrants or expatriates, are haunted by some sense of loss, some urge to reclaim, to look back, even at the risk of being mutated into pillars of salt. But if we do look back, we must do so in the knowledge – which gives way to profound uncertainties – that our physical alienation from India almost inevitably means that we will not be capable of reclaiming precisely the thing that was lost; that we will, in short, create fictions, not actual cities or villages, but invisible ones, imaginary homelands, Indias of the mind.[39]

The case Rushdie elaborates here is posed against the dream of rediscovering and reviving, through fiction, a culturally essentialized, rooted sense of emplacement. For him, it would be heresy to implicate the literary imagination in that 'urge to reclaim' an authentic and singular national history of home. Now in fact spending much of his time in New York, Rushdie calls into question the sovereignty of nationhood, privileging the poetics of displacement as a creative resource. Such rousing sentiments towards the virtues of lifelong exile were horrifically literalized for Rushdie, of course, when in the wake of *The Satanic Verses* (1988) he was forced to seek refuge in Britain from the Fatwa. Under this imposition, his cerebrations on displacement surrendered to the realities of self-concealment. And to withdraw from the public sphere in Britain in the 1980s and 1990s, with its radical waves of social recession and acceleration, seemed like a cruelly ironic penance for writing the novel he himself described as 'a love-song to our mongrel selves' (*Imaginary Homelands*, 394).

If Rushdie 'celebrates' there the lexicon of 'hybridity, impurity, intermingling' (394), he also reiterates a concern which I raised at the outset of this book regarding the relation between particularity, pleasure and critique in contemporary criticism on the novel. Dizzying and polyphonic, despite being historically engaged, texts like *Midnight's Children* and *The Satanic Verses* promote new paradigms for belonging in a world of intercultural flux. But Rushdie's contentions can only be stretched so far between geographical contexts before they are divorced from social history altogether. Claims for the appeal of postmodern migrancy soon turn into velleities, so long as the migrant's condition is romanticized as something available for anyone who feels that their origins are obscure. For Hilary Mantel, writers and critics alike should strive to avoid what is a convenient tendency to mute the actualities of involuntary travel and immigration with the idealized rhetoric of cosmopolitan mobility. In her own memoir, Mantel resists this temptation to transcribe the map of 'how my consciousness as a novelist has evolved' onto landscapes and emigration patterns that proved formative for her contemporaries. By resisting that gesture of elective association as a fellow 'exile' with others from her generation, she declines the liberty to generalize the way her contemporaries were influenced, as writers, by 'the physical and mental journeys which they undertook' ('No Passes or Documents Are Needed', 94). Both Mantel's and Rushdie's personal and professional reflections on belonging serve to caution and advise our study of literary landscapes by forestalling our aestheticization of spatial experiences in the course of engaging aesthetically with narrative form.

Yet there's even a formal dimension at work here too. For these memoirs, by virtue of their personalized, testimonial mode, attest to the very advice they issue implicitly to criticism on literary space. That is to say, Mantel and Rushdie both blend testimony and insistence as a means of dramatizing at the level of style the specific, emanating presence of childhood landscapes lodged in memory. In each case, their refusal to universalize that compulsion to migrate carries with it the metacritical conviction that a writer's memory of place can't simply be used to typify broader claims, trends or speculations about the role of migration in contemporary fiction. We're indeed dissuaded from such abstraction and allegorization, since Mantel and Rushdie leave us with the impression that their desire to leave homelands they now frame as illusory recalls a motivation irreducible to generalization, one that's particular instead unto the memoirist alone.

It is this resolute candour, this insistent personalization of place, which we hear again in memoir of Turkish novelist Orhan Pamuk, recalling his native city after the fall of the Ottoman Empire:

> Conrad, Nabokov, Naipaul – these are writers known for having managed to migrate between languages, cultures, countries, continents, even civilizations. Their imaginations were fed by exile, a nourishment drawn not through roots but rootlessness; mine, however, requires that I stay in the same city, on the same street, in the same house, gazing at the same view. Istanbul's fate is my fate: I am attached to this city because it has made me who I am.[40]

Pamuk's memory of that cityscape is a visceral, intensely gustatory one. The very tense of his commentary pivots between an authoritative, pseudo-documentarian past-perfect, and his present sense of realization and resolve. Cutting in urgently after the semicolon, his intimations of what the present-day 'requires' arrive like the *volta* midway through a Petrarchan sonnet.

In a fleeting interjection, Pamuk poses a reminder to himself of what Istanbul still demands. And over the course of the passage he indeed replaces the lyric sonority of retrospection with the terse repetition of the word *same*: in one fell swoop, Pamuk refuses to embellish remembrance or romanticize that model of voluntary migration he has evaded; instead, he reiterates with this simple adjective the reality that his own imagination has obliged him to 'stay in the same city'. That he *has* stayed is, in part, a purely practical concern – the city as subject-matter is the tool of his trade, fuelling his creative industry. So whereas cultural mobility was a source of 'nourishment' for his famous predecessors, Pamuk has harvested a physiological sense of fortitude from the cityscape of his youth. Creativity finds sustenance there, not in some perpetual search for belonging elsewhere. Pamuk stayed; and in so doing, he honed a style around this place but without monumentalizing it – 'gazing at the same view' of its cityscape without allowing this attachment to reduce urban space to sentimentality. Native familiarity both feeds the indelible 'fate' which he assigns himself, while remaining the lifeblood of his work.

Implicitly at least, Rushdie, Mantel and Pamuk each advocate the need to deal scrupulously with novelists' alternative investments in the artistry of space. Once we start aligning together writers under shared theoretical concerns from overlapping generations but from distinct countries of birth, there is all the more reason to differentiate the priorities behind their spatial poetics. Rushdie himself has nevertheless valorized that 'migrant's-eye view of the world' as an increasingly ubiquitous state of being in today's epoch of global communication and exchange. In his commentary and novels alike he epitomizes the contemporary liberal embrace of mobility, taking migrancy as 'a metaphor for all humanity' (*Imaginary Homelands*, 394). Yet the selections I've made in this book are also sensitive to the ways in which cultural intersections regularly provoke tensions and incompatibilities in actuality that mediate writers' decisions about the creative function of landscapes in their fiction. And by addressing quite different writers through a comparative lens we are also made aware of the stylistic consequences of their decisions to interrogate, rather than celebrate, new paradigms of displacement. Motivating a deeper understanding of the aesthetics of contemporary fiction, British writers are showing how their craft has responded to, and been reconditioned by, the lived realities of landscapes they describe.

Chapter 2

New Horizons for the Regional Novel

British regional fiction saw its 'golden age' with the Brontës' fascination with Yorkshire's remote moorlands; with George Eliot's inquest into the spread of industrialization across the Midlands; and finally with Hardy's Wessex topology on which he plotted his fictions of attachment and estrangement, from Dorset north to Jude's romanticized Oxford, spanning a volatile region where rural traditions and communities are destabilized under the gathering storm of technological modernity – the provincial novel's 'golden age', according to Phyllis Bentley. Yet the canvass of Bentley's pioneering study of English regional prose from 1941 is broader than its favoured line-up of practitioners might suggest. Stretching from 1840–1940, her commentary also encompasses what she calls the capacious 'renaissance' of regional writing between the World Wars. The 1930s was a time of 'fresh impetus': in a period unprecedented for the novel's orientation towards international upheaval, such figures as Winifred Holtby and Storm Jameson wrote of the socio-economic deprivation and working-class unemployment in Yorkshire – a resurgence that affected style as much as setting.[1] Interwar women writers were interested not simply in appropriating the genre towards immediate polemical concerns, but also in mining a seam quite distinct from their predecessors. To novelists in the heyday of late-Victorian regionalism, the very idea of westerliness, of journeying westward out of Wessex, consolidated the equation of seclusion with civility epitomized by Devon and Cornwall – an equation at the heart of these counties' perceived immunity from the kinds of urbanization afflicting England's southeast corner.[2] As though countering the way south-western counties had become idealized as enclaves for vestigial traditions, writers at the latter end of Bentley's spectrum in the 1930s would invert that trajectory: northward they lead us, voyaging past the fortunes of East Anglian agriculture as recorded by Doreen Wallace in *So Long to Learn* (1936); past Walter Greenwood's impoverished Lancashire Cotton mills, and beyond – they convey us to where, 'under the hammer-blow of adversity', industrial depression had caused a whole population to become 'very conscious', as Bentley describes it, 'of the common human occupation on which we all depended, which linked us to our native soil' (*The English Regional Novel*, 37–8).

So conscious were they of these forces that 'linked' regional writers to the upheavals of their 'native soil', that by the 1970s British social historians were

frequently turning back to novelists of the industrial north as spokespersons
for provincial hardship. Cited in empirical research into economic fluctuations,
reduced to talking-heads for demographic patterns, read against the backcloth
of mining and manufacturing towns at a time when indigenous coal and steel
industries were coming under increasing threat – regional realists doubtlessly
sounded prophetic of the latter-day sea-changes to working-class livelihoods
wrought by the upsurge of Britain's free-market economy. Writers following the
generational impulses of 'Angry Young Men' as diverse as Angus Wilson,
Kingsley Amis and Alan Sillitoe, were hailed retrospectively as social documen-
tarians, prescient of a new and virulently divisive era of urban capitalism. As
D. J. Taylor remarks, although this strategy was 'convenient' for sociologists –
insofar as regional fiction offered a sort of affective archive, a literary plight
symptomatic of the need to raise public awareness of the effects of industrial
poverty – 'this kind of approach was highly injurious to the writers themselves'.
Despite the specificity of their respective polemical and stylistic concerns,
northern regionalists from the 1950s and 1960s found themselves 'turned into
a movement whether they liked it or not'. From Stanley Middleton and Alan
Sillitoe in Nottingham, further north still to encompass David Storey's *This
Sporting Life* (1960) and Stan Barstow's Cressley in *A Raging Calm* (1968), their
achievements became variously misrepresented as 'dramatised sociology'.[3]

One key metacritical lesson emerges from this use of realist literature merely
as an adjunctive, sociological resource, co-opted for the purposes of historical
revisionism. In what follows, I want to recover something of what realism's own
narratological evolution has meant for writers exploring alternative conditions
for provincial life. At once operating within while transgressing the criteria for
mimetic narration, Pat Barker and Adam Thorpe both offer an opening here.
Addressed together, they represent a subtle yet experimental advance for the
contemporary British novel, countering received notions of *the provincial* as a
term for habitats characterized by native insularity or regression. While later
sections of this chapter explore their respective techniques in some detail, I will
touch on their concerns throughout, since Barker and Thorpe epitomize the
capacious and innovative way in which postwar regional fiction has developed
in relation to British realism.

Regional realisms

Regional novelists have traditionally been regarded as devotees to a singular
heartland, whose geography seems unique unto its own climate of social and
economic change. Even while borrowing promiscuously from other fictional
modes, the genre today still partially substantiates this customary opinion of
its localized focus and nativist particularism. K. D. M. Snell notes how late-
twentieth-century regional fiction has retained strong attachments to the

specificities of a single town around which its narrative action orbits: detailing a 'region, whether urban or rural, which bears an approximation to a real place', as well as 'characters usually of working or middle-class origin'.[4] The replication of idiolect through direct speech had of course empowered the pioneering characterological innovations of Brontë, Eliot and Hardy. Dialogue was no longer merely functional for later Victorian writers. Instead, it was to be modelled phonetically, writes Snell, 'with some striving for realism; and attempted verisimilitude' (1). Pinpointing and conveying the essence of regional community life becomes here as much a matter of expressive ethnography as scenic depiction – as though rural locations require authentication by way of reported speech. Contemporary writers have refashioned these traits, however, transforming regional fiction's traditional tenets when utilizing the emphases of their nineteenth-century predecessors on social typification, dialectal imitation, or scenic portraiture. By heeding the point that '[e]ach age', as Edward W. Said reminds us, 'has its own method, or optic, for seeing then articulating reality',[5] postwar regionalists have elaborated on the stylistically and politically contingent nature of literary realism, enhancing the novel's imaginative engagement with specific social and ecological concerns.

Barker and Thorpe have become pre-eminent in respect of this formal revival. But it is worth remembering, nevertheless, that their contributions to historical fiction have spanned two particularly capricious decades for the fortunes of British realism. Shrewdly detached from the trends of avid metafictional innovation, Barker and Thorpe have played a crucial role in conveying the affective and intellectual bearing of local knowledges, customs and traditions. As such, they extend the impulse of contemporaries as formally diverse as David Storey and Jim Crace:[6] prophets of emplacement, these writers test but ultimately reciprocate a commitment to projecting 'microcosmic views' of the natural world, views that for naturalists such as Richard Mabey are vital for envisioning the possibilities of ecological salvation. Primed for detecting localized regeneration, these developed modes of viewing make for a new grammar of attention. And according to Mabey, novelists are now contributing to that grammar by discovering vigorous ways of enunciating the land, as it were, crafting spatial plots that delineate 'not just powerful metaphors, but actually the nano-bricks for rebuilding things'.[7] Symbolically and structurally, Barker and Thorpe have met the demands for this grammar of attentiveness at the level of narrative technique, performing a sparer means of registering the multifarious nature of local or enclosed climates. That Barker, for one, has retained a fidelity to English landscapes of the northeast has not prevented her from crossing the boundaries of form. Substantiating Peter Brooks's recent claim that 'realism more than any other mode of literature makes sight paramount',[8] Barker revives for a new century the nineteenth-century naturalist tradition of fastidious landscape portraiture while disclaiming the imperious degree of panoptical authority with which we might associate the venture of intrusive, and all-inclusive, social reportage. Indeed, her three founding novels are crafted in perspectival ways that consciously defy the reader's detection of a stable narratorial provenance. In effect, they afford no objective lens through which the landscape can be perceived. *Union Street* (1982) and *Blow Your House Down* (1984) – both subsequently reissued with *Liza's England* (1986) as a trilogy volume by Virago Press in 1996 – invoke a twin register of unflinching inquest and visionary illumination. These novels achieve a socioecological perspective at once polemical and parabolic of the kind that Thorpe elaborates for various characters across *Ulverton* (1992). Taken together, such writers reform and enrich our appreciation of the vibrancy of recent regional fiction by showing how the genre can operate in prophetic terms – not only for revealing the present constitution of provincial landscapes, but also for envisaging the transformation of everyday existence.

British realism, of course, has had as complex a genesis as the regional novel itself. Both terms have attracted prescriptive categorizations, terms often heavily freighted with value-judgements about the ideology of literary experiment. Such assumptions are so endemic that the specific role of mimesis in capturing regional landscapes requires searching analysis. Formal classifications are always susceptible to generalization, to the idea that 'realism of a kind is essential to all fictional modes'.[9] Indeed, while commenting here as a committed experimentalist in her own right, Christine Brooke-Rose contends that all novelistic discourse possesses mimetic pretensions of some sort, since literature's principal task is to 'mime' a version of the physical world it serves to dramatize through action, character's perceptions and personified setting. As a subsequent decade of criticism would reveal, the reaction to classic realism was not so much a denunciation of the purpose of mimesis in general; rather, it belied a tacitly ideological opposition among structuralists in the 1970s to the kind of impassive and polemically unreflective dictates of utilitarian prose, based on the assumption that realist writers aspire to an unmediated access to the real.

Clearly, making overemphatic claims about the realist novel's renewed powers of intervention today is still problematic. The evolving formal status and terminological definition of realism among the disciplines invites us continually to inspect the varying popularity of certain generic keywords. To chart the role of realist devices in regional fiction today knowing that their appointed classifications are themselves always *in process*, always open to refinement whenever we scrutinize our own preconceptions, remains crucial. Barker's use of third-person narration is exemplary in this respect: eluding any straightforward affinity with that model of the classic realist novelist striving for purely omniscient observations, ever measured, detached, yet unselfconscious when purporting to document the world of social struggle. From the outset of her career, Barker has recognized the ethical integrity of a voice enunciated with impersonal grace, keenly 'aware', she admits, of the extent to which a physical 'setting throws up an image system which is linked to the characters'.[10] Barker doggedly interrogates systemic injustice and poverty through the interior reactions of her allotted focalizers. This narratorial language amply satisfies Elizabeth Bowen's criteria for characterization based on 'perceptions, sense-impressions, desires' (*The Mulberry Tree*, 39). According to Bowen, writers 'must *materialize*' their characters, so that they are 'not only see-able (visualizable)' but expressively 'felt' (38). While in tune with Bowen's subjectivist emphasis on perceptual experience over exterior commentary, Barker herself not only substantiates Dominic Head's point that the 'literary-historical trend' of social realist novelists and playwrights from the 1950s and 1960s is 'longer term', as a heritage, than is so often assumed.[11] When recording provincial geographies, she also dramatizes the extent to which *provincialism* can represent a kind of ontological resource, a productive 'frame of mind', as Snell suggests. It is this strategy of reframing regional realities which so vividly combines the lyrical and reportorial elements in Barker's writing. It is a critical yet emotive strategy that reinvigorates realism's role in re-envisioning the spirit of local places.

A multitude of generic explanations thus accompanies the correlation of realism and regionalism through the contemporary scene. Its properties, its periodicity, its critical project – all are subject to how the regional novel has been measured in terms of its success as a mediator between tradition and provincial change, selfhood and social modernity. Said would no doubt encourage us to revisit Erich Auerbach's understanding of mimeticism as entailing a degree of performance: something of a literary correlative to a re-enactment of the real, comparable to the spirit of theatrical impersonation and metamorphosis. Alive to the way our corporeal, everyday selves pivot between contingency and design, opportunity and stricture, realist art stages the bringing-into-being or actualization of lived experience. Its manner of 'dramatic presentation' provides an occasion, writes Said, for 'staging the transmutation of a coarse reality into language and new life' (*Humanism and Democratic Criticism*, 101). In this appraisal, realism is seen to be a highly visual but also visceral medium, one that echoes Bowen's insistence on novelists dealing scrupulously with quotidian experiences, evoking them through characters' ordinary habits as a means of sensing, *and* reacting to, domestic environments. Auerbach's own mighty effort in *Mimesis* (1957) to advance a more diachronic account of the novel as a socially responsible and reformative mode advances the case for a realist aesthetic that can deal directly yet sensuously with the geography of everyday life.

Refreshing as these unlikely affinities between myriad theorists are, when they enrich our formal appreciation of realism's agility, they succeed at the risk of abstracting its political efficacy from context. For this is a mode whose fortunes have altered across time – nowhere more contentiously than in later twentieth-century Anglophone literaure. Such assumptions consolidated (because they indeed relied upon) the binary view that, in the wake of high-modernist fiction, mimesis and innovation had polarized into formally irreconcilable oppositions.[12] Yet similar forms of contention beset the conjunction of regional particularism and social realism: a sensibility and a genre that together comprise an inherently conservative novelistic mode. Smuggling in recessive fantasies of repair, bucolic literature responds to Jean Baudrillard's typically maudlin verdict that 'when the real is no longer what it used to be, nostalgia assumes its full meaning'.[13] When seen as a latter-day aesthetic solution to the pastoral lyric, rural realist fiction is beholden to a patently nationalistic cause.

The process of classifying genres, then, solely in terms of their putative audience and political pertinence can result in the legitimization of certain modes of 'literary fiction' at the exclusion of others. Fiction from and about the provinces, is equally vulnerable to derogatory preconceptions. When its polemical scope is thus confined to normative ideas of the provincial imaginary as bounded, parochial or largely insensible to the dialectic between local and national concerns, the regional novel emerges as an inherently conservative genre: at best, relevant to indigenous issues and local upheavals alone; at worst, tacitly reviving a host of purely regressive demands. Recent trends in postcolonial criticism have ambivalently consolidated the sense in which regional fiction is conflated with Anglocentric nativism. Canvassing the 'metonymic order of reasoning' underlying the imperial cartographies of John Stuart Mill's *Principles of Political Economy* (invoked by Said when turning to Jane Austen in *Culture and Imperialism*), Ian Baucom points out that the local – hence the regional – invariably connects to the 'contiguous territories' leading out to Empire's seemingly distant dominions. Spaces most emblematic of provincial Englishness thus resonate with those acquired under colonial jurisdiction. Hailed on this model as yet another type of 'region' under English authority, colonial territory loses specificity by becoming figuratively equated with 'little more than a suburb or outlying piece of countryside'.[14] Valuable as this template has been for historians of imperial conquest, following the exemplary work of Said and Homi Bhabha, its vocabulary risks replacing geographical actualities with topographical analogies, reinforcing visions of 'local' Britain as a homogenous enclave of agrarian sensibility. Granted, the melancholic reception of receding colonial sovereignty in the early twentieth century highlights the lingering legacy and salvific pledge of Anglocentric symbolism. But it is critically reductive, nonetheless, to recite the self-governing appearance of England's provincial counties as a native equivalent to the nineteenth-century governance of diasporic colonies – colonies conveniently pictured as an index of 'England's dominion', in Baucom's phrase, 'over the empire's more distant but imaginatively adjacent countryside' (169). To invoke uniform ideas of English pastoral sentiment in this way not only forecloses an analysis of the sentimentalized appeal of regions as timeless heartlands; it also runs the risk of reinstating the nostalgic celebration of pastoral regions as custodians of national decency. Such an approach neglects the idiosyncratic diversity of regional populations and, by extension, those writers who have refused to consolidate that simplified vision of provincial Britain as irrevocably under the duress of industrial modernity.

Paradoxically, then, this unwitting universalization of provincial climates in postcolonial thought can obviate the demographic and geopolitical complexities of regional environments. Despite their dense history, resilience and continuity, such districts fall prey to the same order of abstraction as 'the facts of empire' – those exotic terrains 'fantasized', as Said reminds us, by ethnocentric Victorian imperialists, for whom Archipelagic plantations were merely 'associated with sustained possession, with far-flung and sometimes unknown spaces, with eccentric or unacceptable human beings' (*Culture and Imperialism*, 75). One must be careful, therefore, to avoid the inadvertent rehearsal of these geographic essentialisms when reframing the poetics of native English territory: to avoid the tendency to apprehend regional fiction, past or present, as a naively mimetic aperture for relaying what is, in effect, a highly normative version of regional existence.

Writing in 1941, Phyllis Bentley pioneered a new way of addressing English regional fiction which offers us today something of an instruction. Her study is prescient of the problems of compiling an adequate picture of late-twentieth-century regionalism. What is remarkable about the way Bentley retraces practitioners across time is that she remains acutely aware of subjecting so open-ended a genre to the very procedures of classification in which her survey itself partakes. With this level of interpretative self-reflection, Bentley's commentary helps us not only to periodize the likely Edwardian and late-Modernist influences upon contemporary practitioners, but also to particularize the regional novel's most distinguished aesthetic qualities as a mode that broadens the horizons of literary realism. While concluding that the genre's 'transcendent merit is that of verisimilitude', Bentley took care to qualify her assertion, by highlighting the complex relationship between naturalism and local place. For her, the regional novelist typically displays

> A detailed faithfulness to reality, a conscientious presentation of phenomena as they really happen in ordinary life on a clearly defined spot of earth, a firm rejection of the vague, the high-flown and the sentimental, an equally firm contact with the real: these are the marks of the regional novel, which occupies in fiction the place of the Dutch school painters in art. (*The English Regional Novel*, 45)

Bentley's ensemble here of 'conscientious' traits sounds formidable; in a declarative cascade, her list of 'marks' aspires to infallibility. Yet in spite of the insistency of this catalogue, Bentley remains far from prescriptive. Initially, her criteria appears to suggest that we focus upon a regional writer's 'faithfulness to reality' when evaluating their depiction of a landscape's 'ordinary life'. But this shouldn't be our sole benchmark as readers. Instead, implies Bentley, surveying her selected corpus, all generic prescriptions should become working definitions. That is to say, our prior classification and subsequent judgement of regional fiction should be less about measuring the ability of novelists to replicate a landscape with mimetic precision, than about appreciating how far their use of narrational mimesis enables them to delineate the subtler complexities of rural life. Bentley's implicit suggestion is that realism might enable provincial novelists to achieve something that their metropolitan counterparts cannot – a conjunction of perspectives of the kind precluded from high modernism's defining preoccupations with alienated and entropic urbanism. In contrast to this urban mythopoeia, regional writing practices an unconfined, ex-centric focus, one that counteracts both the English modernists' attraction to the countryside as compensation, and that moves beyond that centrifugal nostalgia for residual traces of marginalized bucolic traditions.

This is the kind of re-visionary perspective endorsed by Pat Barker herself, who has committed, as we shall see later, to 'redressing the balance' where the rural imaginary is concerned: correcting the romanticization of idyllic landscapes by substituting transcendental symbolism with the conscientious depiction of actual social conditions ('An Interview with Pat Barker', 375). At the level of form, this corrective has been implemented by what she calls her fiction's 'compound eye' (379), a scopic mechanism that multiplies the focalizing provenance of her narration to forestall any dominating, panoptical portrait of space, complicating 'the countryside myth' as a stable, Edenic alternative to urban toil (376). By this pluralization of narrative perspective, indebted to predecessors as distinctive as Thomas Hardy and Storm Jameson, Barker pursues a critique of the countryside's susceptibility to mythologization. It is a pursuit that at once interrogates and expands the terms of geographical description, while showing that nativist traditions offer no simple remedies for urban resignation, no enclave for those disillusioned with the modern metropolis as an agent of cultural and spiritual renaissance. From this stance, contemporary regional novelists are hardly unselfconscious heirs of naturalism's cause. Indeed, they refuse to sentimentalize England's provinces, countering the compulsion to idealize rural integrity while evoking the historical density of such localized settings too-often assumed to be self-evident for appearing so secluded.

At the crossroads of native soil and narrative style

Realist strategies in regional writing past and present thus need to be re-evaluated. As Bentley's survey shows, there emerges in provincial fiction a complex yet neglected set of devices for particularizing place – for committing to 'a firm rejection of the vague'. Some pertinent narratological issues arise here as well, concerning the way regional writers navigate between factual and fabulous geographies, distinguishing landscapes of the mind from materially grounded questions of occupancy and local opportunity. For while restoring a more textured account of the stylistic capacities of contemporary realist fiction, we must also consider the extent to which readers evaluate what is 'real' or 'implausible' within any given novelistic setting. The assumption that the realist novel aspires to an unmediated or naïve reflection of our physical environment has disabling consequences. Jeremy Seabrook may be right in claiming that '[i]f the provinces exist now, they are social rather than geographic, a class rather than a place' ('The End of the Provinces', 241). Yet equally, it is crucial to navigate between pressing, demographically measurable changes to a certain location in time and a landscape's wider metaphysical or geopolitical resonance as it is projected by the literary imagination. As we shall see in Chapter 4, we need to remain aware of the distinctions between local settings and their aesthetic elaboration: retaining a sense that the collective ambitions of provincial or suburban populations, living in townscapes often considered peripheral in comparison to their metropolitan counterparts, may not be immediately pertinent for writers who adopt such local climates to dramatize universal concerns. Pat Barker's work calls attention to this fissure between addressing places in light of contemporary demands and re-imagining those same landscapes through the rhetoric of renewal. Like Rose Tremain, Maureen Duffy and Jeanette Winterson, who steer their historical fictions across actual geographies and their proleptic possibilities, Barker blends episodes of topographical realism with more parabolic modes of spatial representation. As Taylor has pointed out, the 'high realism' expected of British regional writers from Barstow and Middleton's generation, 'if worked at long enough and guarded against all extraneous influences, can turn out as stylised as anything in Firbank or Nabokov' ('When the North Invaded Hampstead', 26). And if 'there is one act of salvage', affirms Taylor, 'that ought to be performed in that tribe of 60s provincials', it 'is to stop their novels being regarded solely as pieces of sociological litmus paper, particularly as the sociology was always a great deal more complex than it looked on the surface' (26). No longer is it productive to think of regional space as a monochromatic palate of generic devices, a set of stock traits which writers enlist simply to enhance the authenticity or charm of settings on the metropolitan periphery.

The regional novel's subtlety today lies in its capacity to evoke the resilience of intimate familial and subjective relationships with local environments, without neglecting the impact of wider constitutional changes occurring on a national scale. Barker herself refuses to exploit the realist aspects of her fiction for purely mechanical or instrumental means. Instead, she admits to becoming increasingly conscious as her career progresses of 'the ethics of representation, rather than the ethics of action', and ever more 'concerned with the ethics of using real people' ('An Interview with Pat Barker', 370, 374). With this

heightened awareness, Barker has entered the province of her childhood to
ask whether 'the representation of the region has become slightly more posi-
tive', obligated as she is to 'redressing the balance' between honouring the
legacy of 'derelict areas' while highlighting their 'success' in securing latter-
day redevelopment schemes (375). Emphasizing the ethical premises of literary
realism in these ways has enabled Barker both to refract the social exigencies
under which provincial environments subsist *and* to project their potential for
self-regeneration. Processes of genuine revival are seen to supersede existing
practices of mere survival. Following Barker's example by refusing merely to
mime or anatomize the pressures under which working-class communities
have existed in the past, British regionalist novelists provide us with a more
sensuous, progressive, even optimistic engagement with the brute reality of
everyday spaces.

From early in Alan Sillitoe's career, the imaginative appropriation of
birthplace and its community proved to be a vibrant catalyst. To reanimate
Nottingham's landscape, Sillitoe developed a mode that combined realism and
impressionism, dramatizing the personal side-effects of a town's unstable socio-
economic fortunes. Yet if this was 'dramatised sociology', Sillitoe refused to
abstract the social relations between local people and native traditions in drawing out their universal significance. By refocusing his documentary lens in
luminous and visionary aspects, Sillitoe thwarted expectations of the regional
novel as an impassive record of working-class livelihoods. For many still his most
spirited and inspiring novel, *Saturday Night and Sunday Morning* (1958) shifts
vivaciously between modes in a manner infrequent in his later *oeuvre*. At successive points in this début novel, Sillitoe shadows Arthur Seaton returning from a
heavy night at the pub. On one occasion with Fred, though, after Arthur had
'suggested a short-cut home' the pair are almost run down by a speeding motor-
ist as they cross the road, 'each locked in his separate thoughts'.[15] The car halts,
its drunken driver emerging belligerent. Arthur swiftly retaliates. One punch
alone puts paid to the ensuing confrontation, before Fred joins him, 'locked a
revengeful act', to overturn the stranger's car. It is a moment of 'sublime team-
effort filling their hearts with a radiant light of unique power and value' (116),
and is soon the premise for a pivotal sequence in which Sillitoe's realism
suddenly changes gear. Their joint effort has taken its toll on both men; but
Arthur, exhilarated, 'did not notice the pain'. And in respect of the very genre
in which he serves as a protagonist, Arthur is more than a mere mortal – more
than the typical working-class hero. On the contrary, Arthur becomes a cipher
for Sillitoe's re-envisioning of Nottingham's surrounding region. Now that he
'felt more buoyant and mirthful and stocked with good spirits than for many
months' (116), Arthur walks away, euphoric from the fight. And this is the cue
for Sillitoe to wander astray with the novel's picaresque narrative. Gradually
extricating the point of view from this leading central character, Sillitoe frees

the novel from perspectivism in such a way that fundamentally changes the reader's perception of the regional townscape at its heart:

> The maze of streets sleeping between tobacco factory and bicycle factory drew them into an enormous spread of its suburban bosom and embraced them in sympathetic darkness. Beyond the empires of new red-bricked houses lay fields and woods that rolled on to the Erewash valley and the hills of Derbyshire, and as they entered the house they were talking about the pleasure of cycling to Matlock on the first fine Sunday in spring. (116–17)

Arthur's immediate experience now of walking home provokes a panoramic vision of a landscape, maternal and embalming, projected with a lyricism that seems quite distinct from Arthur's provenance. Even if, by the end of this passage, we can link the landscape back to Arthur (that spreading view over the county resolves his fractious evening by provoking him to anticipate 'the pleasure of cycling to Matlock'), for the majority of this sketch we are lead up and away from the pavement, accompanied by a voice-over whose persona is quite removed from the two men racing home. Sillitoe pans back, tracking across a Nottingham whose physiognomy he painstakingly maps as a resilient domain barely resisting the parasitic 'empires' of suburbia. For panorama facilitates polemic, too. Sillitoe offers an aerial interrogation of the uniformity of 'red-bricked' estates incurring upon his county's rural frontiers, crossing that other frontier between introspection and exteriority, from protagonist to place. The town-centre's 'maze of streets' locates his survey as it moves beyond Nottingham's horizon; local specificity thus embeds Sillitoe's broader critique, lending focus to that prospect-view he climatically assumes.

Sillitoe's imaginative geography works in a double-edged way here, voicing dual priorities which can be traced more generally as an aspect of the regional novel's stylistic evolution in recent years. As the passage above exemplifies, Sillitoe refuses to let his own sensuous prospect of that home-county sentimentalize the townscape it enframes. In embellishing the scenery in *Saturday Night*, he could have merely allowed the sheer *genius* of place, as Raymond Williams describes it, to remain the very making of that place;[16] by prescribing that kind of reverence, though, by enticing us to capture the genius of Nottingham's landscape in a mesh of provincial iconography, Sillitoe would have risked conveying the essence of this place in the 1950s but at the expense of social particularity. Instead, *Saturday Night*'s symbolism complements its scrutiny. Facing an epoch of modernization, Nottingham emerges with resolute precision; under Sillitoe's inspection, its vulnerability is never conflated with the rest of the nation's redevelopment. Oscillating instead between ambient atmospherics and frank dialogue, aerial depictions and street-level conversations, Sillitoe shapes a multivocal method for addressing the lived experience of urban planning and imminent change. Stephen Daniels and Simon Rycroft have noted that by retracing occult pasts alongside immediate socio-economic realities, Sillitoe's work evokes the sense that 'throughout Nottingham's history [. . .] outlaws and rebels sustained a local mythology of a clandestine underworld'.[17] They remark that Sillitoe's precise evocation of provincial traditions and their transformation has confirmed 'his grip on local topography, not just by returning to England, and occasionally to Nottingham, but by sustaining a documentary vision, not sliding from a strictly cartographic to a softly scenic idea of landscape' (268). Offering far from self-evidently *lisible* texts, then, Sillitoe combined verisimilitude with a more mythopoeic approach to visualizing everyday locations, synchronizing empirical and experiential journeys through space.

To me, this movement between two apparently distinct registers is how we might read Sillitoe's own outline for using narrative perception as a bifocal device. 'A sense of place for a writer', he suggests, 'also involves a sense of distance. He has to look at things under a magnifying glass, and from the sky as well.'[18] Equipped with this critical double vision, Sillitoe demonstrates how regional novelists might confront not only the aesthetic problem of writing about indigenous places without romanticizing them, but also the wider question of how to sustain native attachments in the face of rapid modernization. Of how to do justice to a landscape's history without eulogizing its irrevocable past is a task he addresses head on by avoiding the insidious transition from fiction into memoir. Sillitoe summons forth his own personal acquaintance with Nottinghamshire's cartography as a resource for articulating a prospective map of what the county could potentially become. In these parables of spatial attachment and anticipation, visual perceptions give way to intimations of progress, revealing the way such writers bring the exactitude of literary naturalism to the task of envisioning environmental renewal.

Pastoral allegories from Adam Thorpe

Actual and re-envisioned landscapes often merge in the regional novel in ways that complicate the genre's received affinity with documentary realism. In this respect, the synthesis of mimesis and mythopoeia seems essential to understanding how flexibly literary realism functions for contemporary writers as a vehicle for communicating environmental critique. Adam Thorpe's *Ulverton* (1992) is a rich example of this twofold impulse, working within an exclusively rural context. Throughout *Ulverton*, Thorpe invites us to think about the various ways we construct in our mind's eye that provincial scenery about which we read. In one late episode that I pursue in detail below, *Ulverton* thematizes the very intrusion of human perception upon a supposedly impartial documentary of countryside existence. With this self-referential manoeuvre, Thorpe isn't merely resorting to postmodernist devices for parodying the Bucolic tradition. As we shall see, with his nineteenth-century narrator he conjures a precursor to that Orwellian figure of the participant-observer, making us highly conscious of who is mediating the vision we receive of rural progress and environmental vulnerability. Highlighting there the aesthetic sensibility of his own intermediating narrator, Thorpe examines the way distinctive communities poised before impending cultural and geographical change, become romanticized by supposedly authoritative spokespersons enamoured by the countryside's pastoral charm.

On a purely formal level, *Ulverton* offers a set-piece in storytelling technique. Accumulating together an archive of monologues, drawing upon several generations of inhabitants from its eponymous village, Thorpe sustains a dizzying spectrum of idiolects across centuries from this single region. He returns to that region in *Pieces of Light* (1998), the setting this time of Hugh Arkwright's childhood house from where, 70 years on, he conjures the landscape of his adolescence in colonial central Africa. But it was Thorpe's debut novel which showcased his contribution to regional fiction as a genre that can combine ecocritical commentary with a moving, experiential account of place. Constructing the history of its eponymous village as an auditory record, *Ulverton* takes spoken language as something not simply to be transcribed into present-day vocabulary, but replicated lexically throughout its chronicle of village voices. For each of the novel's contrasting chapter-length testimonies, layout, rhythm and diction are brought into concert with one another. This harmonization of syntax, structure and spatial description offers a stylistic correlative for that literal harmony between mankind and nature that Thorpe positions on the brink of disintegration. While signs of domestic and agricultural modernization overtake the seasonal cycles of the land, Thorpe provokes reader to observe the changing ecological attitudes of his observers. We are made aware of how the difference between spatial modification and damage is dependent upon the way in which sceneries are communicated, refracted as they are by alternate characters' perceptions. *Ulverton* certainly exemplifies Snell's assertion that the 'regional dialect novel [. . .] treats language not only as representational, but as a living form integral and distinct to the people using it' (*The Regional Novel in Britain and Ireland*, 32). But Thorpe broadens the horizons further still for dialogue: what Snell described as the genre's 'striving for realism' when evoking speech becomes in *Ulverton* not so much relinquished as recalibrated for the task of replicating that idiolect's variations across time. And Thorpe's reflections on how his technique alters when writing radio-plays seem altogether apposite: 'Radio dialogue has to sound in the mouth, a symphonic pattern-making of offer and response. But the great challenge of dialogue – that it must not be voices in the head but in different heads – is the same whether in a novel or a play'.[19] Densely polyphonic, *Ulverton*'s narration resembles orchestration. Thorpe's account of provincial space becomes texturally contrapuntal, as he subjects the quaint depiction of pastoral unity to that disruptive process of 'symphonic pattern-making' – in effect, matching at the level of form the internal complexity of the rural scenery he describes.

Telescoped across time, Ulverton remains an idea as well as a place, playing host to obsolete hopes and aesthetic obsessions. While evoking a perennially shifting community and a picturesque idyll, Thorpe reveals the vital role that storytelling plays in preserving the indigenous knowledge of ecological processes. His village is a composite realm where social demands don't always synchronize with individual objectives. Dwelling and disenchantment uncomfortably coalesce, and Thorpe's successive oral testimonies turn the novel into a symphony on the pastoral theme of vulnerable provincial space. Together these testimonies drive outward, too: they have distinctly *aural* purchase upon the reader, each broadcasting something of the quintessence of Ulverton's rural geography. With unremitting pride, an eighteenth-century farm owner admits his perfectionism when it comes to attending his crop. Assured that his 'spring-corn field is in good tillage',[20] his visual survey turns inward, as the wintry landscape confirms his long-term investment:

> I rose early and walked it the length around as the church bell gave out the early service. It is my highest field and faces the village, which affords a view but is injurious to the crop as I am southerly to Ulverton. [. . .] This field had been of rye when I ploughed it with a narrow furrow before the first frost. I perceive that the winter has already shattered the furrows, these being narrow, and mellowed them out finely for the first harrowing. I received great pleasure from this observation of good practice. (46)

Knowing it only to be temporary, he overlooks the scenery's austerity, receiving it as a testament instead to human fortitude. So luscious and selfless are his observations of agricultural cycles, that their level of detail seems all the more a substitute for describing his wife's declining mental illness. While occluding little from his piecemeal diary of agricultural routine, he occludes the horror of his wife's growing vacancy. Only by way of spare interludes do we know that she 'walks at night' (68), and that the stress of farm labour has all but 'replaced' that distressing 'loadstone of husbandry' (69). This is surely one of the high points of *Ulverton*'s aural discourse: Thorpe intersperses naturalistic reportage with the irrepressible echoes of interior demands, personal to the speaker and only gradually disclosed.

And yet, as the centuries roll by, Thorpe adds a third, explicitly *visual* dimension to complement *Ulverton*'s oratory: the novel's sequence of *oral* testimonies conveying the landscape's *visual* reception thus build for to the reader into an acoustically rich register. This certainly marks Phyllis Bentley's own warning that '[d]ialect can, frankly, be a bore; apostrophes and misspellings are as difficult to a reader's eye as a ploughed field to his boots' (43). Instead the landscape itself offers its own vocabulary, its own texture for the characters to decipher. Animate, primal, entreating, Thorpe's setting, whether viewed near or at a distance, orients each character towards a triadic process of observation, introspection and testimony. This three-part manner of seeing and relaying the fortunes of rural space accompanies the speakers as they pass from outward perception to consider their own responsibilities towards the landscape. In this respect, *Ulverton* emphasizes the interdependency of natural history and human action, exposing the susceptibility of provincial settings to observers who feign the sentiments of documentary impartiality only to disseminate the landscape in generically pastoral terms.

In respect of his craft, then, Thorpe certainly heeds Hardy's advice from 1867, that the 'poetry of a scene varies with the minds of the perceivers' (*The Life and Work*, 52). The salience of Hardy's dictum is evident in Thorpe's critique of nature-mysticism, especially when we reach his loquacious photographer from the mid-nineteenth century. A kind of rural *flâneuse* alive to Ulverton's most precious charms, she professes a moral devotion to the more startling aspects of provincial existence. Such protean moments of wonderment appear as volatile as the industrial world from which this rural climate has receded. Hence this 'enthusiastic' observer practises the maxim that one 'must always be on the watch for Nature's tiny miracles: those effects which urban dwellers lack, and in their smoky habit grow dulled from, so that the soul remains unmoved by simple glories' (171–2). Hypersensitive to these surroundings, she pursues this environment's weaving together of rustic simplicity and primordial complexity against the timeless backdrop of agricultural routine. The perfect place to await those modest glories as secluded epiphanies is 'Surley Row, at the northern extreme of the village'. Pregnant with ancient significance, ripe for the 'instruction of a spiritual nature', though at first sight seemingly unremarkable, this outcrop 'presents, to the uninitiated observer,

> a most dilapidated and unattractive prospect. But it is in these areas that the photographic artist wanders with most reward: nothing more profoundly salubrious than an old stone wall, nothing richer than a bedraggled plum-tree, nothing more enticing than a raven's discarded feather, or a dust-filled barn spread with ancient sacks, or a pond wherein the weeds lie dank and idly swaying! For upon these surfaces lies a cornucopia of satisfying differences, that the lens, with its unavailing sincerity, and its unjudging eye, captures upon the plate with a fidelity of draughtsmanship the great Leonardo might have envied. (172)

Intensive specification here presides over summary observation. Local colour and affective discernment overtake the stipulative grammar of rural documentary, dissolving the vocabulary of topographical codification into a more personalized, impulsively accretive syntax of appreciation. Note the calculated reiteration of the negative ('nothing'); this euphonic reiteration of the noun serves a rhythmic purpose whose cumulative effect only becomes clear at the end of the passage where, building to a crescendo, the speaker's reverie reaches its finale. Pealing into polysyndeton, that lengthy series of alternate 'areas' offers an exhaustive list of those hypothetical prospects yielding 'most reward'. In the case of each listed perception, the word 'nothing' is cleft to the thematic head of the phrase. Decisive each time, they finally give way to the casual conjunctive: our narrator's racy use of 'or' reflects her eagerness for a word more directly evocative of her sentiment towards Ulverton's richness. It's as though by cataloguing examples of what makes this enclave so rich, the narrator is impatient for us to be convinced by a scene whose beauty requires an act of 'unavailing sincerity' to which only photography can do justice. Thorpe's list gives the effect of accelerating artistic ravishment: his speaker relishes the possibility of not only discovering, but mimetically replicating for all time, one of those treasured sites of 'most reward'. Thorpe here suggests through his rather prolix outsider a more important entreaty, at once ecological and ontological – about the *affects* that come with seeing and being in the countryside. Someone alien to local custom, the photographer contests that her discovery of the rural scene is frequently epiphanic, if not redemptive. As she 'wanders' she affirms that only with felt-experience, with an 'unjudging eye', can we encounter the landscape 'with most reward' as it emerges from such a seemingly 'unattractive prospect'. As the documentary trope of the camera-eye assumes literal form in this episode, Thorpe offers a meditation on his own use of genre. The metaphor of the lens captures here the precise reality of a now-vanishing scene from Ulverton's past and the historical moment of its sensorial apprehension. Thorpe calls into question the reporter's desire for unmediated verisimilitude. With its 'cornucopia' of external surfaces, with its blend of the contingent and the particular, the volatility of the novel's regional setting answers back at the photographer's fallacious thoughts of preserving rural seclusion for all time.

In this self-reflexive respect, *Ulverton* certainly inherits Storm Jameson's sentiments for reshaping narrative form, syntax and diction in an interwar age of literary documentary: 'As the photographer does, so must the writer keep himself out of the picture while working ceaselessly to present the *fact* from a striking (poignant, ironic, penetrating significant) angle'. What Jameson applauded was a writer's ability to capture the social conditions of a place without adornment, focusing on the landscape by a 'seizing of the significant, the revealing word. The emotion should spring directly from the fact'.[21] Thorpe extends this aesthetics of snapshot and seizure, when tracing the susceptibility of Ulverton to intrusion by outside individuals and by industry. The narrative itself seizes upon the significance of rural experience through isolated monologues, confessions and amatory letters, anguished and vituperative in what they disclose or recollect. And the novel's stylization enables its author-figure to 'keep himself out of the picture' of a village becoming an increasingly vulnerable realm. That is to say, Thorpe withdraws, allowing Ulverton, as a community of voices, to speak for itself. By virtue of his withdrawal, Thorpe inspects from afar, as it were, concealed behind *Ulverton*'s testimony register, while his speakers assume their own postures and standpoints.

Thorpe's photographer sets the precedent for such a self-assumed stance of perceptual authority. Blending pastoral portraiture with sentimental introspection, she aspires to a viewpoint on high ground from which Ulverton's peripheral countryside emerges as a hallowed landscape. And Thorpe's concern with perspective here historicizes the very device he deploys. To the enlightened aristocrat with accessible leisure time for adventures onto high ground, it was this kind of open-field prospect which lent something sublime to rural parishes. Margaret Drabble remarks that when re-recorded in writing, the breathtaking experiences afforded by commanding such an elevated viewpoint often results in a place's specificity being subjected to 'effortless profusion, in a gracefully blended mixture of generality, precise location, well-chosen compliment, and patriotic self-congratulation'.[22] Inherited from the Romantics' fascination with rural panoramas, such traits are kindred to Thorpe's photographer, marvelling at Ulverton's rustic particulars in a manner that allows her to marvel at their resolution onto film:

> Until the impossible is gained – and the myriad colours of the universe are arrestable likewise on our silvered plates – we must be content with the play of light and shade, the infinitesimal tremble of texture and tone in a moment's grace, the unencumbered beauty of Nature's pen that brings through our lens, as a richly-laden camel through the eye of the needle, her unsurpassable artistry. (178)

The effort to replicate Nature's inimitability is entertained as a valiant one. And the narrator soon compromises her negative capability with a scenic portrait that builds into mannerism: at once self-depreciating as witness to the sublime wonders of natural processes, while gesturing to her gift for transcribing personal perceptions of the landscape into an authoritative archive. Thorpe takes great pleasure in ironizing this self-contradictory appropriation of the prospect-view. By the very act of self-congratulating wonderment, the narrator asserts herself as professional parasite. By declaring her pretensions to do justice to the natural universe, she also dictates the terms for other aspiring Naturalists seeking her level of mimetic expertise – the terms she awards to herself for attempting 'the impossible' with 'silver plates', for ambitiously embracing the frontiers of documentary technology.

At this later stage in *Ulverton*'s procession across time, Thorpe thus stages and ironizes the imperious appropriation of prospect-visions. Ulverton's surroundings certainly lend themselves to sublime appreciation. J. M. Coetzee has found

it 'worth stressing that, as the word *landscape* is both topographical and
aesthetic in its reference, the word *picturesque* refers to nature and art at the
same time, that is, to physical landscape conceived of pictorially'.[23] Thorpe
elaborates upon this distinction in the 'Shutter, 1859' episode, where the
landscape is seen to attract the languor of Romantic appraisal. By reviving
this sensibility, Thorpe's narrator restores to a position of artistic relevance
and debate the very task of doing justice to picturesque prospects in an advancing age for photographic technology. That debate, of course, can spring only
from personal refinement, mainly conducted 'On fine summer days of good
light' when

> nothing pleases better than to wrap up my machine in brown paper, leaving
> but a slit for aperture, and wander the Village and its environs for human subjects
> that may be caught without the formality of response, that considered design and
> self-conscious air, that the posed picture erstwhile involves. (169)

Spying here is a prerequisite for mimetic reportage, for capturing those in the
community unawares, all-in-the-moment – for capturing, in effect, the essence
of local life in a flawless freeze-frame. As in the previously cited episode, we
might note her strategic insistence on 'nothing' – that blank slate of regional
expanse, upon which the talent of the observer depends on making *something*
out of *nothing* in the course of capturing an idyllically 'posed picture'.

The episode retrieves for us a key moment from the history of artistic perception itself, both as an attitude sensitive to the sublime, and as a series of
conventions to be perfected when bearing witness to rural landscapes. Many of
these conventions Thorpe appropriates throughout *Ulverton* for self-reflexive
purposes. Over the epochs he spans, he shows how, after 'long generations of
observing', as Williams noted, 'the moment came when a different kind of
observer felt he must divide these observations into "practical" and "aesthetic"'
(*The Country and the City*, 120–1). Thorpe's photographer certainly embodies
the traits akin to what Williams calls the 'self-conscious observer'. Self-
consciousness became an object of acclaim; and if the aesthete of the picturesque
could claim it with 'sufficient confidence he could deny to all his predecessors
what he then described in himself, as "elevated sensibility"' (121). This sensibility, however, confers an authority upon the viewer to which our photographer
might not otherwise aspire. That is, she assumes a role usually reserved for the
professional male connoisseur of pastoral iconography; yet the agency this
implies is gained largely by impersonation. Enthralled by her own capacity to
synthesize pleasure and detachment, she adopts a rather imperious set of
criteria for the ideal rural view:

> You may wonder why it is I have no human interest in this picture – no weary
> pilgrim leaning against the tree, or plodding his hedge-shadowed way. It is

imperative to remember that a human interposition subsumes any sublime feeling in a work; there is a kind of sublime melancholia, I suggest, here present, that arises out of the suggestiveness of a presence just around the corner, or about to come into view – for no road is made for anything other than human passage. If that passage be absent, as here, how pure and clean becomes the metaphor! The spectator is drawn towards his own destiny, in which no one truly shares but our watchful Creator. (173–4)

Cleanliness, unblemished and unadulterated Nature, remains the order of the day for achieving the perfect portrait on film. What is altogether significant is her unhesitating invocation of the male pronoun, when imagining how a model-spectator would be 'drawn' into a state of enchantment by a landscape devoid of human presence. In no other way, it seems, can she relish such a masculinized way of observing the natural world, something that in a social environment she would find so discriminatory.

Thorpe charts the ethical implications of this desire for eliminating 'human interposition' from a regional landscape. He uncovers that 'massive discrepancy', as Robert Macfarlane calls it, 'between perception and practice. British parochialism – its strong tradition of interest in the local – leads too often only to general conclusions: to a comfortable sentimentalism'. Something of that sentimentality encroaches upon Thorpe's photographer, whose reeling admiration reminds us 'that wonder is not an automatic guarantor of care'.[24] By declaring herself humbled before Nature's 'unencumbered beauty', the speaker of 'Shutter, 1859' betrays her own false modesty. Gushing self-documentary says more about the perceiver than about the historical specificity of the scenery perceived, so overbearing is that compulsion to 'draw the reader's attention to the minute particulars in our surroundings – whether they be rustic or urban – that serve the photographer so efficaciously' (175). With this cycle of surveillance – increasingly watchful of what it means to watch – Thorpe's photographer deprives herself of vacant fascination, deriding those inattentive to Ulverton's 'minute particulars', only to take pride in her being the first one to highlight the region's vulnerability:

This, then, is the only evidence, dear reader, of all the bustling and moisture and thirst and singing that is harvest-time – but how poignant, how much more poignant, this evidence! And for how long will this precious spill – for precious it is indeed, in the thrifty world of the countryside – be allowed to lie in the dust, to be trampled into oblivion by hooves and cart-wheels? (176)

The posturing rural archivist here reveals a slim threshold indeed between impassioned activism and self-pleasuring aestheticization. Thorpe's narrator initially masquerades as a disinterested source of incontrovertible information about the scenery she records. Yet plate by plate, community ceremonies, such

as harvest-time, protrude into the landscape she initially cherished as an
unpopulated wilderness. While local people serve as a brute reminder of the
progress that befalls them, their 'precious' relationship with the natural world
is obscured by the way they are rendered 'poignant' by the photograph – their
singularity sacrificed to sentimentality. The scenario ultimately affirms Susan
Sontag's remark that a given 'landscape doesn't demand from the spectator his
"understanding", his imputations of significance, his anxieties and sympathies;
it demands, rather, his absence, it asks that he not add anything to *it*' (*Styles of
Radical Will*, 16). Through the 'imputations' and vocal intrusions that charac-
terize his narrator as a participant-observer, Thorpe reveals a subtle duplicity
about her ornamental use of spatial perception. For here, his photographer
confides in the reader not so much a sense of repugnance towards the landscape's visible decline as her motive to extract from Ulverton's topography only
those scenes that can be romanticized as sublime.

What Thorpe achieves here with this intersection of place, perception and
representation is tantamount to allegory, though in a crucially twofold respect.
Ulverton doesn't simply dramatize the impossibility of synthesizing immediate
realities and bucolic ideals, environmental judgements and universal lessons.
Visions of Ulverton's scenery are integrated into our narrator's vocabulary, as
though the complexity of rural life cannot be grasped on its own terms, only
when translated into an enraptured voice-over. Thorpe allegorizes what this
fault line between vision and voice, seeing and knowing, might entail for how
the countryside is relayed and understood. Implanting in the mind of his rhapsodic narrator a volatile dissociation of ambient appreciation and rigorous
documentary, Thorpe raises implications about the way rural places with uncertain futures are described in the present – particularly when description itself is
superseded by the quest for posterity: 'bid adieu to our English village, slumber-
ing on in its quiet valley, far from the city and its peculiar wants' (182). And in
this key episode, *Ulverton* consolidates the critical currency of contemporary
regional fiction. It explores how the efforts of photography to evoke 'the rich
tilth of an unrecorded history' (182) can end in the manipulation of a landscape into primeval mythology. Thorpe's photographer swerves between
spontaneous snapshots and their calculated selection, ultimately favouring
her archive as 'evidence' of what Ulverton stands to lose to the forces of industrialization. An inevitable solemnity thus intones her romanticism. Solemn, too,
is that disunity between the countryside's present-day radiance and its 'poignant' representation in plates that seem set to form a book of remembrance.
And by beginning with this disunion, Thorpe follows the journey of Ulverton's
regional landscape from material existence to idealized essence. Even as he
gestures, then, at the possibility of democratizing the sublime, Thorpe alights
on this tension between sentimentality and development. Forever in danger of
becoming a memorial to an irrevocable age, his chosen setting is marked by
the depletion of ecological self-subsistence. Thorpe implies that our perception

of rural civilization may arise from a variety of representational sources and cannot be reduced to a single, essentializing account. Yet his pastoral allegory also carries the warning that certain embellished visions of regional landscapes still have the power to direct both our understanding of the countryside and of those living within its rapidly evolving boundaries.

Pat Barker's landscapes of illumination

If landforms in the contemporary novel are forever disrupting the dividing line between the way figurative and historical spaces are perceived, they promise to disrupt in turn the theoretical preconceptions with which realist fiction has conventionally been valued. Provoking the reader's cognitive and intuitive response, narrative perception can operate, as we have seen, as a modal device bound up with characterization itself – as integral to *how* a scene is coloured as it is to *what* is conveyed within the actuality of that scene. Pat Barker is situated among a growing body of writers who highlight the broader ethical demands of re-imagining this landscape of common life, while remaining receptive to the discrete conditions under which new social habitats are forged. Alerting her readers to alternative means of self-recognition in everyday spaces, Barker alternates mimesis and visionary prediction, offsetting stark reports of local necessity with panoramic visions of possibility. Her fiction recoils from the piecemeal detailing of interior décor when passing from one narrative location and the next, recoiling from what Roland Barthes considered traditionally to be realism's most rudimentary services: its blank exhibition of domestic routine, its 'ornamental' process of conjuring 'a felicitous backcloth against which the act of thought was thrown into relief'.[25] While her work therefore spotlights the uniqueness of provinces that seem 'bounded, enclosed and self-reliant', in Seabrook's phrase ('The End of the Provinces', 241), she also explores burgeoning kinships with places attuned to those circumstances under which local landscapes might productively evolve.

Engaging with regional settings in this manner, Barker creates a network between the social world and its latent potential, allowing visionary techniques to liberate her fiction from the bounds of geographical verisimilitude. Moreover, her focus on the intimate intersection of between the interior stability of the home and its populated surroundings complicates her status as a chronicler of domestic oppression. Sharon Monteith is right to assert that 'Barker has never been an uncomplicatedly realist writer, despite the temptation for early reviewers to term her novels "gritty social realism" without delving beneath the surface expectations of such epithets'.[26] Optical devices for scenic framing, spectacle and tabulation greatly extend the contemporary realist novel's capacity for environmental critique, aiding its sensory recording of spatial gradients and distances. And together with this fusion of mimesis and mythopoeia, observation and fabulation, recognizing this visual rhetoric in Barker's writing is essential to comprehending how pervasively she, like Sillitoe, re-engineers the investigative *and* affective dynamics of nineteenth-century naturalism.

This is the heritage borne by contemporary writers as they redevelop regional fiction into a genre for articulating familial, ethical and ecological concerns. Though her topographies often appeal beyond their boundaries to universal scenarios, Barker has conceded that to evoke empirical settings entails certain perspectival restrictions. Writers can only attain a partial record of the social environments they scrutinize, not least in Britain, where 'regional dialect and working-class origins go together' ('An Interview with Pat Barker', 374). Encompassing those excluded from personal property or prosperity, Barker allows the scope of her enquiry to breathe. By modulating from social realism to a visionary register for imagining the city otherwise, *Blow Your House Down* exemplifies an impulse running throughout Barker's work: achieving a balance between material places and their interior reception by controlled transitions in tone. Moving between documentary and subjectivist modes of narration, the novel lays claim to a spiritual sense of locality, one that insists that a place's redemption lies residual amid the mundane, awaiting the attentive onlooker.

While Barker's topographic depictions never entirely dispense with social realism, she does complement Robert Macfarlane's warning that 'the natural world becomes far more easily disposable if it is not imaginatively known, and a failure to include it in a literary regard can easily slide into a failure to include it in a moral regard'.[27] Her impulse has been to revive perception as a vehicle for making landscapes known through the imagination: that which her characters gradually perceive, Barker then expands upon, an expansion articulated without authorial interjections. Stressing this intersection of interior subjectivity and physical scenery, she hearkens to Raymond Williams's suggestion that the 'novelty of the naturalist emphasis was its demonstration of the *production* of character or action by a powerful natural or social environment'.[28] Writers who refuse to consolidate these regressive images of provincial life under threat or only visible as a scene of poignant decline offer, in Williams's pioneering view, a 'radically distinct' regional poetics, one that searches the landscape for indications of embryonic yet heterogeneous prosperity. Such novelists share Barker's interest in the imminent progression of rural topographies, likewise eschewing the assumption that realism itself amounts only to stale typification, or ahistorical 'exemplifications of "permanent" human characteristics in an accurately reproduced natural or social "setting"' (*Problems*, 127). In *Blow Your House Down*, Barker is careful to dispute realism's perceived tendency to reduce topography to typicality. Instead, through precise inflections of grammar, syntax and diction, she primes her provincial setting with a new vocabulary for envisioning change.

Blow Your House Down culminates with the ecological coexistence of natural and urban forces within a single regional place. In this regard, Barker echoes Paul de Man's remark that the 'delicate interplay between perception and imagination could nowhere be more intricate than in the representation of the natural scene'.[29] *Blow Your House Down* creates an intriguing symbiosis between immediate perception and proleptic illuminations. What is truly admirable, though, is that despite this elevating, panoptical register, despite her reach towards lyricism and figurative abstraction, Barker never dissociates her narrative from everyday experience. Initially, we shadow Maggie closely as the last member among the novel's cast to whom Barker returns. Periods spent walking spell intimations of recovery, of the chance to re-embed herself in an urban fabric untarnished by regrets that belabour her memories:

> She tried, on these walks, to keep her mind clear: not think, not question, not remember. Sometimes she succeeded and then she brought back images of another reality. Black, untidy birds, rooks, she thought, or they might have been crows, she was too far away to tell, blown across the sky like scraps of burnt paper.[30]

On this occasion, however, Maggie's retrospection subsides as the 'hill rose to a crest'. Her eye is drawn out across the urban sprawl, austere and uneventful, from which she desires so pervasively to escape:

> She looked back the way she had come and saw the whole countryside smudged in the rain, yellow and green and brown all running together into grey, like the colours of a child's painting after the water has been knocked over. (167)

By virtue of this indistinct view, drawn down towards a confluence of spaces, the landscape suddenly re-emerges with renewed definition. From a scene of necessity it morphs into a sphere of promise, as she 'walked to the top of the hill from where she could see the whole city spread out before her' (168). Solitary now, without sanction, Maggie experiences an astonishing sense of elevation over a city rendered uncannily strange. A panoramic version of the existing landscape is irradiated with sunlight now breaking through cloud:

> But then, as she watched, the ridge of black cloud lifted a little, and suddenly there were rays of light, or rather great shafts of golden light, falling onto the city, which looked now like an island raised up out of the sea, for there were still inlets of rain and mist in the surrounding fields.
> This was not the city she knew: back streets, boarded-up houses, the smell of blood in a factory yard. And yet it was the same city. She watched the columns of

light move over it, until the cloud thickened and the veils of rain closed around it once again. (168)

Recast 'as she watched', the scenery thus counteracts its preconceived image as a streetscape deprived of fortune. The city unveils redeeming capabilities about which Maggie earlier 'knew' nothing. Her bird's-eye view synthesizes monumentality with ambitions on a local scale: promoting a broad-reaching, visually sublime prospect in contradistinction to the community's abjection at large that deflates personal hopes of repair.

Barker is not simply indulging here in what Gérard Genette has called a 'new magic of the faraway', whereby the writer compensates for a landscape's depredation by drawing out its picturesque elements, elements made 'at the same time closer and more distinct' against a grimy urban backdrop.[31] Something about Barker's choice of diction counteracts this impulse: something about her restrained use of adjectives, her avoidance of simile – as though denying herself the luxury of authorial adornment – shows her refusal to romanticize this otherworldly prospect to which the city has been 'raised up'. Barker's cumulative ignition of spatial images relies less on assertion than it does upon suspense. Landform and atmosphere alike are conveyed in a manner that seems only reticently decorative: a manner whose fidelity is to a scene that invites fabulous embellishment, making Barker, as a stylist, sound all the more judicious and self-effacing. Rather than adorn physical space with intrusive metaphors, she lists the city's all-too familiar characteristics ('back streets, boarded-up houses, the smell of blood in a factory yard'), announcing them in a plosive catalogue that is made to seem irrelevant before the delicacy of the weather's intervention. It's as though this sentence bristles with adjectives of decay that are no longer substantiated by the sun-smattered cityscape. Maggie's list of accumulated, day-to-day memories, drawn from the grime she witnesses like a routine, can only be attributed to 'the city she knew', not the place now coming into view. It is a list of facts suddenly made to seem fallible: memories of neglect are temporarily deposed, as the 'same' landscape from which they are recalled is recast in 'columns of light'. Barker's lyricism surpasses reportage, appealing to visionary insight but without jarring against the verisimilitude elsewhere in her novel. Balancing, therefore, what seem like contrary conditions of seeing, she carefully indulges in style itself to contest the landscape's corrosion – rekindling urban space with a lush, suasive language of invigoration.

In deploying this spare and sustained mode of description, Barker is not asking us to 'dwell beyond the boundaries of space or life', in de Man's phrase (*The Rhetoric of Temporality*, 132). Neither does she in an exclusively materialist sense revive naturalism's 'transitional phase', as Williams outlines it, when the 'presentation of a specific environment' became merely 'symptomatic or causal' (*Problems*, 130). Instead, Barker encircles the present and the possible, acquiescence and speculation, within a single event where space supports what is half-formed in the perceiver's mind, and where the spatial climate reinforces a latent need to act on personal intuitions. The beauty of a single 'moment only' professes the fragility of Maggie's recovery; yet it also shows that '[t]o understand the city', as Joseph Rykwert insists we must, 'as a dynamic and three-dimensional figure, to follow and inflect its process of self-regeneration, to knit and extend its fabric requires a humane discipline, an understanding of how built forms are transformed into image by experience'.[32] This is a notion I explore over the course of Chapter 4, where we shall see just how crucial the landscape of ordinary life has become for writers concerned with the interrelation of memory and place. For what makes the panorama Maggie achieves so precious is that it frees her from the citadel of habitual scepticism, facilitating a perception of everyday scenery as a sphere of productivity rather than paralysing resignation. It motivates her towards sustaining and personalizing a process of rediscovering the city's hidden vitality.

Barker's environmental and metaphysical registers, then, are intimately bound up with the physicality of her settings. She fuses psychological realism together with a vivid, topographical tracking of the landscape's emergence from wintry hostility. Amid this climate of revival shared by character, mode and setting, Barker never entirely relinquishes her topographical mimesis. Instead, she favours what Ernest Bloch describes as 'artistic illusionism': that 'visible anticipatory illumination' of the material world through the symbolic expression of sensory perception.[33] For Barker, the contemporary regional novel is well capable of hosting these twin aesthetic functions. Likewise, *Blow Your House Down* also aspires to that 'firm rejection of the vague' that Bentley finds so crucial to literature's engagement with provincial environments in all their complexity. Certainly by 'concentrating on a particular part, on a particular region', Barker 'depicts the life of that region in such a way that the reader is conscious of the characteristics which are unique to that region and differentiate it from others in the common motherland' (*The English Regional Novel*, 7). The actual region itself, of course, need not be littered with verifiable place-names. And Barker is less interested in labelling landscapes in her work (merely in order to condemn their industrial decline) than on recuperating such places through the imagination, chronicling what it means for us to know 'a particular region' anew.

This dual-focus on personal and ecological renewal is one for which Raymond Williams himself set new standards in *Border Country* (1960). His protagonist Matthew Price returns from London to his family home in Wales to find his father gravely ill, a switch between settings that intensifies the novel's use of interior perception. This bipolarity between metropolitan centre and marginal heartland seems as far-reaching for the mind as it has been for the nation at large. From his position as an émigré obligated to fulfil a belated home-coming, Matthew arrives once more at the deserted train station of his youth in anticipation of having to 'walk the five miles north to Glynmawr',[34] recalling how 'much of the memory of this country was a memory of walking: walking alone, with the wind ripping at him; alone it seemed always, in memory, though not in fact' (14). Hiking is an everyday necessity here; and Williams utilizes this mobile perspective as a device for engaging autobiographically with the landscape, personalizing the comparison of urban and rural topographies by allowing Matthew to compare the social changes to the Welsh valleys with that of London as a cityscape now relegated to recent memory. It's through this comparative use of settings that *Border Country* prefigures that 'emphasis on the landscape as a personality' which Barker herself considered fundamental to her later novel, *Double Vision* (2003). In this novel's secluded community in northern England, characters find little salvation in withdrawing into solitude. And in Barker's own words, *Double Vision* 'undercut[s] the English pastoral myth – the Forest of Arden – that the rural retreat is inevitably healing'.[35] The insularity of her setting speaks for itself, declaring the psychological perils facing those characters content to recede within its provincial bosom. Barker solicits our anticipation of rupture: her glacial narratorial repose at the outset provides only a discursive calm before the storm, a premonition of later stages in the text, when stark memories begin to quiver for her two protagonists beneath the seeming tranquillity of the novel's 'rural retreat'. Henceforth, Barker ruptures this setting with the recollections it incites; a serene landscape is violated by flashbacks distracting those who survey its pastoral expanse. Under this principle, *Double Vision* heralds the return of one of Barker's earliest devices. As Sharon Monteith describes it in relation to Barker's younger fiction, she

> [c]umulatively builds a sense of character and context from the inside out. One clear narrative strategy is to move out from the home to wider social relations, but Barker never strays far from the interior lives of her subjects; their anxieties and thwarted aspirations leak into even the most descriptive passages. (27)

Barker's agile negotiation between locations and the intellectual reflections they provoke carries shows her keen awareness of how to manipulate a full range of narrative perspectives without diminishing landscape description in a welter of perceptions. Of the *Regeneration* trilogy, she recalls in an interview with Monteith how the 'seemingly simple question' of presenting perception becomes far from self-evident once the writing process begins: 'Point of view is important and the character I focused on when first conceiving of this possible story had much more space within the setting and was much more central to it' (28). This is why we rarely encounter authorial interjections about social space in Barker's work: from one location to the next, she refuses to let exterior commentary upstage those directly participating within the environment in view.

For Barker, this level of vocal restraint is crucial. Always technically demanding, she devotes herself to perspectivism: giving short shrift to exterior commentaries that can only offer landscape descriptions from an imperious distance, or offer proleptic interjections about events yet to take place. As she admitted to John Brannigan, this restraint has compelled her to 'sever the cord' between implied author and focalizer, lest 'something of me might slip in and contaminate the character' ('An Interview with Pat Barker', 378). Yet in light of this commitment, Barker's epilogue to *Blow Your House Down* is peculiarly interesting. Following on from Maggie's journey across town, as '[s]he walked every day now and her walks took her further and further away from the city' (163), the increasingly sonorous episode offers an exceptional instance of Barker taking the initiative to intrude – stepping into the action to convene the novel's closing scene. At this late stage, the landscape once more becomes a crucible for anticipatory illuminations, as Bloch called them. In the novel's concluding sequence, Barker traces a series of limpid impressions of the city:

> There is a moment in every evening when the streets of the city are dark although the sky is still light, almost as if the darkness is exhaled as a vapour from the pavements and cannot reach the sky. At this moment the starlings come. (169)

Barker's initially gnomic commentary gradually diminishes. Tonally, the coda's declarative opening soon attenuates, as might daylight eventually subdue with the settling dusk:

> The sky flames. Then, gradually, as the birds continue to descend, the red gentles through purple and gold to rose, until at last every bird is lodged, and the singing dies away. (170)

The dulcet use of 'gentles' as a verb imputes an audible hush after the concision of 'red', adding a lulling caesura before those consecutive snapshots build up across the passage. Grammatically, too, 'gentles' serves its assonantal sentence as a performative: given the context of what its host phrase is describing about the diminution of the skyline's 'flames', the word 'gentles' works onomatopoeically with the trailing sound of its conjugated syllable. Evoking tonally the very action it denotes, the sibilant of 'gentles' peals across the decelerating sentence, until coming to rest on Barker's succinct and clinching use of 'rose' – a final predicate for the state into which a whole sky has quelled. For now her stage is set. There is a marked sense of anticipation no longer marred by that unremitting tension, hitherto so prevalent amid the novel's household settings:

> Above the hurrying people, above the lighted windows, above the sodium orange of the street lamps, they hump, black and silent; unnoticed, unless some stranger to the city should happen to look up, and be amazed. (170)

This crepuscular scenery moves us because it seems so fleeting, even vulnerable. This illuminated depiction intervenes at this late stage in the novel as a singular, arresting event. Predominantly visual, the episode nevertheless intensifies our relationship to syntax itself. For Barker's ocular mode arrives like something rare and unprecedented in the context of the novel's prevailing realism. Her customary concision, epitomized elsewhere in the narrative by her reportorial snapshots, modulates here into impressionism. It offers a linguistically innovative move, one that seems as fleetingly creative as the scene it evokes, suspending the descriptive brevity prevailing for the text up to this point. Barker's repetition of the word 'above' protracts her series of conditional clauses like a mantra – collectively elevating, their euphonic iterations perform the very impetus to gaze skyward that they describe. Matching Sillitoe's capacity for aerial panoramas that reveal the embedded histories of immediate spaces, Barker's scene-sketch imposes itself urgently upon the reader as an onlooker observing an ordinary world rendered unknown. Stimulating without prescribing, the episode implies that substantive possibilities do persist amid everyday spaces even if they pass too easily 'unnoticed'.

As readers, then, we're frequently summoned to partake in the parabolic aspects of regional fiction. Writers like Barker and Thorpe, extending the work of Williams and Sillitoe, imply that alternative spaces remain latent yet inferable amid the demands of the present, spaces which seem imperceptible to those who greet their local environments with cynical disenchantment instead of spirited engagement. Barker's own distinction among other regional novelists today lies in her navigation of the legacy of British social realism from the 1950s and 1960s, while building on the assets of a much earlier paradigm of landscape approximation by inheriting a Naturalist aptitude for texture and scale. By lucidly stressing the ecological bases upon which workaday habitats operate and evolve, she lends support to Salman Rushdie's recent claim that 'fiction does retain the occasional surprising ability to initiate social change',[36] framing new versions of existing topographies as a challenge to inattention, ignorance or careless pessimism. And by using the language of perception to embellish and irradiate events which seem at first so ordinary, Barker gives something remarkable back to the landscape of everyday life.

Chapter 3

Urban Visionaries

Now a century on, it is worth marking Ford Madox Ford's bewilderment when reflecting on the British capital:

> One may sail easily round England, or circumnavigate the globe. But not the most enthusiastic geographer [. . .] ever memorised a map of London. Certainly one never walks round it. For England is a small island, the world is infinitesimal amongst the planets. But London is illimitable.[1]

The terse finality of his qualifying, unequivocal 'But' sets the last sentence here apart with ominous aplomb. In *The Soul of London* (1905) London withholds its spirit from definition, thwarting expectations, rapidly appearing inestimable to ambitious inquisitors who, like Ford, encounter it firsthand. Even his subtitle (*A Survey of a Modern City*) chimes-in like the preterition of an implausible task. At once announcing and ironizing the very idea of surveying the capital's 'soul', the ephemeral subject of Ford's main title pulls against the pragmatic task indicted by his subtitle, stipulating precisely the kind of phenomenological investigation that a factual 'survey' could never achieve. Witnessing the hub of London's workaday life, Ford in effect concedes that writers hoping to depict this city in its entirety will themselves be unable to find a prose style adequate to the variety of the scenes they perceive. His implication is that aspiring chroniclers of the city are forced to develop ever more mobile forms of perceptual representation that can somehow reflect the provisionality of cartographic knowledge. What we observe in the urban here-and-now, implies Ford, often compromises all that we assume to know about the London we construe from a map. In the swell and onrush of the moment, he affirms the sense in which landmarks seem all the more elusive not only because of the vicissitudes of human perception, but also because of the illusive influence of his own preconceptions upon his ability to chart a city for which place-names seem redundant. 'Is this again London that comes to one at a distance?' (15), wonders Ford, withdrawing into that impersonal pronoun to voice a mysterious, disconcerting appeal that declares its own irresolution.

Unwritten yet immemorial terrains return time and again for contemporary novelists, too, for whom the simultaneous concreteness and intangibility of

London's expanse inspires a rich vocabulary. Ford's project anticipates the adventures of a host of formally and thematically experimental writers including Peter Ackroyd, J. G. Ballard and Michael Moorcock, to whom he bequeaths an approach to the cityscape driven by decipherment. Understandings of urban space as a foreboding labyrinth, as no less than 'Infinite London', as Ackroyd concluded in his Millennial *Biography* of the capital,[2] continue to resound in that trope of the city as curiously *illimitable*. In suggesting that there exists a 'cartography of hidden or unexplored places' obscured from everyday perception, Steve Pile has maintained that 'the important thing about the "unknown city" is not so much that there are parts of the city that are unknown, but that urban space vacillates between the reassuring solidity of knowingness and the sinister voids of unknowingness'.[3] It is indeed the unending mission of fathoming the unfathomable which attracts a compulsive refrain from London writers like Ackroyd, writers for whom suspicion and seduction, unanchored fears and artistic fanaticism, are braided together in the course of observing those 'sinister voids'.

For these practitioners, chance intuitions preside over cherished expectations. They exhibit a dedication to *dérive*, to rendering legible the mobile experience of viewing London firsthand, while simultaneously acknowledging the impossibility of assuming a totalizing documentary viewpoint over so famous a city. This is an approach epitomized by Iain Sinclair, whose later work I consider alongside Ballard below. In his documentary best-seller *Lights Out for the Territory* (1997), Sinclair asserts that '[w]alking is the best way to explore and exploit the city' (4), thereby endorsing the same quest for an ecstatic yet watchful means of experiencing the capital that Jack London entertained in 1902, here recalling the prospect of a documentary excursion into the East End:

> I went down into the under-world of London with an attitude of mind which I best liken to that of the explorer. I was open to be convinced by the evidence of my eyes, rather than by the teachings of those who had not seen, or by the words of those who had seen and gone before.[4]

Preparing to enter the *fin de siècle* capital, Jack London predicts Edward Said's point that we need look no further than the Victorian novel for testimonies to an overinscribed city, forever deciphered in advance. Nineteenth-century predecessors of Ballard and Sinclair had already noted that London could be the site of creative anxieties; it remained a dizzying constellation of hieroglyphics for which any new account was rendered unoriginal. To Said, 'all Dickens's fiction testifies' to the status of 'metropolitan space' as a phenomenon 'meticulously charted, spoken for, inhabited by a hierarchy of metropolitan personages' (*Culture and Imperialism*, xvii). Precisely because 'London' is such a famous yet illusive denomination, the contrary tropes of overwriting and illimitability still resound in the work of Sinclair, on whom I have focused this chapter – resounding in his prosodic intertwinement of bewilderment and speculation as he confronts the spectacle of everyday routine. Sinclair's migratory inquests suggest, at the level of form, that only by going *in search of* London beneath the everyday rhythms that submerse it, can one begin to research the city's most elusive and illusive inner realms. And by extension, only in committing to searching its social environment at first experientially might the cityscape be re-searched imaginatively, in an effort to prospect the possibilities for dwelling within it anew.

'Is this London?'

This imperative encapsulates what many London novelists still find so sinister yet seductive about the capital's topography, for which nothing can be taken at face value. Lending primacy to intuitive, transient modes of inquiry, Sinclair's work blends factual depictions and sensory reactions. He is dedicated, as we shall see, to relaying the exploration of places that cannot be encoded in advance simply by referring to aerial maps. Recent London writers have indeed followed Sinclair's emphasis on the creative dissemination of street-level urban experience. For this new generation of novelists, recording the changing cityscape has entailed a perpetual reconnaissance between stylistic innovation and the ethical demands of representation. Broadly, two principal modes have emerged, observing the city from different temporal directions: millennial fictions of hybridity and belonging; and self-styled visionaries who seemed compelled to unearth the city's occult, subterranean pasts. Thus while in *White Teeth* (2000) and *Brick Lane* (2003), respectively, Zadie Smith and Monica Ali have evoked London's social, ethnic and demographic constitution, by contrast such impassioned and often perplexing works as Michael Moorcock's *Mother London* (1988) and Maureen Duffy's *Capital* (1975) reveal a psychogeographic strategy of excavating urban histories, forgotten or diffused amid the onrush of commercial modernity. Treating London as a sentient being, Sinclair and Ballard join this latter group of visionary chroniclers. Like Moorcock and Duffy, they are similarly compulsive in their scrutiny of the improbable behind the façade of everyday routine. Since they retain as a principal focus the significance of chance encounters and shock impressions, it is certainly tempting again to associate Ballard and Sinclair with that key ancestor of contemporary urban visionaries, Walter Benjamin, and in whom Theodor Adorno celebrated an 'inordinate ability to give himself over to his object. By permitting thought to get, as it were, too close to its object, the object becomes as foreign as an everyday, familiar thing under a microscope'.[5] Superimposing versions of the cityscape across time, they extend Benjamin's insistence that the most familiar worlds should always be presented as the least real. Evoking the duplicity of urban experience, Sinclair and Ballard, as we shall see, obsess over the eventfulness of place – entering the cityscape as an orchard of surprise.

Alongside such postcolonial novelists as Ali and Smith who have dramatized the brute implications of racial assimilation and reconstitution, Ballard and Sinclair pose as London's most relevant and acute commentators on urban change of an architectural and socio-economic kind. These formally industrious novelists have posed both as spokespersons of the city's present, and as prophets of its uncertain fortunes. Tracing London's subterranean histories, they accept in their own ways that Blakean invitation for readers to question their empirical assumptions about a place that undermines settled knowledge, and whose surface expansionism detracts from its multilayered social, cultural and industrial histories. For his part, Sinclair has stated clear preferences with regard to this defamiliarizing impulse, favouring those writers who reveal how government redevelopment schemes privilege London's reformation solely in material terms at the expense of understanding the city's past: 'The London novelists I admire shift between dystopian visions of the city as an enclosed system, complex and treacherous, and open-field narratives that try to invent ways of escaping the pull of this gravitational centre'.[6] He implies that such writers compel us to suspend our habits, to entreat new ways of apprehending the physical world precisely in order to observe what is usually passed over. London-based novelist Nicolas Shakespeare satisfies these criteria, by showing the extent to which the capital's potential remains latent within the workaday: diluted or occluded within the present, London's spiritual renaissance waiting to be initiated. Only by substituting general knowledge with felt-knowledge can one become attuned to those zones of possibility veiled by the city's routines. Switching modes into a personalized travelogue-cum-memoir, Shakespeare offers the pertinent reminder that London can seem at once '[a]n unobvious city, and also a cosmopolitan one'.[7] In personal accounts from many famous incomers, says Shakespeare, from Henry James to Dostoevsky, London's brio is altogether disarming. These visitors serve to remind us of the city as the numinous scene of the unforeseen, while its image as 'a foreign capital' is all but taken for granted by its native populace: 'Each minute of their visit, they have come to terms with something strange. We who live here are often blinded by familiarity' (18). With their anticipation piqued, such visitors have in the past recalled the everyday landscape as deceptively benign. Their pilgrimages to the capital navigate its tourist spots from the margins, as it were: participating in a psychogeographical mode of defamiliarization by practising what appealed to Viktor Shklovsky as the virtue of turning familiar space into 'something strange'.[8]

This method of sifting through the plethora of one's ordinary experiences in an effort to grasp and particularize London's strangeness has become a working principle for novelists today. As this chapter considers, Sinclair takes that principle to a fervent level, turning it into a catalyst for experimenting with style. His work privileges spontaneous insights to develop narratives in which perambulation gives way to polemic, writing under the assumption that spatial

sensations are always more penetrating than any form of sociological delibera-
tion. An ensemble of cartographical journals, Sinclair's later *oeuvre* tracks the
descent of London's social spaces under Thatcherite policy into zones of alienation, inhospitable and malign. Even as he brings this journal up to date, tropes
of bewilderment persist. An early encounter in *Liquid City* (1999), a volume
written collaboratively with photographer Marc Atkins, exhibits the extent to
which London's writers face an exhaustively mapped terrain, a terrain whose
topological indeterminacy conspires to discredit the way they choose to represent it. Accompanied by Atkins, Sinclair sees that after skirting Greenwich via
Shooter's Hill 'there's still plenty of ground to cover and most of it is unknown'.[9]
Catching them hence, 'in mid-stride' (40), a French visitor apparently overwhelmed by this estuarial landscape stops Atkins and Sinclair in their tracks.
The man appears to them 'deranged', disorientated by a prospect before him
that resists definition as a province of London's domain:

> There's something wrong with the landscape. Nothing fits. His compass has
> gone haywire. 'Is this London?' he demands, very politely. Up close, he's excited
> rather than mad. Not a runaway. It's just that he's been working a route through
> undifferentiated suburbs for hours, without reward. None of the landmarks –
> Tower Bridge, the Tower of London, Harrod's, the Virgin megastore – that would
> confirm, or justify, his sense of the metropolis.
>
> But his question is brute. '*Is* this London?' Not in my book. London is whatever
> can be reached in a one-hour walk. The rest is fictional. (40)

In this scenario London is not simply ungraspable, but an incredulous terrain
actively defying any definitive denomination. Consolidated by the caesural
break between those two paragraphs, Sinclair affords himself a sense of retrospective distance from the encounter. His pruned qualification opens with the
conjunctive 'But' in a self-checking manner; its labial correspondence with
'brute' contracts the sentence from both ends as if to arrest the narrative's forward momentum, urging the commentating voice to pause and reassess that
encounter with the tourist as something which cannot be passed over unanalysed. Sinclair's reportage is thus suspended by a sudden authorial interjection:
it's as though he is forced to ponder the stranger's question in the reflective
privacy of his fallout from the meeting. Sinclair elides the distance between recollection and his present knowledge. Telescoping back, he resumes his pose as
a competent observer standing beside a bewildered visitor. In so doing, Sinclair
retains something of the surprise and wonder in confronting London as an
object of ceaseless interpretation that invites ever-conflicting readings. The
French visitor's query recurs itself *after* the event: a haunting incantation to
'landmarks' unanchored, devoid of reference. And that semi-desperate phrase,
'Is this London?', resounds and rebounds like a rhetorical warning-shot, one

fired across the bow of any writer pretending to define the boundaries of its terrain with precision. For the man's question here is 'brute' inasmuch as it remains irresolvable, and results from the sense of foreboding that London conspires to incubate in the minds of those crossing its 'undifferentiated' boundaries.

This concern with re-examining in ever increasing persistence London's topographic indeterminacy furnishes Sinclair's work with a compulsive, rhythmically demotic mode of urban representation. Sinclair aims not only to encode the transience of urban life, but also to allow his ludic artistry of perception to mould the very structural, grammatical and phonetic properties of narrative form. Yet he takes a risk here by courting the aestheticization of physical space, confronting London as an opportunity for stylistic showmanship rather than frank reportage. Indeed, for Roger Luckhurst, Sinclair's work sentimentalizes the very topographical ruins whose causes it seeks to satirize, hyperbolizing the effects of New Labour's regeneration plans with passages of Gothic symbolism. While facing a city beset in the late 1990s by corporate regulation, 'Sinclair's advocacy of London's hidden cabal of lunatic scribblers and dowsers might well hold off "the violent pressure of central powers", but it does so only by reifying and repeating the hierarchies it ostensibly opposes'.[10] It is that 'buried Gothic fragment', as Luckhurst pertinently describes it, which 'operates as the emblem of resistance to the tyranny of planned space, but this resistance is necessarily occluded and interstitial, passed on only between initiates' (532). Given its alternation between oneiric photographs and lyrical documentary, Sinclair and Atkins's *Liquid City* certainly raises the issue of whether the 'London' they represent is a London their readers can recognize for themselves. At what point, the text inquires, might experimental writers over-embellish narrated perceptions, only to bombard us with highly subjectivist, sensual travelogues which we, as readers, cannot relate to our personal notions of the city? To what extent, in other words, does literary style begin to detract from, rather than enhance, the writer's representation of such a famous landscape?

Settling in an illimitable metropolis

Nowhere more insistent are these dilemmas of observation and alienation than for writers of metropolitan immigration, racial difference and settlement. Black and Asian novelists as technically distinctive as Zadie Smith, Hanif Kureishi and Hari Kunzru have not simply engaged thematically with issues of identification and incorporation, but have also raised formal questions about how to avoid aestheticizing hybridity *tout court*, and about writing an adequate response to a city that both fosters ethnic diversity while perpetuating conditions of displacement. Monica Ali dramatizes this equivocal and difficult search for belonging in scenes that encircle ethnic multiplicities and divisions in *Brick Lane* (2003). An understated novel, it evokes Nanzeen's experience its eponymous borough where many Bengali residents stem from the Sylhet province of Bangladesh. And by Ali's stylistic restraint, her reticence to embellish her chosen setting, she complements the narrative's intimate discernment of personal mobility with the very register in which perceptions of Brick Lane are relayed. So although Sukhdev Sandhu sees that Ali's 'manner is flatly compendious . . . or pointlessly accretive',[11] it is precisely the tempered, unobtrusive style in which she conveys her heroine's thoughts in open space that allows the reader to witness through an intimate lens the consequences of Nanzeen's racial self-consciousness.

As a practitioner, Ali herself has admitted her preference for discretion over 'momentous' display – a withheld style that facilitates her depiction of Nanzeen's quiet resilience amid the magnitude of the metropolis. *Brick Lane* embodies Ali's warning that

> Accustomed as we are these days to the 'big' novel, the novel of ideas and of information that soars across continents, spans decades or centuries, dazzles with science, flirts even-handedly with glamour and gore and expostulates on the causes of war and terror . . . all too often in the big novel, beneath the glitz there is a nullity.[12]

Episodes in *Brick Lane* that travel alongside Nanzeen under a public gaze are especially effective in offering a corrective to that stylistic 'glitz'. Ordinary routines acquire salvific appeal for Nanzeen: shopping is often more of a release than simply a chore. Ali thus leads us out of the flat, into a far from unremarkable commercial district awaiting evening trade. In a series of accelerating snapshots she acquaints us with the drifting, peripatetic perspective of the silent Nanzeen, following in the wake of her husband Chanu's own purposeful strides:

> Nanzeen walked a step behind her husband down Brick Lane. The bright green and red pendants that fluttered from the lamp-posts advertised the Bangla colours and basmati rice. In the restaurant windows were clippings from newspapers and magazines with the name of the restaurant highlighted in yellow or pink. There were smart places with starched white tablecloths with multitudes of shining silver cutlery. In these places the newspaper clippings were framed. The tables were far apart and there was an absence of decoration that Nanzeen knew to be a style.[13]

Nanzeen continues to follow in tow; but fissures develop between them. Her passage before shops, from one frontage to the next, is refracted by sudden self-observations, interrupting the principal momentum of their route set by Chanu. Ali intervenes in consecutive events, telescoping in to align with

Nanzeen's viewpoint as she captures a sudden portrait of herself in submission:

> He began to move again. Nanzeen followed. For a moment she saw herself clearly, following her husband, head bowed, hair covered, and she was pleased. In the next instant her feet became heavy and her shoulders ached.
>
> 'From a sociological standpoint, it is very interesting.'
>
> A young woman with hair cropped like a man's pointed an impressive camera at a waiter in a restaurant doorway. She wore trousers, and had she been wearing a shirt her sex would have been obscured. To alleviate this difficulty she had dispensed with a shirt and come out in underwear. She turned round and pointed the camera at Nanzeen.
>
> 'You see,' said Chanu to the street, 'in their minds they have become an oppressed minority.'
>
> Nanzeen adjusted her headscarf. She was conscious of being watched. Everything she did, everything she had done since the day of her birth, was recorded. (210)

At first, what we as readers witness of Nanzeen's surroundings isn't quite the same at what she's able to perceive for herself. This makes the subsequent, interiorizing switch to the Nanzeen's momentary epiphany all the more arresting. Ali's move from exterior commentary to focalized reflection enhances the immediacy of the episode step by step, intensifying our acquaintance with Nanzeen's reaction to inhabiting an environment in which self-recognitions arrive without warning. Ali incites her reader's self-awareness as observers tempted to speculate outside Nanzeen's immediate frame of perception. It's as though Ali factors us into the scene as one of the reasons why our vulnerable heroine 'was conscious of being watched'. The episode culminates in a tableau, striking Nanzeen in an opaque repose, as bereft of agency in public as she is habitually within the home. Any capacity for self-assertion seems as banished from her outward appearance here in public as it is silenced by her private role as an unquestioning wife. Authorial commentator and focalizer merge at the point at which that tableau is first distilled *for*, then finally interpreted *by*, Nanzeen as she imagines how others would see her everyday self in this place where 'white working-class culture', as Chanu generalizes it, has now 'become an oppressed minority' (*Brick Lane*, 209). Ali encapsulates the wider implications of Nanzeen's resignation that 'everything she had done' had been 'recorded' by the camera-eye of propriety. The limits of personal fulfilment are reaffirmed by the persona she exhibits in public space. Private restrictions of faith are rehearsed outside in Brick Lane itself, where Nanzeen remains susceptible to the curiosity of tourists who patronize her as an exemplar of the district's ethnic concentration. Amid the tensions of social and familial interaction, that which Nanzeen perceives outwardly in Tower Hamlets thus comes to shape how she reflects inwardly – a reciprocity between seeing and feeling that mandates the possibility of her negotiating such scenes of racial objectification.

The public perception and prescription of personal opportunities is a subject of Iain Sinclair's urban polemic as well. His thematic use of perception alone, though, often turns inward, as he interrogates his own tactics for discerning, recording and monumentalizing the spectacle of metropolitan decline. Sinclair poses the problem – to himself as incisively as to his audience – of how to do justice to such fleeting experiences of space when transposing them into narrative art. And his fascination with what London seems to conceal fuels an innovative use of perception that allows him to retain a capacity for materialist reflection, even as he aspires to new heights of verbal abstraction. This self-reflexivity furnishes a style that often unfolds like a parodic rendition of its key tropes and traits, a style that chimes with Raymond Williams's suggestion, nevertheless, that 'a commitment to examining our most settled commitments might be the most literate thing we could attempt'.[14] Yet Sinclair's art of self-abnegation sits uneasily with the polemical or oppositional imperatives of urban representation. His solution is to adapt this language of self-demotion to his own strategic advantage. *Lights Out for the Territory* is the epitome of this watchful, nomadic style, where improvisatory statements are more often forensic than merely indiscriminate: 'Drifting purposefully is the recommended mode', since 'the born again *flaneur* is a stubborn creature, less interested in texture and fabric, eavesdropping on philosophical conversation pieces, than in noticing *everything*' (4). Reworking this resolution across his *oeuvre*, Sinclair's priorities compete between a duty to material facts and their fabulation for satirical purposes, compelling us to examine how that underlying conflict between polemical and artistic impulses informs the way he chooses to experiment with style.

Indeed because of their contrary imperatives, Sinclair's topographic narratives reward close attention in this comparative sense. His project matches the agility of Ballard's own 'mapping enterprise' which, as Andrzej Gasiorek remarks, develops a twin-trajectory for *deciphering* the landscape on social and subliminal levels, 'committed to forging connections between phenomena that for most observers are unrelated'.[15] Both historically investigative and attuned to the contemporary landscape, Ballard complements Sinclair's satire insofar his approach unfolds at once vertically and laterally, allowing a diachronic account of the city's past to inform his synoptic intuitions of all that is yet to come. Yet in contrast to Ballard's s otherworldly cartographies in *Concrete Island* (1973) and *High-Rise* (1975), or in the prophetic *Millennium People* (2003), there is something more personal, if not confessional, about Sinclair's dialogue with London – a dialogue that integrates hostility and endearment. Indeed, we find a striking epigraph for this alternating posture, detectable throughout his London *oeuvre*, in the way *Lights Out for the Territory* characterizes Patrick Wright: the cultural historian in whose documentaries Sinclair infers a fusion of 'scepticism, celebration of Englishness, the polemic that is half in love with the thing it denounces' (*Lights Out*, 303). Using style itself as a sounding-board for his own episodes of reverie and denunciation, Sinclair considers that a commitment to neo-modernist experiment is coeval with the demands of social critique. As such, he refutes the equivalence of innovation and insularity, amplifying instead, *through* his formal pyrotechnics, an alternating voice of appeal and mistrust with which to re-envision contemporary London.

Stalking the city with Iain Sinclair

At once seduced and disarmed by this task of representing an illusive cityscape, Sinclair allows his stylized images of London to push at the frontiers of the novel-form. Richard Todd aptly remarks that '[w]here Sinclair departs from Ackroyd is in his evident view that the past is embedded in the present at a much more fantastic, even futuristic level' (*Consuming Fictions*, 176). From the feverish séances of *White Chappell, Scarlet Tracings* (1987) to the memorial foray across England's southeast in *Dining on Stones* (2004), Sinclair works astride history and the contemporary, offsetting his archival approach to London's occult relics against a visceral engagement with regions in the custody of late-capitalism. In his search for an expressive mode that at once honours and distrusts the metropolis, place-names are pinpointed, savoured and discarded, their cartographic value rendered useless if not deceptive. Such is the performative wariness with which Sinclair often casts his narratorial self in the role of a *stalker*: a role trained-up for sleuth-like inquests beneath the illusory comforts of everyday routine. In his 'nine excursions' across a terrain of social degradation in *Lights Out for the Territory*, Sinclair portrays himself subject to exilic quests in which the satirist is liable to enmesh a prey too vicious to handle, approaching the city as if it were a persistent threat. When hunting down the legacies of enterprise culture, '[d]ebt corruptions and creative poverty assault the narrator as he stalks his "pillar to the dispossessed"' (*Lights Out*, 75). A sceptical prowler who envisages a London yearning for an architectural and socio-economic renaissance, Sinclair presents us with an emaciated realm whose inner-city 'past is an optional landscape', and whose waterfront industries are sat 'waiting for investment to catch up with imagination' (208).

Downriver (1991) takes this poetics of prowling to a metanarrational level, as though harassing the creative persona behind the text. Particularly in its Isle of Dogs section, the novel exemplifies Sinclair's tendency to morph from mystic narrator to shrewd self-parodist. As irony supersedes impressionism, his mythopoeic register is less simply diminished so much as trumped by sober, materialist interjections: the visionary stands back to give the satirist centre-stage, whenever the surrounding deprivation necessitates critique. Sinclair's posse mounts a foray into a Vatican Docklands; once a prime redevelopment zone, the site is sardonically refocalized in the novel as a realm put to waste by investors Olympia and York. This postindustrial scenery, however, serves primarily as a backdrop for Sinclair's self-inspection as a fetishist of ruin, for whom the 'occult logic of "market forces" dictated a new geography' (*Downriver*, 265). Enervating spaces thus stage an interrogation of the stalker's susceptibility to becoming an aesthete of urban degeneration. In the character of Davy Locke, with his penchant for striking cute comparisons as analytic parallels, Sinclair finds a mouthpiece for critiquing his own ability to comment usefully on social space:

> You realize we may actually have been flung back into an historical anomaly: a confirmation of Hawking's absence of boundaries, a liquid matrix, a schizophrenic actuality that contains the fascinating possibility of finding ourselves placed in postmodern docklands and *quattrocento* Florence, *at the same time*. So all those greedy pastiches have become the only available reality, 'real fakes', if you like. We arrived here by an act of will: *was it our own?* (297)

The hyperbolic sarcasm here echoes the equally garrulous self-satire that Sinclair inflicts upon himself elsewhere in the novel, when shadowing this bizarre entourage into London's East End. Likewise at the level of plot, this scenario encapsulates Sinclair's hallmark obsession with the conspiratorial nature of public terrains that appear – as they did for Ford Madox Ford – to retain functions so curiously incongruous with their given place-names. *Downriver* feasts on such incongruities between observation and depiction; and by skewering reality through arcane analogy (whereby 'postmodern docklands' transpires as '*quattrocento* Florence'), Sinclair defamiliarizes the Wharf as an insidious monument to the incursions of corporate planning. He plays up his own perspectival myopia, disarmed of satiric resources by the scarred landscape itself. The novel diagnoses how the human imagination can be annulled by the realization of multinational plans: 'We had lost the capacity for experiencing surprise' (265). Stalling hesitantly, Davy's own sardonic questions epitomize Sinclair's grammar of mistaken sighting – so central to his use of narration as misperception. And in this prosaic vision of a prime location now 'inoperative' to the multinationals that conjured it, the reader is made privy to the volatility of Sinclair's demystification of everyday space. For the satirist here so despairs before the banality of 'a much photographed frontage' (266) as to appear unable to provide a redeeming version of the Greenwich Peninsula. Fractious denunciation is offered in place of any lasting alternative. It's as though the once-inspired writer, now shading from scepticism into pessimism, has contracted the same infectious resignation afflicting his characters. Of this affliction, Sinclair's style bears the first symptoms. Wildly disintegrative before the space it describes, *Downriver* implies that this 'schizophrenic actuality', with which its very form affiliates, remains 'the only available reality' for apprehending contemporary London.

Tirelessly sardonic, this narrative practice invites the reader to partake in the decipherment of urban space through the very estranging contortions of style itself. The reader is also invited to participate viscerally in Sinclair's process of exceeding to new formal and discursive horizons for articulating urban experience. Shunning mimetic scene-setting, he never allows us to become immersed in depictions of a place against whose spiritual and economic atrophy he joins us in remonstrating. Instead, he takes every opportunity to mend the perceived separation of public debate from the contemporary avant-garde, forever morphing between roles as experimental novelist and ludic reporter. In fact, the slimmer format of weekend broadsheet reviews has allowed him access to a wider audience. As here, in *The Guardian*, the media article draws the appeal of Sinclair's combat into a more urgent, public forum of exchange than his literary fiction might otherwise allow. That is, within the confines and deceptive geniality of the review column, his vociferous demonstrations sound even more impetuous, new-minted; they are exercises in writing for London's present while highly attuned to its resonant past. Sinclair's hyperbolic language of perception seems fashioned from the heat of the moment, as though informed by the most recent experiences:

> Fearful we try to understand where we are, before we give ourselves up to the drift, the deceptive counter currents of the labyrinth. There are fleets of miniaturised vessels, blackened, carbonised, dressing the walls of financial institutions: fetishes of superstition. Even the dullest pedestrian, burdened with everyday panic and non-specific terror, will acknowledge the presence of underground rivers: Walbrook, Fleet. Liquid prompts guide our steps towards the scintillae of the supremely visible Thames.[16]

Those sinewy, sibilant-loaded accretions of participial adjectives and abstract nouns some essential to Sinclair's assault. There is a distinctly aural quality to this prose. The plosive present tense here; that sudden adverbial catalogue ('blackened, carbonised, dressing') interjecting mid-clause; the ethereal personification of subterranean waterways as a 'guide' to the present-day spectacle of the Thames, looming forth from time immemorial – Sinclair poses as a stylist acknowledging the impossibility of indexing all that he perceives amid London's estuarial landscape. Yet this language of dissection seems no less than required, scarcely excessive before the 'currents of the labyrinth'. For it is with this level of adjectivally heightened, angular description that Sinclair presides over an oscillatory poetics: swerving between the indefinite anxieties of 'Even the dullest pedestrian', and the specific seething of a satirist well versed in the 'fetishes of superstition'. His oscillations furnish a mode of forensic realism, one that obsesses over its ability to paint a malevolent portrait of London as a city half-deciphered yet undefeated. Sinclair turns into prophetic grammar this ongoing 'difficulty with representing a force that resists representation' ('Paint Me a River', 16), summoning it hence to imagine the city's salvation.

What is notable is the way Sinclair has reacted to this environment at the level of rhetorical address. Throughout his work he condemns the casual observer as a narratorial prototype. Peripatetic descriptions of indefinite peril remain a key resource, since the whole

> concept of 'strolling', aimless urban wandering, the *flâneur*, had been superseded. We had moved into the age of the stalker; journeys made with intent – sharp-eyed and unsponsored. The stalker was our role-model: purposed hiking, not dawdling, nor browsing. [. . .] This was walking with a thesis. With a prey. (*Lights Out*, 75)

What has 'been superseded' in Sinclair's later work is the reliance on accrued knowledge. He has dispensed with posterity, with the critical usefulness of rehearsing, as *Downriver* did as a concluding reprise, '[a]ll those years picking at the scabs of Whitechapel, fondling safe (confessed) images, visiting the butchered sites as if they were shrines: paddling in mysteries'.[17] When 'trapped' in *Lights Out for the Territory* 'in an isthmus of signs, not language. A field of force deliberately set-up to eliminate the freelancer, the walker, the visionary' (41), it seems that only immediate observations can sustain his understanding of the landscape.

The implication that such fleeting perceptions can elicit valuable responses from the cognitive intellect informs the perspectival poetics of *Liquid City*. As a writer travelling alongside a photographer, Sinclair lays claim to all that film cannot grasp. Thus he confesses to being continually afflicted by

> that impulse to sketch, note, improvise, revise, double back, bifurcate, split like an amoeba. My rampant schizophrenia expressed itself in the act of transcribing the speech of dogs, watching cloud-streets advance across the mouth of the Medway, listening to the shapeless buzz of cafes, trains, supermarkets – until I arrived at that nanosecond when the pattern was revealed, before it vanished forever. (8)

The adjacent rhyming of 'improvise, revise' here offers us a phonetic analogue to the double-pronged imperative running throughout Sinclair's work. It is his will-to create *and* critique, to remain an improviser and revisionist without letting either compulsion dominate. A logorrhoeic catalogue of verbs peals across this passage, giving the sense that documenting London is a physiologically demanding mission: as much a test for the writer as it is a quest for his participating characters. According to Tim Adams, Sinclair's impulsive swerving between semantic and semiotic priorities amounts to a sort of 'desperation prose': 'Perhaps it is the book dealer in him, but the almost visceral fear in every sentence of this writing seems to be that of being pulped or remaindered', with 'each individual phrase clamouring for attention'.[18] Motivating Sinclair's 'rampant schizophrenia' is something more assured, however. It reveals a compulsion to seek out London's runic spaces, to decipher 'the pattern' in and through the perceptual moment of its revelation, while acknowledging how inadequately felt-perceptions can be articulated through language. Operating therefore at the very limits of referential discourse, Sinclair offers writing-as-sketching in laying claim to the totality of the erupting image 'before it vanished for ever'. This generates a savagely paratactic syntax whose phrasal compressions encapsulate the demand Sinclair makes of himself to maintain the utmost attention to a demotic world where unanticipated runes are often noticeable only by their elusive trace.

London only begins to make sense, in Sinclair's account, when appreciated as an arena for encounters at once threatening and enthralling. Sinclair reiterates the importance of relying on intuitive rather than accrued experience in his serial documentations of the cityscape. In a candid epilogue to *Liquid City*, Sinclair ponders whether his joint-project with Atkins was less a systematic collaboration than '[a] series of accidents that occasionally fused discrete worlds' (223). London writers have exploited that fusion, when advancing new accounts of urban experience, revelling in the perpetual traffic between sight and spectacle. Acts of viewing reveal much about the level of volition enjoyed by the viewer: Sinclair distinguishes between areas of a terrain he can apprehend intuitively, under his own directive, and those areas that impose upon him because of the institutional ways in which they have been arrayed. Sinclair makes us acutely aware that so many of our perceptions of London are heavily mediated, almost preordained; so much so, in fact, that his search for premonitions of the capital's future also predicts the inconceivability of ever attaining such a prophetic vocabulary once and for all. London seems to confound a complete glossary of its various fates and fortunes. As committed, nevertheless, as Ford Madox Ford was to researching the urban interior, Sinclair works in *Lights Out for the Territory* with heuristic impulsiveness, proceeding with the notion that the 'stalker is a stroller who sweats, a stroller who knows where he is going, but not why or how' (75).

Such is the self-satirizing character of Sinclair's work that it reveals much about conditions for novelists working through and against a literary marketplace hostile to experimentalism. His commitment to formal innovation through the late 1980s and early 1990s can be seen as an incisive reaction from within London's stifled counter-cultural artistic sphere. Neatly summarizing this temporal correspondence between Sinclair's antagonistic craftsmanship and the Tory's hegemonic reign, Robert Bond reminds us that 'Sinclair is of course no opponent of feverish prose and was writing it long before Thatcher came to power'. And Bond's careful delineation between context and intentionality here is worth mentioning at length, since he refuses to defer to social history as a convenient background for speculating on Sinclair's formal judgements and decisions:

> His objection is to a particular contemporary variety, the feverishness of which is simply a by-product of the reactive description of a fevered social regime. Naturalistic discourse is seen to derive its codes from a limited repertoire of strategies that are enforced and preordained by what is reported upon. Sinclair therefore views naturalistic accounts of galloping social decay as little more than abstract, contentless stylistic exercises, because they replicate the meaninglessness of the social experience that they represent.[19]

More recently, Sinclair seems aware that the networks of truly reactionary artists that once united against Thatcherism have waned. All that is left are the visible scars of the enterprise culture that they fought against, scars of underinvestment etched into the cityscape. Qualifying Patrick Wright's report in *Living in an Old Country* (1985) on the ailing health of Britain's heritage-sector industries, stripped by the Tories of independent funds, Hilda Kean notes how this impending 'oblivion was seen by the Conservatives as the rightful abode of all those anachronistic forces that resisted the rationalization of social relations around market forces and new technology'.[20] In *Downriver* remnants of those market forces become personified as assailants. The novel opens replete with tropes of the chase, tracking a posse of documentary filmmakers who remain on guard against the workaday fabric of the city, fearful of the visible depredation now reified as everyday space, as here, in the port district of Tilbury:

> Pensioned trading hulks rusted in the docks: fantastic voyages that would never be consummated. The cranes had become another forest to be culled for their scrap value, another location for 'Dempsey and Makepeace.' The rampant dereliction of the present site was as much an invitation to the manipulators of venture capital as the original marshlands had been to the speculators and promoters who dug out the deepwater basins, and laid thirty miles of railway track in 1886. When artists walk through a wilderness in epiphanous 'bliss-out,' fiddling with polaroids, grim estate agents dog their footsteps [. . .] The visionary reclaims the ground of his nightmares only to present it framed in perspex, to the Docklands Development Board. (16–17)

Frequently in Sinclair's excursions, London emerges thus as a presence plaguing the author as observer, overwhelming his best efforts to implement a distanced critique. If outward suspicions make Sinclair inwardly sceptical towards his own oppositional stance, then often it's as though the topography itself is to blame. Bond indeed returns to this episode from *Downriver* when suggesting that 'Sinclair recognizes the complicity of artists in interestedness when he shows the intertwining of contemporary artistic production with capitalist processes'. Insofar as 'the colonization of urban territory by artists is seen to ease the way for mainstream property development', then the incursion and perennial residence of writers 'either act as a springboard to seduce new residents [. . .] or else literally blaze the development trail themselves' (*Iain Sinclair*, 154–5). It is notable, therefore, that Sinclair not only defamiliarizes his own residential terrain as a means of acknowledging this authorial complicity, but actively turns that inevitable sense of implication into a creative practice based on the displacement of artistic authority.

Sinclair journeys into the capital, then, as an environment existing not as inert and malleable by humankind. Rather, London is a place that continually rewrites its own apertures of entrapment and release, provoking intimations of peril that seem both justified and self-induced, at once actual and illusory. It's with evident enthusiasm that he declares in an appraisal of H. G. Wells that we are now entering 'an era when fiction and documentary will be inseparable'.[21] Yet Sinclair is again concerned with how this suffusion of literary modes might tempt writers to hyperbolize their perception of the metropolis, effacing the material scenery by privileging its solely mesmerising qualities. This tendency confirms James Donald's notion that urban representation has to negotiate between the cityscape's double-apparel, framing it as 'an economy of symbolic constructs which have material consequences that are manifested in an enduring reality'.[22] And it is this interanimation, this osmosis between material place and metaphorical space, which raises questions about the critical and ethical commitments that writers like Sinclair profess when evoking London's malaise. From *Downriver*'s invective towards Thatcherism's policies of selective and mercenary investment, to New Labour's benign Millennium Dome met with scorn in *Sorry Meniscus* (1999), Sinclair's inquests exemplify Wright's assertion that 'you have to accept that narrative and fiction are part of the urban texture – and you can use them without being untruthful'; not least in order 'to close the gap between the onlooking rhetoric and urban reality it exploits'.[23]

In reconciling that exploited distinction between perception and imagination, place and prose, *Liquid City* lauded the possibility that '[t]here is a world out there that isn't London and that belongs to no particular time or period' (*Liquid City*, 223). Sinclair indeed brought to light in that text the way London's appearance could be metamorphosed, transcribed into something almost immaterial, in switching from matter to fabrication. *Liquid City* privileges the transfusion of modes over chronological delineation, allowing its ostensible setting to alternate between forensic photography and florid commentary. Such formal oscillations prompt us to query whether the 'London' portrayed is indeed as unanchored from 'time or period' as Atkins and Sinclair portray it. Sinclair's misgivings towards London as an indistinct image, abstracted from history, are perhaps more instructive than they sound. In the light of trying to convey a cityscape where so many histories compete and intersect, his reservations justify a method of interrupting his documentary's self-consistency with perceptually relayed moments of insight. Reminding us of Ford's admission of the city's resistance to representation in *The Soul of London*, Sinclair demonstrates how immediate perceptions alter our prior understanding of landscapes we have come intimately to know. Where '[s]unlight, space and movement present real difficulties' (10), only the visceral reception of London matters. Documenting such episodes of heightened receptivity offers a new mode of seeing the city's present-day condition, while speculating about its destiny; at least, that is the hope Sinclair discovers in Atkins's album:

> Struggling with these difficulties for so many years has left Atkins with a monumental archive of prints: a displaced autobiography, portraits of vanished writers, demolished buildings, unique epiphanies of light that can be re-imagined but never experienced for the first time. You can't rebuild London from this formidable catalogue, but you are free to work your own combinations. You can conjure up the grid-patterns of a shining city from these loud particulars. (10–11)

Sinclair is mindful of the fate that awaits the vitality of perceptions when they enter written form. But as a writer, his ongoing concerns are less about what is lost in communicating ephemeral epiphanies, than about finding new ways of articulating perceptions in a language that evokes something of their singularity. The aim is do justice to recovering 'grid-patterns' inferred by chance while recording London's surface 'particulars'. He thus focuses upon insights yielded unexpectedly and never to be preserved afterwards in prose: premonitions snatched when recording spatial sensations of a kind that can only be 'experienced for the first time'. By utilizing perceptual experience as a device for decryption rather than description, Sinclair claims to foresee the capital's uncertain destiny, because working with pure instinct has allowed him to work at some remove from London's present-day routines. To this extent, his writing acquires a presaging force. *Liquid City* is exceptional in revealing that an instinctual, phenomenological inspection of everyday places to which we feel so utterly attached can challenge what we assumed to know about their socio-spatial organization.

The self-satirizing force of Sinclair's recent work is such that it motivates him to stitch personal interventions into the fabric of social commentary. Coruscating, impetuous, equally sardonic, *London Orbital* (2002) circles the M25 only to circumvent the motorway's onward rush. Here again his appetite for encrypted runes emblematic of the actual causes of urban ruin remains insatiable. Yet as an appetite, too, for innovation, it acknowledges the ethical dilemmas facing writers who fetishize occult imagery when evoking the city's apocalyptic decline. From a compelling reflection on the role of literary style in conveying memories of war-torn Europe, W. G. Sebald's concern comes to mind, that 'the construction of aesthetic or pseudo-aesthetic effects from the ruins of an annihilated world is a process depriving literature of its right to exist'.[24]

Heeding this kind of caution, Sinclair's aspirations render him knowingly complicit, particularly when '[t]he temptation, as always, stood firm: to inflate a day's wandering, out in the weather, into something that could be described as a "quest"' (*Lights Out*, 113). As we have seen, this highly practised form of knowing self-chastisement can digress precariously in the direction of its scrutiny, compelling Sinclair to ransack his own false modesty at the expense of social critique. But it also has the potential to be a richly self-implicating repose, whose broad spectrum of rhetorical interrogations makes every performance of it different for each new quest.

J. G. Ballard's oracle of entropy: Middle-England and after

In Sinclair's urgent, caustic prose, stylistic equivocations form part of his effort to seek out the prospects for London's spiritual benediction. With the insatiability of an urban stalker, Sinclair hunts for hints of spiritual and social effulgence that emerge in opposition to metropolitan decline. Sanguinity often shimmers just beneath his scorching satire. By contrast, Ballard's most prophetic work has nothing of this blend of obstinacy and optimism. Throughout his work, Ballard has subjected elegant urban lifestyles to a distinctly irascible kind of scrutiny, while predicting their imminent demise. Chaotic urban territories are often deliberately anthropomorphized, their workaday rhythms dictated by the psychic instability and amorality of self-pleasuring inhabitants. The dystopic universe in *Crash* (1973), where all bodily desire is galvanized to the machine, recapitulates in the similarly erotic dependence of marina populations in *Super-Cannes* (2000) on the gaudy opulence of their villas, whose 'walls and balconies moulded into biomorphic forms'.[25] Both of these texts offer parables of jaded spectacle, whereby the reign of supreme appearances is suddenly curtailed. Ballard seems fascinated with encroaching banality, with foretelling the propensity of the elite to act as the instigators of their own implosion. They reside in an insular world under the totalizing seizure of excess, a self-dominating community whose luxury settlements impact upon the natural landscape only in so far as they render it invisible. Incarcerated within a zone of their own making, it's as if the occupants of Port-la-Galère no longer have the ability, even if they wanted to, to perceive any landform beyond their own fabrications:

> Rather than sit on their balconies with an evening drink, enjoying one of the world's most striking views, the owners of these exclusive villas preferred to slump in the dark of their rumpus rooms, watching Hitchcock films and English league football. (140)

No other space seems relevant beyond this self-regarding 'enclave of luxury houses' (140). Eden-Olympia provides its population with a sort of environmental conceit, a false, uterine sphere wedged into the coastline. In a self-deluding exercise of power over physical space, indifferent to its natural climate, Ballard's wealthy Britons have reoccupied a landscape without compromise so as to meet their every satisfaction.

It's in this apocalyptic mood that Ballard uses urban space to stage the impending combustion of middle-England. His settings play host to a growing anarchism half-concealed, half-repressed behind the systemic veneer of consumerist frivolity. When we enter the claustrophobic setting of *High-Rise* (1975), for instance, we confront a primitivist emporium, echoing an order of existence to which Robert Maitland submits yet acclimatizes in *Concrete Island* (1974), eventually presiding over his miniature, motorway-embankment manor. Inherently mechanized yet free from systemic rule or decorum, Ballard's London often seems at once monochrome and manic. It has become a primeval yet prophetic setting for his fiction, and his characters often can't help themselves from detecting in their firsthand perceptions proleptic intimations of disorder still to come. As we shall see, *Millennium People* (2003) is Ballard's most pertinent and agitated version of this oracular aesthetic. For the novel offers us not so much a definitive reflection of London's social ills as they persist today as an ominous prediction of just how entropic the social sphere will imminently become.

That Ballard makes his readers feel like active participants in this prophetic project might be expected: instrumental responses are implicit to the function that oracles themselves perform. An oracle's cryptic message impels the enquirer to translate into action what they hear of the future, entreating our interaction before issuing prophecy. Michael Wood has noted that an 'oracle is the surest thing in the world, and also the most ambiguous'; if this is so, as Wood goes on to point out, then the 'corollary of the suggestion that all oracles could be ambiguous is that there is no oracle that cannot be reinterpreted, one way or another'.[26] Oracles may provide a possible solution; but they rarely encourage the listener make a quick decision. Prophecies breed hesitancy. Implied predictions insinuate rather than suggest personal changes, never forcing us to renegotiate immediate plans right away or without considerable equivocation.

The ambiguity of an oracle's mode of instruction precisely complements Ballard's prophetic pursuits. As he implies to Will Self, his London narratives are attuned to the ambivalence of the city's everyday terrain. Familiar spaces always have the capacity to deceive Londoners who claim know them best, areas 'which a true native takes totally for granted and is unaware of'. In which case, the job of contemporary novelists, in Ballard's view, is to remedy our ignorance while preserving what seems so numinous about landscapes assumed to be overinscribed:

J. G. B.: [. . .] there is still an underlying strangeness for me about the English landscape and there is even about this little town of Shepperton where I have lived for thirty-four years. If you settle in a country after a certain age, after your early teens, then it will always seem slightly strange. In my case this has probably been a good thing, it has urged me to look beyond Little England for the source of what interested me as a writer.

W. S.: This is certainly what you have said, the proleptic quality of your fiction through the sixties and into the early seventies, that anticipation of England as a motorway-dominated culture. Do you think that is a function of that hard-wiring coming into this environment, that you simply didn't see England the way other people were seeing it at the time?

J. G. B.: I think that it is true, absolutely.[27]

Tracing how those ominous strategies of control are rehearsed in the domestic partitioning of an inner-city tower block, *High-Rise* offers its own version of that 'proleptic quality' by allegorizing London's terminal segregation in advance. Anarchic events within the building comprise a metonym for the force with which core mechanisms fail. As everyday social divisions begin to atrophy, the novel exposes the way the British 'class system', as Ballard tells Will Self, 'has always served a political function as an instrument or expression of political control' (*Junk Mail*, 340). In *Millennium People*, he is again more preoccupied with the destiny of middle-classes in an inner-city context, probing the fault-lines of a gentrified community colonizing the banks of the Thames. For Self, these voyages into the interior of a certain socio-economic strata are what inform the most polemical aspects of Ballard's urban fiction:

> Ballard has always defined himself as a chronicler of 'inner space' and attempted to imagine what the parameters of the human psyche will be like in the not-so-distant future. The irony is that the works he has produced have turned out to be far more accurate predictions of the character of evolving modern life, than those written with that intention.[28]

Millennium People offers an apotheosis of this oracular technique. Yet at the same time, the novel's intimations of dissolution reveal an altogether more elegiac aspect of Ballard's concern with urban space, when predictions of London's fate at the hands of its wealthy citizens subside into pessimism in light of what the city has already become.

For psychologist David Markham, it comes as no surprise that Heathrow is the target of what seems like another terrorist bomb. As with the towering mon-olith in *High-Rise*, Ballard is ever keen to anthropomorphize his chosen setting. Using Markham's gradual approach to the crime scene, Ballard unveils Heathrow piecemeal, so industrious in his ascription of metaphor as to render the airport in a catalogue of analogies:

> Heathrow approached, a beached sky-city, half space station and half shanty town. We left the motorway and moved along the Great West Road, entering a zone of

two-storey factories, car-rental offices and giant reservoirs. We were part of an invisible marine world that managed to combine mystery and boredom.[29]

Somewhere as malevolent for newcomers as the high-rise, this platform for international travel is equally as mundane for those who regularly use it.

On learning that his ex-wife Laura has joined the casualty list, Markham mounts his own inquest, collating the conjectures of initial police reports with his own hunch speculations about the rise of disparate protest groups from within London's bourgeois hinterland. And after discovering the extent to which '[p]rotest movements, sane and insane, sensible and absurd, touched almost every aspect of life in London, a vast web of demonstrations that tapped a desperate need for a more meaningful world' (37), Markham himself detects the lure of anarchism. His quest elides his conscience, soon finding himself enveloped in the world of factions working from the immodest Thameside development of Chelsea Marina. As the instigator of a movement against the banalities of corporate life, the seductive Richard Gould becomes Ballard's mouthpiece, as Markham is coaxed into serving in their impending revolt. Despite his charisma, Gould is a mere cipher for the novel. Two-dimensional and impersonal, he operates with economy as a humanoid oracle, prospecting the salvation of Chelsea Marina from self-mystifying contentment. Gould anticipates the eagerness with which London's entrepreneurial sector will foster the desecration of its own directionless lifestyle, a rebel leader confident of his own unanimous election by '[c]ongregations [. . .] hungry for a charismatic figure who would emerge sooner or later from the wilderness of a suburban shopping mall and scent a promising wind of passion and credulity' (38). Through Gould, Ballard exercises his fascination with the possibility of wholesale psychosocial change. Yet if *Millennium People* intimates anything, it is merely the retrenchment rather than refusal of modern urbanism, projecting a city nullified by the sensibilities of its most settled inhabitants, a city in stasis beckoning the remedy of shock violence.

For Ballard, then, the saturation of contemporary Western society in routines of its own making should occasion our collective panic. His panoptic perception of London's spiritual and systemic crystallization implies that complacency has bred apathy to an abhorrent and ubiquitous degree. This late Ballard seems repulsed by the way mobile, global lifestyles sanction our voluntary submission to the repetitiveness of occupational demands, annulling any critical response to new technological advances. As part and parcel of 'a more needy and impetuous era', he writes, transatlantic flight has become little more than a chore.[30] Long-haul flying is now lacklustre, devoid of the wonderment it once provoked. This is not simply because 'millions of us take to the air as casually as we board a bus or train', but because of the repetitive services accompanying those uniform places of departure and arrival: 'We wait in nondescript boarding lounges, walk down metal tunnels and lever ourselves into the narrow seats

of a small cinema where we watch Hollywood films on a low definition screen'
('Up with the Celestial Helmsman', 9). Aircraft terminals, for Ballard, epitomize if not exacerbate the termination of flight's stimulations:

> After a few hours we leave the cinema and make our way through another
> steel tunnel into an identical airport in the suburb of a more or less identical city.
> We may have flown thousands of miles but none of us has seen the outside of the
> aircraft, and could not even say if it had two, three or four engines. All this is
> called air travel. (9)

Repetitiveness lies everywhere in our contemporary midst, warns Ballard,
a stultifying malaise from whose clutches we cannot entirely take flight.

It is tempting to read *Millennium People* as a fictional meditation on these concerns, only that Ballard's diagnosis of present-day lifestyles, crippled by
uniformity, turns into a *prognosis* of London's fate in the face of lamentable
alternatives. Appropriately for a novel with one eye on this uninviting future,
Ballard's pathology shades into prophecy. *Millennium People* prospects the reluc-
tance of middle-class sectors to oppose their inertia in banal corporate existence.
One of the significant structural outcomes for the novel of Markham's choice
to view *in person* Chelsea's dissidents at play is that he relocates Ballard's critique, leading the action away from the river into a kind of virtual, resituated
suburbia, proximate to the City. Here the schedule of commuting and expendi-
ture has smothered the landscape like an anaesthetizing haze. Ballard enframes
a population so self-absorbed in routine as to be unaware that they are hosts of
an urban scene where personal money sponsors public monotony – a population summoning forth London's communal dystopia through the negligent
tastes of the wealthy individual. In his growing complicity with the rebels,
Markham lends prophetic weight to recurrent signs of mutiny elsewhere in
highly public locations, developing an ambiguous empathy towards indiscriminate violence. The miasma of *repetition* once more sets the tone for Ballard's
sardonic critique. Surveying his own *oeuvre*, Ballard admits the prevalence of
both tropological and topographical forms of recurrence, seeing repetition as
a working method overarching his preoccupation with urban chaos:

> J. G. B.: I go in for a lot of deliberate repetition, I don't see why not. I like that.
> They are signifiers for the reader to cross-reference them.

> W. S.: To go back to the idea of fictional topography, I was wondering if you felt
> there was a sense in which a writer's body of work, taken as a whole, is a kind of
> aerial shot of a foreign territory through which you are conducting the reader.
> And further, a sense in which all these topographies join up into some other,
> numinous parallel world.

J. G. B.: They do.

W. S.: And the repetitions are, therefore, the switches directing the reader back into this world.

J. G. B.: They are road signs. They point to possible destinations. (*Junk Mail*, 341)

The repetitions Ballard finds so attractive unwind like a proleptic code in *Millennium People*. The novel gestures at many 'possible destinations' for Markham between complicity and virtue, willing seduction and undercover prosecution. And for the remainder of this section, I want to invoke Ballard's use of 'deliberate repetition' as a basis for reading the novel's oracular focus and reach.

The cityscape of *Millennium People* is one in which the duplication of suburban development is the source of middle-England's uniformity and stoic self-repair. Markham understands that the futility of the rebels' cause and the inevitability with which their rebellion falters seems insisted upon, as though in advance, by Chelsea Marina itself. The district repeatedly states its own social continuity; a self-healing arena, it returns the urban elite to the consumer luxuries to which they are accustomed: 'The street was on fire, but Chelsea Marina had begun to transcend itself, its rent arrears and credit card debts. Already I could see London burning, a bonfire of bank statements as cleansing as the Great Fire' (228). The Marina is soon revamped; just like a set is struck after the heated final act of a stage-play strewn with props. Indeed, Ballard reverts to this figure of the stage set, whose imagery chimes throughout the novel, to offer a tableau of capitalistic self-subsistence. The vision of 'an avenue of three-storey houses with large gardens, labradors and Land cruisers' (86) is a set-piece vision that remains open to replication, available to those with ample wealth and complacence. Markham is repeatedly reminded of this when travelling undercover with Kay Churchill, reminded that '[t]he disdain of metropolitan intellectuals was heaped on these bricky piles, but the lifestyle had been copied throughout the world' (87). His journey through West London is mnemonic. Reminded of his 'grandmother's place in Guildford', Markham recalls how '[t]hose big houses in Twickenham were an eye-opener. Civilized people, golden retrievers, but each of those homes was a stage set. All they do is inhabit the scenery' (109–10). Ballard turns into replicable pastiche the image of upper-middle-class existence based exclusively on consumer purchase.

Gould tries to convince Markham that as an impassive inhabitant of civic life he already is a seasoned campaigner for this staged world, where kitsch accoutrements are reified as necessities. Always the first to read other people in prophetic ways, though, Gould also insists that it might have been Markham's destiny to join the anarchists after all. The contention is that Markham joined them in heartfelt truth, not in disguise, when 'disenchantment set in' upon reaching 30:

> Already the future was receding, the bright dreams were slipping below the horizon. By now you're a stage set, one push and the whole thing could collapse at your feet. At times you feel you're living someone else's life, in a strange house you've rented by accident. The 'you' you've become isn't your real self. (138)

In *Millennium People* the repetition of the 'stage set' as an analogy for middle-class aspirations becomes a geographic reality when Chelsea comes to rest after the revolt. It's as if the development appears, literally, to be resetting itself following temporary disturbance:

> The second barricade was hosed and breached. The police advanced through the cloud of steam and a black, almost liquid smoke lay over Chelsea Marina, drifting across the Thames to the Battersea shore [. . .] The kingdom of the double yellow line would be restored, and the realm of sanity and exorbitant school fees would return. (229)

The estate's demographic status as a 'kingdom' recovers: ruled by the consensus of an elite and individuated community of suburban professionals. The area has returned to a stage whose domestic props are now more than ever resistant to the pretensions of those eager to strike them away from within:

> Only by cutting short their exile and returning to the estate could they make it clear that their revolution was indeed meaningless, that the sacrifices were absurd and the gains negligible. A heroic failure redefined itself as a success. Chelsea Marina was the blueprint for the social protests of the future, for pointless armed uprisings and doomed revolutions, for unmotivated violence and senseless demonstrations. (292–3)

Through Markham we hear the echo of Ballard's faint resignation. *Millennium People* prophesies London's spiral into a sphere of inaction in which the most radically conscientious among its population are ridiculed. Markham has had to experience for himself how, thanks to its repetitive and recuperative topography, Chelsea has been able to patronize and quell the revolt as a 'heroic failure'. His accumulated experience of the city so far could not have foretold this outcome; but now it is a 'failure' that will linger in the mind, hindering his willingness to act purely on instinct. It adds to his growing knowledge of how far public space can and cannot be reformed, only to dull his eagerness to know that space anew. It is thus defeat against which any future intimation of London's constitutional change will be soberly measured. Pacifying his

oppositional desires, memories of Chelsea will merely return him to conven-
tion, restoring his acceptance of what the capital can never collectively achieve.
Harmonizing with that rhetoric of apocalypse so pervasive in *High-Rise*, where
the city's dissolution is miniaturized and scaled in proportion to a single,
emblematic building, Adorno's melancholic claim rings true that the 'world is
no longer habitable' insofar as 'the heavy shadow of instability bears upon built
form'.[31] Yet the paradox of *Millennium People* as a story about dwelling stems from
Ballard's effort to give an account of urban modernity as all but uninhabitable
yet without refusing to care about the possibilities of inhabiting the city anew.

It would seem, therefore, that Ballard's oracle coils in upon itself by adopting
a double stance. *Millennium People* partly answers the question – posed incisively
to Ballard's earlier work by Roger Luckhurst – of 'What happens when the
contemporary itself is projected as a ruin *of the future?*'[32] Diagnosing, through
present conditions, an impending storm of social retrenchment, *Millennium
People* resorts to generic type: rehearsing a ceremony in commemoration of
prophetic strategies now well established by urban visionaries. For no longer
does it seem so pertinent to stress that today's insecurities merely confirm our
suspicions that the city of tomorrow is already cast in doubt. This novel exhausts
its purpose as an oracle because the future it anticipates is so grey, dropping
back into that derivative tenor of malign portent. Sinclair himself recently
avowed that 'London anticipates disaster. And, in that fearful anticipation,
incubates it'.[33] Ballard, though, somewhat dispels the combative logic of
Sinclair's anthropomorphism: his millennial omen turns away from a London
that 'anticipates' to face one that merely stagnates. Shaped by Markham's
own personal account of rebellion from naivety to sceptical knowledge, the
novel's closing divination is that of a city already in regression. It's as if the
potential for local communities to redeem themselves has already been dispelled. London emerges as a place scarcely in need of more prophecies.
Fracturing its predictive lens with the nihilism of the scenario it predicts,
Millennium People stages a version of inner-suburbia where the predictability of
public desires makes any idea of personal intervention seem redundant. In this
sense, the novel is a mouthpiece for its author's driving concern, voiced in the
early 1980s, about the exhaustion of a future whose mundanity has yet to arrive
and be fully experienced in daily life:

> I would sum up my fear about the future in one word: boring. And that's my one
> fear: that everything has happened; nothing exciting is ever going to happen
> again [. . .] the future is just going to be a vast, conforming *suburb of the soul* [. . .]
> nothing new will happen, no break outs will take place.[34]

In *Millennium People* Ballard follows Ford Madox Ford's entreaty: going in
search of whether anything 'new will happen' to the capital, only to find
that a 'conforming suburb' has stolen in to replace London's soul. Nearly

20 years on, the novel is an ominous effort to offset Ballard's fears of a soulless city, and to envisage the radical kinds of consciousness-raising conditions that might compel middle-class Londoners to react against their fate.

Ballard implies that London's plenitude will only beget uniform lifestyles, becoming a place stalled by the scarcity of original thought. No mending of this malaise is forecast; instead, he remains an unapologetic antagonist of reparation, a prodigal diviner of spiritual bewilderment who outstrips the present by inclining towards the future's emaciation. But his latest novel's prognosis has been cast in grave light in years since by the rise of international terrorism. Fears of a 'boring' future have been succeeded by Londoners' present fears of the bomb. By imploring readers, in *Millennium People*, to resist the stultification of urban life at the dawn of a new century, Ballard's oracle twists unexpectedly on its axis: an oracle today whose anticipations of violence have newly acquired an appalling and unanticipated validity.

Cryptographers of the commonplace

As an epigraph to the opening part of his kaleidoscopic *Mother London*, Michael Moorcock directs us to the city's veteran inquisitor, H. V. Morton, reflecting here in 1941:

> The people of London, having developed a technique of living in the face of repeated danger, now accept the preposterous, and what was until so recently the incredible, as the normal background of existence. I often think that the ability to reduce the preposterous and the incredible to the level of commonplace is a singularly English gift.[35]

As Sinclair and Ballard exemplify in their own urban inquests, the goal of writers seeking to re-imagine the public sphere is to rescind that 'gift' of blinkered acceptance. To negotiate precarious distinctions between figurative and factual landscapes, and to entertain famous landmarks as sites of conspiracy and mediation, has become their way of retrieving incredible sights and sounds from everyday urban experience. For his part, Sinclair is certainly poised to turn the novel, as Jeanette Winterson might applaud, into 'a bringer of realities beyond the commonplace' (*Art Objects*, 136). In both his fiction and journalistic commentary alike, successive representations of London's brute actuality get 'combined', in Peter Ackroyd's phrase, 'with a unique ability to divine the mythic and fabulous within images of the contemporary city, and an extraordinary attention to colour, sensation and the narrative possibilities of urban life' (*The Collection*, 349). Seemingly unproblematic facts emerge as fabulous, unfamiliar, only provisionally decipherable for such visionaries – a sensitivity to undiscovered zones that refuses to 'accept the preposterous' as an everyday social background. Finding new methods for pursuing an anthropomorphized city radically out of sync with its commercial centre, they evoke a metropolis that when encountered in person feels uncoordinated with its public image.

Stripping away the everydayness from everyday life becomes a laudable conceit for such novelists. Sinclair is adamant that '[w]e have to recognise the fundamental untrustworthiness of maps'. *Lights Out for the Territory* plays on this paranoiac sense in which the most familiar maps 'are always pressure group publications', at best 'a futile compromise between information and knowledge. They require a powerful dose of fiction to bring them to life' (142). Sinclair epitomizes visionary writers who develop the anxieties of perceiving urban space as a catalyst for experimenting with narrative form. They exploit the hazards of experiencing a city in actuality whose potential has only previously been tested in the mind. Evoking sensations of space at the level of style, they imply that radical changes to our physical world can only occur by harnessing new connections between topography and perception; that our built environment remains somehow too encrypted to be apprehended solely in terms of its visible present; and that our mineral universe can only be redeemed with 'a powerful dose of fiction'.

Chapter 4

Cartographers of Memory

When Kazuo Ishiguro won the Winifred Holtby memorial prize for the most compelling expression of place in 1982, his novel *A Pale View of Hills* brought into the Royal Society's spotlight of literary acclaim the fundamental interrelationship between memory, movement and place. Their infusion pervades *The Remains of the Day* (1989) as well. Standing before the secluded Mortimer's Pond near Dorset's Wiltshire border, Stevens senses that it is 'no doubt the quiet of these surroundings that has enabled me to ponder all the more thoroughly these thoughts which have entered my mind over this past half-hour or so'.[1] While associated with that immediate place in which they are recalled, memories are retrieved along more unlikely paths, sparked by topographical features discovered unexpectedly in enclaves that seem at first so serene. Stevens admits that 'but for the tranquillity of the present setting' (128), his recollections would never have been examined with quite the same scrupulous wonder. And by exploring these unanticipated mental allegiances between place and the past, Ishiguro stages an uncanny yet highly self-conscious process, one that activates within the perceiver what Suzanne Nalbantian has described as a kind of personal '"reconnaissance" or conscious recognition'.[2] In the mode of its retrospective unfoldment, *The Remains of the Day* performs this very process, whereby a material terrain outside the reflecting subject stimulates what Nalbantian calls 'the mind's conscious recognition in the operation of memory' (8). In so doing, the novel typifies Ishiguro's technique of furnishing everyday landscapes with powerful mnemonics.

Stylizing remembrance

Memory has had an altogether significant role in shaping the imaginative geographies of contemporary British fiction. As Peter Middleton and Tim Woods argue, writers have aspired in recent decades to respond directly to the historical evolution of everyday life, experimenting with the depiction of mundane territories that occasion our workaday routines. They propose that contemporary fiction can engage us in 'a space or matrix of confluence where the status of textuality is constantly being articulated and tested'. And because it can inspect the quiddity of ordinary places and the diverse habits they induce, '[f]iction is able to represent those sites/spaces of the everyday which escape the purview of social control. Like the alleyways, backstreets, nooks and crannies and the "heterotopias" of the city, so fiction has within itself similar investigations and spaces' (*Literatures of Memory*, 281). Ishiguro's work has long underscored the intensity with which our movement through everyday spaces can trigger-off phases of uncanny retrospection. His work can be set among other contemporary novelists who use remembrance to implement certain *formal* effects just as they *dramatize* the cognitive and emotional upheavals of recollection. While incorporating this synergy of the *showing* and the *telling*, such fictions of remembrance also reveal much about the way striking memories arise spontaneously from everyday environments with disarming consequences.

Involuntary memories also epitomize the extent to which retrieving past experience influences immediate perception, altering the priorities governing what the recollecting mind chooses to perceive in the historic present. In *Thinks . . .* (2001), David Lodge capitalizes upon the introspective detours of his middle-age neuroscientist, Ralph Messenger, remapping the territory of the campus-novel format. Lodge complements his thematization of consciousness on a stylistic level, dividing the narrative between first-person reflections and free-indirect discourse. Where the former prevails in the novel's first half, Ralph's convoluted meditations navigate between *mind* and *brain* while highlighting the inaccuracy of the rhetoric he invokes to articulate their respective differences. Henceforth, everyday journeys and their accompanying frustrations spur his digressive yet playful inspection of his own pathological jargon. In a 'painfully slow' Monday morning trip to his Gloucester department,[3] the Ring Road itself prompts Ralph to run rings around the language he uses to tape-record what his mind is doing. It's as though the very passage of commonplace routine in the physical environment calls into question how he describes himself there. By sitting before this mundane scenery, Ralph ponders whether or not his viewing this place is the same thing as understanding it, a discrepancy between seeing and knowing that prompts him into a verbal tirade. Railing partly against the outside world, partly against himself, he verbalizes inner thoughts that oscillate between the workaday and the profound:

> I interrupted the recording on the Inner Ring because I noticed a passenger in the front seat of a Mondeo level with my car in the traffic jam was staring at me and I became a bit self-conscious, especially given what I was . . . interesting that usage, by the way, 'to become self-conscious,' as if we're not self conscious all the time . . . (149)

Lodge's series of interceding ellipses self-consciously satirize the novelist's ambition to render thought processes mimetically through the undulating shape and fragmentation of narrative phrases. Ralph is an apt spokesperson too for the ways in which retrieving memory, as Paul W. Burgess and Tim Shallice point out, reveals recollection itself to be 'a computationally complex multi-stage process'.[4] Acts of remembrance are composite and interiorized, yet also peculiarly responsive to environmental events that incite retrospection. And as Burgess and Shallice conclude, by virtue of what happens in the spaces occupied about us, any process of remembrance must to some extent 'correspond to the moment-to-moment retrieval of the humdrum happenings of daily life' (385). Lodge offers a satirical take on that correspondence. *Thinks* . . . shadows a rather vain narrator enjoying life under a microscope of his own making – never more self-admiring than when unleashing neuroscience on his own reactions to 'humdrum happenings'. The fact that he is sat 'in a layby on the A435' stimulates the memory of recent incidents, diverting him into a style of abstract inner-thought comically incongruous with his outer surroundings:

> What it really means is second-order consciousness, or you could call it reflected self-consciousness . . . when we become conscious of ourselves as perceived by others, or rather we feel others are conscious of our self-consciousness, as they've accessed what is usually private and known only to ourselves . . . I wondered if this bloke could lip-read he looked so interested, twisting round in his seat to stare at me dictating . . . I gave him a cold fuck-off look and he hastily turned his head away, but I didn't feel like going on with the dictation, so I closed down the Pearlcorder . . . and quite soon the traffic cleared and I was on my way . . . (149)

In a layout so visually explicit for the reader, Lodge mounts a forensic self-inquest of his own here comparable to that of his speaker. The splintering of sentence structure becomes somewhat contentious, as Lodge poses the question as to whether syntax can ever be used as a correlative to memory's unpredictable rhythms, zigzagging from one recalled experience to the next. Lodge splices together typographic fragments while conceding their imperfections: words on a page, however deftly arranged, could never mirror the precise tempo of Ralph's successive deliberations. A sly metalinguistic commentary thus ensues. We can detect Lodge's self-consciousness in his character's verbal vacillation between everyday statements and existential meditation – between immediate spatial perceptions and the intellectual reflections they provoke. Incorporating these fluctuations into the text itself, Lodge moves a step further. For he entertains the possibility of grammatically embodying his protagonist's thoughts by encoding internal monologue at the level of the novel's typography. As its aposiopetic incisions increase, *Thinks* . . . registers graphically the way human thought accelerates in uneven cycles of observation and recollection, cycles that ultimately resist being reproduced in written form.

Aside from this gesture of self-referentiality on Lodge's part, an important notion arises in *Thinks . . . .* What the novel reveals is that memory is circular rather than linear, and that multiple pasts resound in the chamber of one's present-day consciousness, re-echoing like an ensemble of episodes contrapuntally arranged and rarely played in tune with one another. And on behalf of the role that literature plays in portraying this peculiar yet precious logic, A. S. Byatt requests our attention. She points to the capacity of creative writing to evoke memories by recovering and revivifying that '"glittering" quality about certain experiences'. Traced back to their singular context, they could now be as 'tormenting as they were delightful'; yet narrative language alone, for Byatt, captures and transmits the enduring significance of past impressions, for 'only the act of writing gave them place, a form and an order which made sense of them. And which they seemed to ask for'.[5] It's this quality of encapsulation and form-giving, exemplified by narrative fiction's capacity to become a custodian of memory's affective afterlife, which the present chapter explores. I address several novelists who formally embrace the need to understand that memory is never in stasis even where recollections seem so tied to everyday places, so conditional upon the specificities of a memory's originary provenance. Alongside Graham Swift's late fiction, I'll be turning to a more recent generation of writers by exploring the poetics of spatial memory in Trezza Azzopardi and A. L. Kennedy. As we shall see, they present their readers with mnemonic environments where daily routines spur chance recapitulations, qualifying Nicola King's assertion that from within the quotidian tasks we habitually complete 'memory does not lie dormant in the past, awaiting resurrection'.[6] In the context of everyday landscapes, the writers I consider here don't simply dramatize the experience of negotiating places of remorse. Equally, their narratives often refuse to tolerate the consolations of self-pity or obsolescence, disallowing the wishful sort of 'forgetting', as King describes it, 'that assumes that remembering is finished' (180). Agitating the insecurity of recollection, they guarantee the inefficacy of casual denial. Pointing to the unpredictability of recollections occurring amid the apparent mundanity of everyday spaces, they map unlikely, overlooked, or chancy sites of solace and reprieve.

Ancestral zones

The rapid expansion of Nottingham's outskirts, where 'countryside . . . turned into suburbia', left Alan Sillitoe with clear priorities as to how the novelist should approach the depiction of remembered places. In charting the evolution of his local communities before the forces of domestic and industrial change, Sillitoe asserts that ultimately for the novelist, personal '[m]emory is not enough. It needs the lever of imagination to make it real. While memory may make it real to yourself, only imagination can make it live for others' (*Mountains and Caverns*, 67). Graham Swift's own preoccupation with the poetics of memory and everyday space in south London has inherited precisely this imperative in recent years. For just as Nottingham's suburban expansionism compelled Sillitoe to reconsider the extent to which he might aesthetically appropriate his home city, so Swift's early work implicitly resisted the creative use of autobiographical settings. Instead, Swift seemed lured afar for resources, drawn to evocative places where he had never even been in person.

After the success of *Waterland* (1983), for instance, Swift surprised (and indeed disappointed) many by denying he had grown up as a child of the East Anglian Fens. Of late, in fact, Swift still seems bemused as to why he originally chose *Waterland*'s locale: 'Why did I set it in that peculiar region', he remarks, 'having no connection with that region? I have no idea. But I did and I explored it and it became the territory'.[7] This disparity between authorial biography and narrative space appears all the more 'peculiar' itself, given the intimacy of Swift's connection to the South London of his youth; to move a short distance from the Bermondsey backdrop of *Last Orders* (1996) is to discover Swift's own birthplace on the fringe between Sydenham and Catford. In the Jubilee edition of *Granta* magazine 2004, Swift assumes the role of memoirist to navigate his enduring attachment to suburbia's quotidian terrain. In what follows, I want to trace the implications of turning Swift's statement about *Waterland* around, as suburban South London itself 'became the territory' for his recent *The Light of Day* (2003). For his gesture of geographical retraction and relocalization marks a significant turn in Swift's craft, registering at the level of scene-setting his reinvestment in distinctly everyday spaces. And with its own grammar of peripatetic recollection, Swift's *Granta* memoir, 'Making an Elephant', rehearses through its laconic self-commentary the voice he deploys in this novel, whose narrator not only enunciates but also exploits a crystalline rhetoric of remembrance. Each of these commemorative narratives serves to render the mundane strange, each affirming Paul Ricoeur's assertion that an 'investigation into what "place" means finds support in ordinary language'.[8] In a comparable respect, Swift's work radically elaborates upon a quotidian, seemingly unyielding topography to transform the imperatives of the *quest* motif in which he invests, an organizing motif that witnesses the intersection of urban scenery and narrative style. And by charting here his respective excursions across South London as a defamiliarized landscape replete with mnemonic cues, I want to suggest that Swift dramatizes for his readers the extent to which a literary navigation of public place and the literal rejuvenation of personal history interpenetrate one another, providing an insight into the way recent writers have expressed ontological concerns through the subtleties of everyday discourse.

On a personal level for Swift, South London today is less a composite landscape of distinct districts than a fabric into which his childhood sense of home was rewoven several times in the wake of the Second World War. His *Granta* memoir, 'Making an Elephant', is highly self-exposing; in tone, it evinces a passionate determination to re-encounter personal history, while acknowledging that remembrance is subject to fabrication. Swift's memoir is punctuated with candid self-commentaries of the kind that he has honed for his fictional characters over the past two decades. Swift returns to south-east London as his father Allen had known it from the 1920s and beyond, re-entering a house whose 'conspicuous dereliction' meant that it 'wasn't just ordinary and anonymous. It was singled out, even by that crooked angle, from its unremarkable neighbours, and that ivy and wreckage . . . were like some mock-portentous, tongue-in-cheek acknowledgement of mortality and the grave'. For Swift, his childhood 'Lower Sydenham' was a place of endless discovery, multifaceted beneath its everyday façade – even its 'name embodies more than one kind of stratification'.[9]

Recurring here is the fascination exercised in *The Light of Day*. Swift is interested in how we negotiate the tendency for recollections to embellish our mental image of a place as it may have once appeared – especially when such places are overlaid with the intimate memory of siblings who once inhabited them. Occupying various narratorial stances across his memoir, Swift navigates the palimpsest of childhood memories by transposing several narrative perspectives at once. The most prominent transposition centres on his late father. Reassimilated through the eyes of Allen Swift, south-east London reappears as a highly provincial terrain, 'just unsuspecting countryside colonized by the gentry' ('Making an Elephant', 303). By deferring the provenance of his commentary onto Allen, while retaining the agility of intruding with the occasional gnomic gloss, Swift is thus able to retrieve something of the essence across time of the way these 'suburbs can be very strange' through a twin perception of how far suburban boundaries have since expanded, their street-maps extensively redrawn (303).

'Making an Elephant' therefore provides the reader some 2 years on with a sincere authorial equivalent to the narrator's meditations in *The Light of Day*. Compared to that novel, as we shall see, Swift's memoir is richly informed by his remarks on the metaphoricity that native places attain when drawn through childhood memories. King has attributed Toni Morrison's notion of *rememory* to the kind of fiction-writing that 'testifies to the impossibility of forgetting without adequate remembering, while recognizing that remembering – or finding form and expression for one's memories – may never be complete' (153). This idea that personal history is fundamentally open-ended and incomplete, resonating on into the fluctuations of the present moment, remains both a guiding assumption and rhetorical principle behind Swift's memoir. For here, remembrance scarcely angles towards completion, because certain locations recalled have themselves been transformed. Rather than simply being memorialized, London's historic south-east corner is revived as a fellow character.

On a voyage in which that region is periodically personified, Swift's lyrical recollection of the landscape in terms of how it once appeared is able to mourn certain places without manipulating them into sentimentality.

One episode is particularly assured in striking this balance between geographical descriptions and their endearing memorialization. The scene concerned focuses on Swift, as a boy, being driven behind Crystal Palace in his father's Vauxhall Wyvern – a vehicle treated 'with a coaxing sensitivity as if it were a sentient being' ('Making an Elephant', 305). Swift quickly distinguishes here the actuality of urban space from its sumptuous fabulation. After ascribing an anthropomorphic simile to the car, Swift turns out towards the cityscape, choosing to figure 'central London, London proper' in saline dimensions: it looms forth as a vast watery presence punctuated by incalculable illuminations (304). Despite the City appearing as 'a sea of lights, a black bowl of jewels' (304), Swift concedes that '[n]o doubt that view from the Palace would seem commonplace now' (305). But Swift's deftly crafted comparison between 'that view' and 'now' seems to avoid the normalization to which his vision of the capital as a 'sea of lights' has been subjected by present-day life. Opulent recollection works here to preserve the strangeness that no longer appears topographically self-evident for London's contemporary scenery, preserving the wonderment that younger generations today may not sense with quite the same intensity. Following on from this aside, Swift confesses how his striking boyhood perceptions can scarcely be attributed to the present-day apparel of the realm he now inhabits as his own: 'London itself, the inner core, was unknown to me then. I know it now, but I still have a sense of it – elusive, glamorous, a dark phosphorescent lake – that comes from those journeys, sitting behind my dad in the marvel of our car' (305). What visual memories alleviate here is the absence of irrevocable experiences; they permit Swift to divulge an adult admission that at once consoles for the loss it concedes – the loss of that luminous sensation of once finding a city 'unknown'.

Swift's slight memoir, then, offers a reprise of the compulsion that *The Light of Day* so intensely embodies in the texture of its retrospective narrative, that compulsion to retrace and personalize the quirky yet sensuous aspects of this unremarkable region of so famous a capital city. Swift maintains that the *provincial* should be seen as coeval with rather than culturally or geographically distinct from the metropolis. Guiding us towards the social and cultural possibilities of perceiving London and its south-eastern provinces as mutually defining zones, his memoir indeed questions the assumption that densely populated urban centres are devoid of local idiosyncrasy. Following his next move to South Croydon, Swift recalls how communities there aspired to an 'absolute paradigm: the new house in the outer suburbs, the job in town, the train to and from' (312). But in a state of flux and only '[a] short distance away in one direction were open fields and farmland: the literal edge of the country. London was moving outwards and behind all the bland domestic trappings of suburbia there was an odd spit-on-the-palms pioneering spirit' (313). Swift reminds us that the ethos of provincialism itself – when conceived as a series of social customs and domestic values to which people attune their every-day lives – not only survived but intensified amid the demographic transitions that propelled south-east England into a phase of rapid urban expansion.

This is certainly a sentiment that *Waterland* endorses. By shifting between metropolitan and riparian worlds, Swift evidently relished London's marginal frontiers in this earlier novel, restoring to prominence many sidelined histories of the capital's evolution from the marshes. Prefacing an episode in which he describes his usual Sunday routine of tramping up to Greenwich Observatory to get a better view of his former self as much as of the westward City, Crick slips from the first-person to an externalized third-person commentary. At the summit, in front of the Observatory, overlooking the river's 'steel serpent coiling through clutter', he reassesses his own genealogical path from the Fens along-side the capital's industrial growth, knitting personal history to a sweeping archaeology of London's genesis as a merchant city born out of the Thames:

> From the top of Greenwich Hill it is possible to not only to scan the inscrutable heavens but to peel back past panoramas (wind-jammers in the India Dock; royal barges, under Dutch-Master skies, bound for the Palace), to imagine these river approaches to London as the wild water-country they once were. Deptford, Millwall, Blackwall, Woolwich . . . And, away, out of sight to the east, the former marshes where, in 1980, they are building a flood barrier.[10]

That ability 'to peel back past panoramas' is something Swift exercises for his native Wandsworth Common. To its terrain he confesses

> a certain inescapable attachment. If you are born somewhere and circumstances don't take you away from it, then you grow up and remain within it. Of course there are times when I hate London, but equally there are times when I can walk round a corner and I really feel that this is my place. ('Triumph of the Common Man')

Swift's characterization of George in *The Light of Day* elaborates upon this love-hate affinity. For by the end of this itinerant novel suburbia has become a threateningly mnemonic terrain, in spite of the narrator assuming to know virtually every corner of its streetscape.

Graham Swift's quotidian quests

Swift's concern with the way places invoke perceptions of the past yields certain principles in common with the genre of the quest. Most explicitly his fiction expresses the need to retrace personal memories to their contexts in an act of reconstructing, and making sense of, actions once committed there; secondly, his narratives are driven by the impulsiveness of characters who long to return to originary sites, literally or imaginatively. Likewise, Sarah Dunnigan has indeed noted how '[t]he typologies of longing so embedded' throughout A. L. Kennedy's work serve to *spatialize* her voyages into an uncertain past, lending her more extended narratives 'the structure of a quest'.[11] A more ornamental stylist than either Kennedy or Swift, Candida Clark has also worked with the quest genre in *The Mariner's Star* (2002), a voyage-based narrative in which the suicidal widow of a drowned fisherman travels alone into the sea with the intention of joining him by way of the same fate. Here Clark's quest-plot coils into introspection. *The Mariner's Star* launches into the sea, and into its narrator's elaborate meditation on questions unanswered about whether her husband's death was accidental or self-intended. Clark, however, harvests from the blankness of this ocean setting an unexpected opulence; lavishly punctuated by metaphor, her first-person narration turns into an act of stylistic compensation for its vacant surroundings. Clark evokes her seascape with negative pronouns that reiterate its vacancy, while leaving the novel's heroine adrift in a briny realm not altogether evacuated of mnemonics that reignite her mourning. She senses that

> With no other life anywhere on the horizon or in the sky, without even sunlight as a reminder of the land's location, I am reduced in an instant to nothing more than a solitary woman in a fragile boat, rocked towards night on a slippery heave of sea.[12]

Gradually, of course, it is that same extreme isolation that becomes the redeeming agent in the novel. That the narrator is unable to 'call it a place, because how can it be real' (23) is the catalyst for a reassessment of her former life, married yet often left alone on shore. This interiorized assessment is directed straight at a version of 'me who's back on land' (14), setting off a chain reaction of self-recovery. That is to say, once she leaves the shoreline behind, the most important events occurring there return more accurately in her mind. For the voyage has turned the 'grey hopelessness' (14) of the present into an arena of spiritual reparation, an arena in which 'the sparkled surface of the great sea of memory' stages a spectral visitation of the husband in whom she had lost faith and whose death she misconstrued as suicide, the husband of whom her '[m]emory, now, is more than enough' (87–8). By activating this chain of reassessment and repair, it's as though the sea has acted as a mnemonic for understanding life on its topographic opposite: by going to sea she returns to the land now out of sight beyond the horizon. Appearing impartial in its immensity, the ocean seems less judgemental for being so limitless; its grand scale allows her to make small-scale evaluations of the life she led back on shore.

Clark's voyage in *The Mariner's Star* across a desolate seascape uses novelistic setting itself to reorientate its heroine's recital of mourning, leading away from self-insulation towards the preservation of experiences too precious to be extinguished in her own suicide.

This infusion of personal searching and private recollection is precisely what enhances the description of place in *Waterland, Out of this World* (1988) and *Ever After* (1992) alike. Nevertheless, Swift's idiosyncratically unadorned manner of address has across his career divided critical opinion. Reviewing *The Light of Day*, Hermione Lee remarked on how far the 'plot of this book is bounded by the postal district of SW19'. For Lee, though, by indulging this restricted setting, Swift had discovered the *mis-en-scène* for honing his 'colloquial style, short on verbs, thick with question-marks'.[13] James Wood labelled Swift's meticulous spareness as specifically 'Folkestone tradition', expressed by the novel's 'self-conscious, deliberate drives into the sublime banal'.[14] Wood warned that 'there may be readers so incredulous at the even grey of its stylistic climate that they feel the need to take a warmer holiday after only a few pages, convinced that some cold literary game is being played on them' (28). Out of the novel's circular mnemonic journey that dour 'climate' flourishes, however, with the text embarking on a suburban quest whose completion underscores the importance surviving the past by holding remembrance and prediction in a delicate balance.

Swift's ostensibly suburban settings host such reciprocal relationships between personal memory, populated landscape and the impress of anticipation or longing. What I want to show here is the way that recollection and location work dramatically in *The Light of Day* while also affecting the novel's formal organization, even its typographical layout. While sustaining this sense of cohesion between *space* as a trope and the spatial nature of textual form, Swift incorporates the priorities that distinguish a certain genre of 'suburban' fiction, a genre that, according to Lynne Hapgood, evinces a 'need for harmony between individual, culture and place', while at the same time emphasizing 'the intrinsic value of the ordinary'.[15] Swift's moderately anthropomorphic descriptions of urban territory incorporate this drama of memory and recuperation, presenting Wimbledon as a highly animate hometown that provokes its native George to become something of a pioneer of his own conscience.

Swift himself asserted in 2003 that 'I do my thinking while I walk', and that walking across Wandsworth Common 'just loosens up the mind in a way that you don't get when you are sitting at a desk' ('Triumph of the Common Man'). *The Light of Day* offers an exemplary exposition of walking as an ignition for thought. And, again, it is the *quest* conventions of contemporary urban fiction which are at once rehearsed and reformed by Swift's concern with places as catalysts for remembrance. Typically, these conventions dramatize a twin-imperative: first, a character's attempt to indulge private memories in order to atone for, or make fresh sense of, actions he or she once undertook there; and, secondly, that character's ongoing search for belonging in a chaotic and bewildering metropolis. *The Light of Day* inherits much of this joint impetus from B. S. Johnson's *Trawl* (1966). Just as Swift departs from the conventional inner-London setting, so Johnson isolates his narrator aboard a deep-sea trawler, whose alien workaday routines will help 'shoot the narrow trawl of my mind into the vasty sea of my past'.[16] Swift, too, revitalizes the cityscape as an environment populated by cues for involuntary recollections. In tune with his memoir's rhapsody of retrospection and self-scrutiny, *The Light of Day* somewhat dispenses with that trope of London as an inherently impersonal realm – a realm of aggressive progress, orientated towards a future of individuated consumption, ever hostile to the sensibilities of private reflection and repair. For despite their dissimilar approaches to novelistic experiment, what Johnson and Swift have both sought to dramatize is the sense in which memories are induced by our contact with the physical world and in ways that also influence our most deep-seated attitudes to the past.

It is this degree of circularity, this reciprocity between cognition and recognition, which has lead Edward S. Reed to advance what he calls an 'ecological' approach to remembrance. In this framework, the act of remembering lived experiences involves our reflective perception of how we inspect the past in the course of navigating present-day locations. Memories thus return amid, and are frequently provoked by, the current rhythms of social space. 'Through memory', writes Reed, 'we not only encounter the past environment, but more importantly, we keep in contact with our past selves in their surroundings'.[17] As we shall see, Swift's own use of quest conventions highlights the necessity of keeping in touch with those environments from which memories challenge and enrich one's sense of self-knowledge. His excursion into suburbia for *The Light of Day* was not simply a conceit, a manoeuvre restoring to view the hidden metaphoricity of the local and the mundane. Rather, he charts the narrator's quest for personal reparation through a network of quotidian routines in order to complicate the conjunction of private memory and local place, revealing just how peculiarly past experience can disrupt the manner in which one negotiates daily habits. Extending the model of narrative memory which I have been formulating thus far, James Olney offers a similarly circular template for autobiography: 'the winding round and round in present memory is the precise linguistic and structural analogue of the going round in a circle of errors of the past, and a narrative that would be adequate to the experience of present memory as well as the experience of past erring must display that one same structure that is responsible . . . for the continuity of identity between past experience and present memory of that experience'.[18] On this recursive model, landscapes provoke sensations that in turn invoke memories whose originary context can either seem directly related to, or quite distinct from, the immediate environment. As it does for the recitation of memories across decades in Ishiguro's novels, this place–perception–recollection trigger operates in an internally cyclical, self-perpetuating way in *The Light of Day*. For Swift's concern is with the power of landscapes to wield legacies that counsel against our temptation to forget. Surviving the regret such places reinvoke is achieved only by restoring one's faith in the continuity of quotidian existence.

From the outset, Swift delineates the novel's Wimbledon setting with thriving precision: exhibiting a pristine attention to an initially unremarkable townscape, while refusing to embellish it with the help of flashbacks or dream sequences. Again as Wood remarked when reviewing the novel, 'what better place, full of its own "effects", for the literalization of cliché, than Wimbledon' ('How's the Empress?', 29). This might sound a little dismissive of Swift's choice of diction; but what Wood is really saying is that we should remain alert to the colloquial vocabulary with which Swift broadcasts his narrative of memorialization. In *The Light of Day*, he refuses to sensationalize this experiential portrait of suburbia made strange; neither does he embroider its appearance with effusive cartographical metaphors. Instead, Wimbledon's everyday demeanour is traced with a descriptive patience that is worth quoting in full for its judicious reticence and poise:

> The sun feels warm through the windscreen, but the street's full of people hunched in coats, chins buried in scarves. I drive along the Broadway, past the station, towards the Hill. From Wimbledon's lower end (my end) to the snooty Village on the hill. Past Worple Road. Then at Woodside I turn right, and then left into St Mary's Road, and I'm into the leafy, looked-after, quiet zone of houses set back from the street, of lawns and drives and hedges and burglar alarms. Rooftops backed by trees.[19]

Appearing as a 'quiet zone', the secluded street cues up an inner zone of turmoil. The next paragraph slices in upon the outward depiction of this familiar neighbourhood like a filmic intercut. George's previously measured account of his journey is suddenly suspended, superseded by a series of percussive self-justifications issued in a declarative present tense:

> I have to do it. I didn't say – nor did she. But I have to do it, today. Beecham Close. Number fourteen. Someone else lives there now. Another world, another planet. I could find out all about them, check them out. It's how I make my living, after all. (19)

Then, Swift blends these two registers together by compressing two phrases – as he did when figuring that childhood memory of central London as a glittering seascape in his *Granta* memoir. In this instance from *The Light of Day*, Swift foregrounds in that modal switch George's compulsive reversion from external reportage back to contracted, Senecan self-inspection; this time it occurs in even quicker succession, too, switching in the space of two consecutive sentences:

> A zone, as you climb the hill, of verges and double garages and wrought iron and speed bumps and private nursery schools. But don't knock it. If you make your living how I do, then make it where they'll pay your fees, and where – with all they've got – they can still (you'd be surprised) do the strangest things.
>
> And don't knock it anyway. This home-and-garden land, this never-never land where nothing much is ever meant to happen. These Wimbledons and Chislehursts. What else is civilization for? (19)

As these curt rhetorical questions angle insistently towards the townscape (generalized here as a 'never-never-land' of suburban habituation and security) Swift marks the starting point of George's own orbit of remembrance as atonement, an orbit that follows him round a 'safe-as-houses land where nothing is meant to disturb the peace' (21). Moment by moment these familiar backstreets, cul-de-sacs and shortcuts become malevolent mnemonics; encompassing the novel, they play host to a circular voyage throughout which personal insecurities proliferate suburbia's most uneventful scenery.

Structurally shaped, then, around the principle of voluntary delay, complementing the amount of '[t]ime to kill' before George's impending prison visit (115), borne out by its narrator's retreat into zones for contemplating past actions – *The Light of Day* leads us on a route orientated by calculated digressions. Time and again, every new street demands that he re-explore those hidden territories within himself where guilt still finds refuge. Repeated roadnames punctuate the narrative as it unfolds episodically. Noted streets anchor the contextuality of the action between our narrator's digressive flashbacks. Mundane sidings, pathways, alleys and parkland perimeters are reassessed by the novel; such sites are rehabilitated as valuable zones of solace, zones of recess that reciprocate '[s]omething I see in myself these days: I don't mind waiting . . . I've lost the knack of impatience' (139). The uneventful, ostensible functionality, of everyday places approximates George's halting self-scrutiny. Mundane locations peel into view, realms where nothing out of the ordinary occurs because all the action is occurring psychically within.

The very form of *The Light of Day* thus engages with this temporal process of projection and anticipation. Sidestepping and stalling alongside his narrator's passage of remembrance across town, Swift juxtaposes episodes of self-remonstration, hesitation and tentative resolution. In a structural sense, the novel's tripartite system of indirection, suspension and delay is evidenced when George is about to visit his beloved Sarah, jailed for murdering her husband in avenging his affair with their fostered Croatian postgraduate. This instance encapsulates at a dramatic level what Swift is attempting formally throughout.

That is, the text's diegetic circumnavigations and circular digressions mirror the chronology of its narrative action. From within the novel's oblique and episodic manner of recounting, a recurring pattern emerges that amounts to a

> usual routine: park in the side road, walk first in a different direction. Not that I'm ashamed. Ashamed to be seen to be a visitor, a prison visitor. For God's sake, I'd be over that by now.
>
> And anyway: the most precious moments of my life.
>
> Twice a month they see me. An old hand by now, a regular. His home from home. A woman's prison. (115)

In limbo now, contented to pursue this 'precious' routine until her eventual release, George proceeds to recall the investigative mission assigned by Sarah '[t]wo years ago and a little more. October still, but a day like today, blue and clear and crisp. Rita opened my door and said, "Mrs Nash"' (12). From that meeting on the entreaty seems set, the quest's map unfolded. Sarah is resolute:

> You see, it's all over. It's all over. Kristina is going back to Croatia – in maybe three, four weeks. Do you follow the news? It's agreed, She's getting a plane. What I want you to do is follow them to the airport. Watch them. That's all. (15)

At this point the landscape against which the novel is set changes ominously. No longer representing a reliable emotional or physical *A–Z* with which George can map his course to expiation now in the present, Swift rewrites the street-plan of south-west London as a deceptively banal zone of routine that actively protects the past from being deciphered in a way that will enable George's self-acquittal. Swift anthropomorphizes Wimbledon and Putney: they stand between George and his idealized versions of the past, intruding as fellow interlocutors with whom he must convene when retrieving memories in which the question of culpability remains unanswered.

In attempting such answers so as to appease his remorse, George gives his detour to the scene of the crime itself legitimacy as a kind of anniversary rite. It's as though his heightened reception of familiar zones has intensified that need to defamiliarize his own habitual manner of recollecting and disseminating the contexts of guilt. Sense-impressions from the streetscape serve to accelerate his voyage of self-analysis within:

> The sun flashes off the road where the frost has turned to a black dew. I reach the corner of Beecham Close, as if a magnet has pulled me. I didn't say I would, she didn't say I should (and I won't tell her I did). Though it's hardly a detour. It's even a short cut, avoiding the Village. Wimbledon Broadway to Putney Vale.

But now I'm almost there I have to pull up. I taste the dark taste again, like a gush
of oil in the throat. I have to stop. It's even hard to look.

Two years and everything is quiet. Frozen. The simple turn into a quiet street.
A cul-de-sac with verges and chain-links and houses screened by autumn trees.
It could almost be a private road. Private, keep out: not for you. (26)

The anticipatory aside in parentheses here reveals another of Swift's linguistic
traits for interanimating the detours of recollection with detours through urban
space. Other idiosyncratic speech-effects familiar from *Ever After* – such as the
use of intransitive and gerundial verbs, the sudden aposiopesis and declama-
tory, single-word sentences – are reiterated throughout *The Light of Day*, too.
By depicting George's epigrammatic flashbacks as if they are incited by the
most particular of places, Swift complicates Richard Hoggart's recent distinction between quotidian and abstract speech. Hoggart argues that '[a]phorisms
on Time prove to divide easily into two main groups: the practical, the everyday,
the hortatory; and the more numinous and brooding'.[20] In *The Light of Day*, the
universal and the banal resonate with one another contrapuntally.

Moreover, it is the sudden intrusion of such marked parentheses, enclosing
George's aphorisms, which lend emotional content to the very typographical
space around and between the text's printed words. That the novel is typeset in
Monotype Dante certainly harmonizes with Swift's verbal concision: the chiselled serifs and plinths visually complement the frugality with which Swift
records both George's extended reflections and spoken dialogue. Pages in the
first edition script from Hamish Hamilton indeed seem proportionally whiter.
And within generous outer margins, the printed words are inset like fugitive
marks of adamant self-accusation; they are like the stains that George carries
home from the forensic frontline. Odorous reminders of his previous job with
police, his undercover travels across Wimbledon and Putney always leave him
with something of that 'taint – that everyday, workaday taint' (135). Smattered
across the page, grouped only in short paragraphs spaciously aligned, the
printed words themselves appear as indelible as those suburban mnemonics
reminding George that being a prying-eye is '[a] dirty job sometimes' (135).
It's as though the novel's typesetting offers a graphic correlative to the ingrained,
olfactory mnemonics strewn so pungently across present-day suburbia. In this
sense, Swift's hallmark spareness exemplifies Susan Stewart's remark that 'space
between letters, the space between words, bears no relation to the stutters and
pauses of the body. Writing has none of the hesitations of the body; it only has
the hesitations of knowing'.[21] For if the townscape appears, to George, like a
place '[s]tudded with detentions', then so, to the reader, do the letters on the
page. Isolated letters are placed like typographic indicators of our narrator's
retrospection – markers of the suddenness with which public spaces compel
him to retrieve past events whose aura of trauma persists undiminished.

Central to *The Light of Day* is precisely this notion of self-knowledge endlessly deferred, just beyond reach, its deferral caused by the dispersal of memories within the immediate cityscape. And this mutual confirmation of memory as a theme and as something that organizes syntactic form implicates the reader in the novel's choreography of recollection. Swift's request is not simply that we tolerate the text's periodical digressions as it sidetracks into memory and regret; he entreats, instead, our empathic interaction with its divagations and intercessions, whereby we may learn something of the duties we prioritize for our own mourning selves. Because the novel's setting is so confined, because it pursues the implication that 'in this quiet corner of the civilised world there are no safe houses', as Hermione Lee reviewed it, Swift's narrative geography 'alerts you, as the reader, to be as attentive as any sleuth' ('Someone to Watch Over You', 9). Even the neighbourhood itself invites us to remain sceptical of George's anecdotes, of his susceptibility to offhand self-pity over the more progressive challenge of self-doubt. More than a muted domestic backdrop, the setting of *The Light of Day* visibly responds to Georges's self-condemnation with its own inevitable and irrepressible advancement: 'The house looks calm, calm and safe. Can houses be acquitted, let off? It wasn't *their* fault. Someone looking out from one of those lit windows might see it all the other way round: I'm the sinister element round here' (233). So little can be remedial, implies Swift, about our longing for what a landscape no longer contains; little is restored long-term simply by committing to an unrelieved vigil in which mourning is succeeded by the self-insularity of regret.

Swift's novel rehearses a trope used by Hanif Kureishi in his celebrated suburban *Bildungsroman* fictions such as *The Buddha of Suburbia* (1990) and *Gabriel's Gift* (2001), a trope bisecting narrative temporality and the characterization of perception itself. That is, when narrators like George, Karim or Gabriel stop and stand still in the street, the presented relationship between memory and place changes like quicksilver. As a result of their drawing to a halt amid the urban scenery, impassive introjection twists into a more considered form of self-inspection out of which unforeseen resolutions emerge. Everyday space lives on, bustling around these inwardly gazing figures – a brute reminder of the social sphere that inaugurates their responsibility to survive the pull of memory's aftermath. And, as in his memoir, Swift's *The Light of Day* is concerned less with the way quotidian locations can play host to a purely individualistic confrontation with the past; despite the interiority of its first-person narration, the novel gestures outward towards zones of public encounter, dramatizing a more protracted emotional *and* social challenge. It concerns our capacity to face recollections that render us accountable to others, recollections that we cannot prevent ordinary places from provoking.

Mnemonic narratives of this kind exhibit some of Swift's most innovative yet discreet syntactic techniques. Practising the virtues of a kind of scrupulous concision, he advises novelists today that the 'real art is not to come with extraordinary clever words but to make ordinary words do extraordinary things. To use the language that we all use and to make amazing things occur. This may be a very strange thing for a writer to say, but I don't think that writing is about words' ('Triumph of the Common Man'). Not about words, no, but about spaces – the spaces *between* words. With *Last Orders* as its precedent, *The Light of Day* epitomizes Swift's devotion to the neglected possibilities of 'ordinary words', dealing comprehensively with minimal, staccato diction. For it is this attraction to apparently mundane moments of contemplation and reminiscence which has allowed him to develop, through impulsively self-vigilant narrators, the tonal range and affective nuances of a quotidian lexis, from offhand anecdotes to idiomatic dialects.

Experimenting with these deceptively simple materials, Swift's latest novel unfolds a mind-map of just how differently memory can work between separate landscapes. By revising our understanding of *remembrance as enactment*, rarely depicting it as a voluntary endeavour, his first-person register offers a lyrical medium for expressing this aspect of 'memory as performing history', a dynamic which Matthew Campbell, Jacqueline M. Labbe and Sally Shuttle-worth see 'as essential to defining our understanding of the past and the future'.[22] Complementing Lodge's priorities in *Thinks . . .*, of paramount significance to Swift is the extent to which memory's circularity impacts upon textual composition. Swift makes use of memory on formal and figurative levels, leading us to the forefront of the past's unexpected recapitulations where remembrance becomes the occasion for self-examination. In this respect, *The Light of Day* sanctions against the reader's uncritical immersion, summoning us to the breach of its inquiry over and above passive observance. Counselling against our purely genial response to events, the novel shows Swift's serious intellectual investment in the quotidian dramas of reparation. Suburban spheres swell with history in Swift's world. And by setting the fluctuations of personal memory against the diurnal patterns of public routine, he coordinates and contrasts the pressures of remembrance with the everyday demands of inhabiting community space.

A. L. Kennedy's mind-maps of habitation

Park bench, train carriage, high street and kitchen, all take their turn as sites of momentary recollection in A. L. Kennedy's fiction. Seemingly unremarkable yet suddenly mnemonic, the ambience of such places becomes all the more uncanny for intensifying the unforeseen demands of hindsight that cannot easily be assuaged. At a compositional level in *Looking for the Possible Dance* (1993), Kennedy invokes the standard definition of a *mnemonic* as a practised tool or technique for improving memory, using a free-indirect discourse to shadow her heroine's progress through successive memory-tests staged in between states of transition between dwellings. In *Looking for the Possible Dance* Kennedy uses Margaret's train carriage as an anchoring mechanism for the narrative as a whole: it returns time and again at the head of large sectional digressions into recollection. As Margaret sleeps, dreaming the dreams that provide the material for our voyage into childhood memories summoned and reanalysed, an exterior narrator continually leads us back to the trope of the train window. One comes to associate it with the onset of each new episode of mnemonic retrieval. It's as though Kennedy ensures that reader and narrator both arrive from a common, recognizable starting point in space and time before the novel's excursion into remembrance unfurls apace. For the narrative soon becomes unanchored from any one setting, accumulating urban scenarios in which each new interpretation of personal memory spells our heroine's cautious submission to bewildering self-inspection. Kennedy tracks Margaret's propensity to relive past decisions while lamenting their ramifications, plotting across environmental borders the way our conscious recollections have the power to deny us the comfort of passive reminiscence.

In pursuing what seem like ordinary spaces as settings for provoking retrospection, Kennedy simultaneously heeds King's warning that '[i]n everyday social discourse, narratives tend to elide memory as a process' (*Memory, Narrative, Identity,* 3). What is significant is that the revaluation of this process influences the very style of Kennedy's landscape descriptions. In *Looking for the Possible Dance,* she refuses to see memories as relics, archived and inactive, by allowing her exterior narrator to become our guide to the furrowed mindscape of Margaret's past, a narrator with the freedom to intervene in Margaret's journey through the novel's implied present. With the novel proceeding slowly and incrementally onward from its opening, an agile, prominently depersonalized commentator informs us of circumstances preceding the action's present domestic context – circumstances also influencing the journey coming next:

> Margaret is sleeping now.
> It is three o'clock in the morning and the sparrows and dunnocks are trying out their songs. Windows along the street have full dawn against them and Margaret Hamilton lies behind the dark of her curtains asleep.
> A week ago, Margaret was still employed and today she is not. Because she was prepared for this, she had her railway ticket ready and this morning she will travel away from here. Probably she will come back, but this is not certain. She is going away to think about things like that.[23]

As the prevailing mode in *Looking for the Possible Dance,* the narrative's chiastic procession from retrospection to the historic present-tense complements Margaret's cyclical flux of retrieval and dissemination. Narrating becomes rehearsing. Kennedy's impartial narratorial persona oversees a voyage punctuated by *elaborative rehearsals*. From psychological parlance, elaborative rehearsal denotes a person's purposive attempt to organize life-experiences in order to comprehend how the very act of retrieving such experiences might benefit his or her sense of dwelling in the present. Something comparable to this process of organized retrieval happens in the passage above, yet in such a way that also inflects the narrative mode conveying it. Kennedy rehearses that set of events leading up to Margaret's decision to leave Scotland for London. But in so doing she also insinuates the sense in which Margaret's leaving seems contrived, precisely too organized: too clinical as a way of obviating memories of events '[a] week ago', the causes of which she has indeed yet to rehearse and thereby address. And what adds to the portentous atmosphere, above all, is Kennedy's own austerity as a removed spokesperson for preceding events, sitting back merely to imply that all will not be well thanks to Margaret's over-hasty departure. Thus in her documentarian address to the reader at the novel's outset, Kennedy denies our inclination to assume that Margaret has either faced up to the past or by any means 'prepared for this' journey south:

> Asleep, she is surrounded by waiting. In her kitchen, her half-packed holdall is waiting to be filled, the kettle waits to be boiled and the curtains are waiting to be drawn. In a street a mile away, the sleepy taxi driver who will take Margaret to the station is waiting by a hamburger van with his radio turned off. And away in the city the railway station is expecting her. (7)

That this voyage beckons so imminently, as if programmed onto an English landscape yet to come, serves merely to intensify the urgency of remembering the landscape being left behind.

By the very reportorial register with which Margaret's departure is hastily relayed to the reader, the novel's opening episode reveals a vocabulary peculiar to Kennedy's work. Elaborated to pristine effect in her short stories from *Indelible Acts* (2003) and *Original Bliss* (1997), a certain rhetorical reticence has become Kennedy's trademark. Like Graham Swift, she is committed to the virtues of a kind of scrupulous concision, practising Swift's advice for novelists today that the challenge is 'to make ordinary words do extraordinary things'. For Kennedy too deals comprehensively with simple, staccato diction, choicely positioned between relative clauses. Such rhetorical choices are often deployed for strategic effect, negotiating exterior and interior spaces to accentuate the interrelationship of material landscapes and mental reflections. In her latest novel *Day* (2007), the manipulation of narrative tense highlights the provoca-tive impact of terrestrial features upon the direction and reach of represented thoughts. By narrating in the second person, Kennedy invites us to collude with the bouts of digressive retrospection that affront Alfred Day, a former RAF tail-gunner in the Second World War, who has now (on the eve of the fifties) volunteered as a minor extra in a POW movie. Not surprisingly, the film-set

itself provides Day with a stage-set for recollection, the role-playing alone facilitating his retrospective scrutiny of military and emotional conflict. From the
outset, Kennedy moves between past and present tenses, the second-person
commentary serving to implicate her readers by making them privy to Day's
traumatic memories of active service. While the novel often seems to ironize its
own elegiac tone, on a more candid level Kennedy's use of the second-person
'you' in episodes of involuntary recollection includes us as direct witnesses to
the human physique at war. In *Day* the characterization thus soon divides along
mental and physiological lines, compelling us to occupy the ethically contentious position of an audience watching a body enduring abject states. Certain
scenes, often drawn from everyday duties, depersonalize Day's limbs, soiled
and dissociated from their owner's introspection: 'And the dust, you might
say, was so distant there at the far end of his body and nothing to do with up
here and the neat, clean secrecy of private thought, invented thought.'[24] Self-
removed yet descriptively fastidious, Kennedy herself redefines what it means to
be a 'distant' observer, using distance itself as a leitmotif to link Day's spatial
and cerebral perceptions. As often happens in her work, memories pervade the
way places are presently understood. Objects belonging to or crossing a landscape elicit thought-experiments which in turn anthropomorphize the very
sceneries that ignite them. This animating and animistic strategy affects the way
we interpret the wider personal and historical significance of the locations that
Kennedy maps. What may at first seem like endearing memories become
freighted with prophetic implications:

> Circling in from the north-west came a single Lanc, big-chinned, blunt
> as a whale and open-armed and singing. When you heard them like that, far off,
> you could think they were trying to speak, words hidden underneath the roar, and
> if you could only work them out, you would understand everything, you would be
> saved. Except you were always too near to your own, half deafened with her, and
> someone else's Lanc would never quite talk for you. So you'd never know.
> (73–4)

Like a feature born out of the horizon itself, the bomber here appears at once
distinct from, yet intimately bound up with, Day's portentous reflections.
Detected aurally first, only later spotted at some range, the plane remains an
object sensed in momentary suspension, physically distanced from the anxieties
it provokes within. Yet Kennedy offsets these two perceptual scales here only to
emphasize their dramatic interdependency – showing, in effect, how an apparently routine, 'far off' spectacle can incite thoughts that seem entirely more
ominous and irresolvable.

It is this attraction to the prophetic richness of mundane sightings and
settings that Kennedy has explored from her earliest work. In this younger
phase, we find the verbal inflections of her highly self-vigilant narrators

extending the tonal range and affective nuances of quotidian language. Kennedy's combination of composure and improvised intrusion is central to a kind of narrative authority with which she choreographs events in space. Her grammatical and figurative innovations are understated in *Looking for the Possible Dance*, precisely because of the humane sensitivity with which she elucidates the mind of her focalizing heroine. Kennedy is undoubtedly a background engineer who knows when to stand away from her invention at work. Indeed, when recalling Margaret's fondness for her telescope as a child, the account of how it used to alter her everyday vision of the night's sky – itself an ancient landscape of surprises – serves as an analogy for Kennedy's poise as a shrewd curator-like figure overseeing and occasionally ironizing the novel's arena of remembrance: 'She loved to disappear into watching, to be nothing but eyes [. . .] Two of you couldn't watch; it was impossible for you to see the exact same things' (14). On a stylistic level, too, instances such as Margaret's leaving town, where our narrator disappears into pure watchfulness, reveal much about Kennedy's idiosyncratic choice of diction and tense. Across the novel, it is her rhetorically fastidious attention to the import of recollections however, short or unexceptional, which allows her to explore the fissures between memory and anticipation by emplacing them in everyday settings.

Kennedy's self-monitoring repose, her coolness as a stylist, draws our attention to how dynamic her sentence construction can be. Slight tonal inflections are scarcely functional. Specific grammatical devices offer not only a syntactic complement to the character's reaction to time and space; their construction mirrors the mechanisms of memory. At various stages in *Looking*, sentences rotate chiastically between retrospection and prediction. Certain phrases pivot in their temporal direction; often without severing into a subordinate clause, prepositions hinge from the past-perfect to the explicitly proleptic. When describing, for example, Margaret's recollection of her father's suit at a Methodist dance – the piercing memory of which opens the novel – Kennedy returns us to the event in its vivid actuality. Whenever waltzing like this, '[h]e drew her eye; surely, everyone's eye' (2). The sight of his outfit back then seems more eventful than the here-and-now; but in a more tragic respect, its vitality as a memory is precisely what betrays the vacancy it affirms in the present. By recalling her father's grace she confirms his absence, latching onto the image of an object that foresees its own return in a mournful acknowledgement that this was a 'suit she had never seen before and would not see again until after her father was dead' (2). Kennedy's transition in tense between verbs is devastating; it shuttles us rapidly on from a singular moment in years previous, towards its posthumous bereavement. With no dividing clause to offer pause between Margaret's past and present, between mourning and reparation, the sentence subjects the scene of memory to subsequent history in one fell swoop. Indeed, the caesural placement of the word 'before' marks a threshold past which Kennedy unleashes her knowing prediction. Following on from 'before', the anapaestic tetrameter accelerates away from remembrance, the clause racing onward to its foretelling closure. Aided by this pacey foot, Kennedy dislodges the status of the suit once belonging to Margaret's late father, telescoping it across time from being an object of admiration into an artefact – from that which 'drew . . . everyone's eye' into one of a few surviving things she can remember him by. Such is Kennedy's distinction in utilizing the space and rhythmic pace of syntactic inflections so as to achieve pathos; such is her courageous poise so portentously to 'disappear into watching'.

To similar effect, as the voyage southward unfolds in *Looking*, the pictorial rendering of memory's sudden revival influences the rhythm and tense of syntactic composition. The mutual stimulation of verbal repetition and involuntary remembrance is one of Kennedy's quintessential traits. Her laconic reiteration of adverbs across the novel frequently attests to that which is retrieved intermittently and without warning. And repetition in itself activates a verbal mnemonic for human absence. Words are feeble substitutes for human touch; they attempt to occupy the place of Margaret's lover as she herself is propelled through alien countryside. 'Even now, on her train, Margaret closes her eyes to imagine Colin in his yellow hospital bed [. . .] She misses him. She misses her daddy and she misses Colin more' (236). Those transitive verbs build through hissing *gradatio*, giving an effect of acceleration equivalent to the very voyage away from what she 'misses'. Cruelly ironic in this sense, the passing scenery merely accentuates her loss. The train leaves in its wake a trail of mnemonics on the trackside flashing past, triggering memories that confirm the absence of a homeland fast receding in this journey south:

> The walls by the side of the track are very strange now, grey brick and black brick and honey brick. Margaret has entered a foreign country. She remembers seeing waxwings searching the grass when she was at university and suddenly feeling homesick because they were not Scottish birds. (236)

Kennedy's dexterity proves itself here, in that sudden switch from outward description to recollections clutched and closely observed. Seized in single clause, held in the present-tense, Kennedy handles the flashback like porcelain – as though memories flare up from the landscape with a fugitive radiance, easily missed. And by tracing this ephemeral exchange between perception and retrospection, Kennedy certainly substantiates James Wood's claim that '[t]he delicacy of stream of consciousness is that it both discloses the movement of the mind and also gestures to what cannot be said, to what is unrepresentable; it is the soul's stutter'.[25] Kennedy's manner of *oratio oblique* offers such a prism. She adopts the accusative case in everyday language with lightness and precision; and for free-indirect discourse, this sensibility provides a verbal idiom in which characters reveal their faulting attempts at self-inquiry to us without ever being aware that their own daily habits of denial are being so thoroughly exposed. For as in the episode above, by being able to observe Margaret's inner recollections as an unsuspecting presence, the reader catches her unawares under the stimuli of associations that transfer late-teenage homesickness to the present. Using the most ordinary diction, Kennedy marks each flash of reminiscence with a new splash of tonal colour. *Looking for the Possible Dance* shifts unpredictably in style to affirm the unpredictable tendency for involuntary memories to lend both security and disenchantment.

Paradise (2004) inherits much of this impetus from *Looking*, equally immersing though couched in the first-person. As in that earlier novel, everyday settings in *Paradise* are transfigured from deserts of routine into vineyards of resurrection. The workaday world looms forth as a context replete with associations. As in Kazuo Ishiguro's work, we find a single character crossing an everyday environment where he or she is forced to reinhabit memories in the intensity of their originating circumstances. In *Paradise* past experience viscerally reignites the lived present for Hannah Luckraft, and for whom '[o]ne of the many pleasures of forgetting is, as we all of us know, remembering. You trot from room to room and can't imagine where you left your keys the night before: without them, you're locked in your house'.[26] Hannah is our perilously inebriated guide to the everyday, ever prepared to pass into coruscating self-analysis: 'I am delicate and the world is impossibly wrong, is unthinkable and I am not forewarned, forearmed, equipped. I cannot manage. If there was something useful I could do, I would – but there isn't. So I drink' (240). Kennedy uses that slide into intoxication to stage Hannah's dislocation from ordinary public places, places surrealistically recast into zones of violent fluctuation between past and present.

This temporal vacillation avails a mode of psychological inquiry that builds across successive settings. As she leads between urban realm and the interior mind, Kennedy 'represents the paradox of self', in John A. Dussinger's phrase, induced when selfhood feels at once ephemeral and secure – as an 'object caught in the momentary flux of consciousness and as the subject, freed from time, viewing discriminately past experience'.[27] *Paradise* reveals here a superior aspect of Kennedy's technique. We see it at work from the very opening chapter of *Looking*. Dunnigan has described it as the recurrence in her fiction of an '"expendable" temporal framework', a structuring device exploiting 'the instability of tense which renders the past and present lives of characters in intimate proximity' ('A. L. Kennedy's Longer Fiction', 145). In *Paradise* this frame assumes a new prominence in proportion to Hannah's decline. Hannah alleviates the pressure on the family who have despaired with her only to exacerbate the pressure of recalling the reasons for their mutual grievances, eventually forced by another relapse into a rehabilitation clinic in Montreal. After she relents to this enclosed, hospitalized place, the past recurs condemningly for Hannah by compelling her to question her very reasons for condemning her own siblings. That pastoral expanse around her in Montreal generates an abundance of more local memories; its foreignness repels her desire to wipe England from the mind's eye. Spoiling every moment of contemplation before its scenery, it's as though this landscape exports her back to the English province of her grief. No place for recession or wishful elimination, the terrain alone refuses her penitence. Hannah finds she is unable to repent simply by retreating into the fold of Nature's rustic yet foreign beauty here, a beauty which itself intensifies in a new climate her dissection of ugly regrets:

> I take the path through the floral borders: azaleas, the blue glow of rhododendrons, deep, broad ferns, honeysuckle trained against a maple, everything live, eating up the sun – my mother would love it here, the beauty of a garden edging into woods, into forest, into mountain: the only scar, the road that brought me here.
>
> I remember my mother. There are other people, details, items of importance that I have misplaced. I'm aware of that. (336)

Kennedy directs our attention here to the hidden side-effects of courting oblivion out in the open, of embarking into the landscape in the hope of abnegating one's self by surrendering to Nature's bosom. For Hannah, that path she wanders in the present cannot be detached from the mnemonic 'road that brought me here'. Encircled at the perimeter by pastoral 'floral borders', this is less a resting place for tranquil intellection than a zone of intense self-exposition. Kennedy manoeuvres us into a territory across which the sources of Hannah regret acquire fresh clarity with each step. Dispersed 'items of importance' are scarcely expected, never invited; their nagging recurrence thwarts her wish to enter this landscape merely as an 'abyss of remembering', in Anthony Vilder's phrase, which 'erases as much as it traces'.[28] Among this opulent fauna, so distinct from home, her childhood garden still intrudes. The landscape itself presents an insurmountable hurdle to forgetting: dispassionate in provoking her to recall that which she longs to diffuse most, the scenery alone acts as an obstinate failsafe guarding against voluntary amnesia. Proleptic conjectures intrude upon her isolation, denying Hannah any chance of erasing the prediction of how much her 'mother *would* love it here'. And again, Kennedy's shift between narrative tenses says it all. Switching from present-perfect to speculation and back again, Kennedy dramatizes how involuntary recollection switches tactics within the mind, leaving Hannah at the mercy here of a terrain whose mnemonic cues she cannot avoid. The conditions of dwelling may have outwardly changed, but they only accentuate the persistence of interior remorse.

In addressing issues of belonging, Kennedy shows how habitation is both a spatial and temporal phenomenon. At once immediate and inherited, our claim to habitability is conditioned by the values we attribute not only to privacy and permanence, but also to memories of places freighted with personal and familial history. Behind their discursive irony and self-reflexivity, Kennedy's narratives retain a humane poise, as she dramatizes the relationship between memorialization and displacement, filial attachments and physical motion.

Trezza Azzopardi's poetics of belonging

The search for a sense of belonging filtered through characters consumed with retrospective longing has become a common feature for contemporary novelists who dramatize the experiences of fugitive or marginal spaces. From a younger generation of British writers, Trezza Azzopardi has worked in this subgenre of narratives that evoke the tension between the idealization of mobility and the contrary desire for physical stability and ontological emplacement. In *Remember Me* (2004), Azzopardi's pitiable heroine is unwanted by her nuclear family in the wake of her mother's oblivion, and is freighted between relatives throughout her adolescence. For Winnie, the present can only be understood, it seems, as an indefinable landscape across which childhood traumas are placed at every turn. Tragically in this fashion, Azzopardi reterritorializes Winnie's past, staking it out as a series of mnemonic trapdoors through which she re-encounters personal actions that can only be recalled with despair. Memories are encoded across the novel into Winnie's story of unbelonging, a story that extends into her seventies. Awaiting bouts of more considered, evaluative forms of remembrance, memories taunt the uneventfulness she would prefer in old age:

> Sometimes there's an event, like a snow, or a funfair, or Christmas lights going on in the city, and it reminds you how the year rolls over. But mostly there's no edge, just tumbling days, which is how I like it. I have a routine which is rarely spoiled; it stops me having to think.[29]

Scenes from a whole lifetime soon disrupt narrative continuity as *Remember Me* unfolds, intermediating its chronology over seven decades. Her Booker-shortlisted debut *The Hiding Place* (2000) attested to Azzopardi's ability to navigate between interiority and external event. We also find this formal strategy in Kennedy and Swift, by which the subjectivist dimensions of the voyage trope are turned out to the social world via represented perceptions of public space. And in each of these writers, the very narrative conventions of mobility and self-scrutiny, walking and reflection, are mediated by quests for belonging. As in *The Light of Day*, retrospection becomes a literal as well as cerebral journey for Azzopardi's narrator. In *Remember Me* that haunting progress through uncharted memories complements Winnie's progress through communal places. Her past seems bound up with bodily movement in ways that militate against the prospect of repair that personal mobility might promise. As a child,

Winnie soon finds that she can't circumnavigate recollections as she might an obstacle in the street. No less in old age. For even here, looking back, 'all the other versions' of the childhood she remembers, including those of her mother's debilitating mental illness, are revised by every step she takes in the present built environment (68). In hindsight this reveals she had

> yet to learn that memories aren't real, that nothing except the thing itself is real, not an image of a pencil-thin woman lying flat on the bed, not the smell of sunlight baking a room, or the shape a life makes when it spills across the floor. But a handkerchief, a ribbon, a heart-shaped locket speckled with rust; these are objects, artefacts, proof of life. (68)

Like a collection of personal objects defying classification, or documents shuffled into disarray, separate points in family history refuse to be assimilated.

This sense of dissimilated retrospection and fabrication also affects narrative form. Azzopardi's use of paragraphical scissions to convey flashes of retrospection seemed less successful in *The Hiding Place*. Our immersion as readers can often be compromised across that novel by the intrusion of focalized thoughts, thoughts that branch off in recollections so dispersing as to elide the singularity of the locations that triggered them. By contrast, the sudden digressions in *Remember Me* seem more assured. For here Azzopardi uses recollection not only as a point of departure into remorse, but also retaining the essence of memory as situation. *Remember Me* rarely abandons the brute presence of landscapes in the here-and-now by allowing its narrator's memorial voyage to obscure the material impact of places that return to her mind. Azzopardi also thwarts any inkling we might have of *Remember Me* being a conventional *Bildungsroman*: by no means does her narrator labour across an inhospitable landscape of remembrance only to reach the frontiers of redemption. Instead the novel unfolds like an unkempt archive, a disordered accretion of artefacts, mirroring the uneven accumulation of its heroine's self-knowledge. As the passage above typifies, personal memories – apocryphal, perhaps unreal – refuse to synthesize. Lodging in objects, acts of remembrance establish an all but fragile 'proof of life', scarcely resilient before public eyes. Memories refuse to cohere in the novel within landscapes whose workaday spheres seem so incoherent; past experiences are assailed, if not diluted, while inhabiting radiant yet overwhelming public spaces. Such are the consequences, implies Azzopardi, of searching for portals between everyday demands through which to enter the winding vistas of irreparable events. One such event surrounds Winnie's sorrowful assumption that she could have done more to aid her anguished father:

> I balance his memories, all the same, storing them on top of mine, carefully leaning one against the other like a stack of playing cards. I am building a tower without bells. Later I will bring them down, in an earthquake of my own. (68)

Winnie proceeds solitarily towards this cataclysm. *Remember Me* is a journey both of isolating retrieval and chthonic prediction, branching backward and forward before the distractions of routine in old age. From one provincial corner of England to the next, Azzopardi's lexicon of absences – elaborating on words like 'nothing' and 'without' recurring throughout the text – offers a grammatical correlative to the emotional side-effects of encountering mnemonics in unremarkable landscapes. Between sceneries *Remember Me* flourishes with these negative epiphanies. In mental voyages from London to Yarmouth, the vacuums left by indefinite personal memories are merely exacerbated by the vacancy of public spaces, a mutuality that breeds distrust in the narrator posing as navigator: 'Clocks and mirrors: liars both, but it was all I had to go on' (69). Azzopardi dramatizes one's effort in retrospection to avoid the influence of invented memories, especially those fabricated by extended family members across the years, now freighted with deception and selective erasure.

Across *Remember Me*, that repeated vocabulary of pronouns each bereft of a specified object – 'nothing', 'nowhere', 'everything' – serve as sensory receptors to its narrator's disorienting process of remembrance. One to add to this list is the generic 'you': it beckons out between recounted events to Azzopardi's implied readers, summoning them as co-witnesses to Winnie's distress. The repetition of 'you', along with those other indefinite pronouns beckons to our participation in that process by which remembrance can become resuscitation. By occasionally shifting into this second-person narration, the novel obliges the reader to ponder in ways comparable to our uncertain narrator – to wonder at the probability of recovery beneath the lived weight of all that has passed and been lost. Azzopardi attributes those indeterminate pronouns as epithets for the uncertain provenance of Winnie's memories: pronouns that chime with the unreliability of retrieved experiences, while denoting the absences left by periods in her life that defy recollection altogether. Throughout *Remember Me*, these hanging pronouns recur like incantations to memories whose doubtful veracity requires a degree of settled, measured, analytic retrospection of which Winnie is barely capable. Much of this disorder is once more imposed by place itself. After shortly being rejected by the austere aunt in whose isolated farm she seeks refuge in the novel's mid-section, Winnie is exiled back to suburbia. Packed off again unwanted, she foresees herself 'shrivelling to nothing in the middle of the dead brown land' (*Remember Me*, 128). What drives the wider family severally to desert her is a habitual neglect Winnie soon normalizes as mundane. Much like the passing fields outwardly 'skimming into a muzzy blur' (128), she gives up trying to calculate the motives for these incessant expulsions that throughout childhood have guaranteed her sense that displacement is part and parcel of everyday life: 'I stopped counting, looked the other way. I was going back to Chapelfield; there was nowhere else' (128). And in the course of this return journey, Azzopardi's lexicon of indefinite pronouns furnishes a vocabulary for expressing personal memory as elusive, yet tangible too and multilayered. It also conveys the emotional consequences of memory's fabrication and subsequent metamorphosis. The multiplication of indefinite pronouns in Winnie's narration reflects her bewilderment, especially when a flood of associations are triggered by her hometown now in the wake of war. Azzopardi uses this indefinite grammar to complement the past's apparent immunity to any kind of definitive verification.

One episode exemplary of this condition is reminiscent of the menacing Regency Park in Elizabeth Bowen's opening to *The Heat of the Day* (1949). Closing the novel's first chapter is an unerring description of the way the Park's perimeter-terraces have hunkered down beneath 'bronzy' twilight: 'the indifference of their vacant black windows fell on the scene, the movement, the park, the evening they overlooked but did not seem to behold'. Emblematic of London's increasingly unoccupied centre, 'their semi-ruin' bears witness to a city awaiting night-raids, pinioned in the vice of expectancy.[30] Azzopardi offers a more literally embattled townscape. Interspersed with ruins, Chapelfield's patchwork of familiar landmarks causes Winnie to interrogate what she once assumed to be her most valid and valuable recollections:

> It was a long walk from the station. The streets looked ordinary at first, just as I remembered them, and then I turned a corner, and there was a pile of smoking rubble, a spume of dust, as if the earth had split its belly. More ordinary streets, then the sky where there used to be a factory; a hole in the ground for a church; a tumble of bricks, burnt wood, bent wire where a row of shops once stood. A cottage with its face peeled off and the furniture inside turned over and broken, like a ransacked doll's house. On and on through the city; the same and different at every turn. (128)

With the narrator glancing round in bewilderment, indefinite articles take over this time. They punch out emotive stills in clauses shorn of deixis. In a chorus of phrases unanchored in tense from the past-perfect, description peals forth in a nominative case, icy, uninflected, forensically precise. Azzopardi reverts to a depersonalized imperfect-present tense so as to convey the volatile suspension of urban space between memory and reality. With every successive sentence, Winnie's mentally preserved image of the town clashes more insistently with its present destruction. And in each case, the appetitive repetition of that declarative 'a' carries the urgency of her desire to document changes all the more overwhelming for being so close to home. Hurriedly tracing this fabric of erasures, allowing herself only the occasional simile, Azzopardi finds no need for topographical analogies beyond the frankness of pure reportage. Sheer spectacle forestalls measured elegy, since the violent proximity of absence after absence where buildings once stood ('the sky', 'a hole in the ground') prevents Winnie from pausing in nostalgic remembrance of what is no longer there. Those unadorned sentences tumble thus into a list of snapshot remarks, accelerating with every street corner. The landscape is seemingly transformed in actuality to such an extent that makes it impossible for Winnie to keep pace with the rapid transformation of its image held previously in her memory.

By invoking the trope of the exile's return here, Azzopardi maintains a closely knitted relationship between memory, place and the contradictions entailed by a desire to preserve both. She offers a humane dissemination of how memory is predicated on painful paradoxes, elucidating Scott McQuire's notion that remembrance 'faces a double injunction: the imperative of preserving, bringing close, and making familiar what must nevertheless remain unfamiliar, alien, discontinuous'.[31] In *Remember Me*, exterior stimuli from altering landscapes induce sudden insights into an uncharted mindscape. Therein unfurls a psychic terrain of self-doubt, across which our narrator voyages to question retrospectively the circumstances of her own origins and upbringing. 'Like my name', she concedes, 'staying made no difference to me. It was just another place' (135). The novel initially seems to epitomize Marc Augé's claim that narrative fiction is 'the fruit of memory and oblivion, of a work of compensation and recomposition that translates the tension exerted by the expectation of the future upon the interpretation of the past'.[32] Yet Azzopardi's work only partly substantiates this claim, giving more emphasis to the lived experience of recomposing the past over any prospect of recompense. In *Remember Me*, social spaces themselves perpetuate a dismembering routine, a routine that compels Winnie's genealogical self-inquest into a search for recognition within a world in which to be unnamed is synonymous with unsettlement.

As her plot unwinds, Azzopardi foregrounds the way memories intervene, with both comforting and disruptive consequences, in personal quests for belonging pursued through public space. Often it seems as if the novel is unfolding in spite of its heroine's sentiments – embodying the memorial voyage she claims never to have embarked upon. Winnie's repeated consideration of the validity of her own name gradually provokes her to reconsider the everyday landscapes she moves through, diverting her from inhabiting spaces of complete resignation and despair. This is where rhetorical repetition recalibrates the very texture of the novel by the time Winnie takes refuge in an austere Bethel Street boarding house, sheltering from all those who have 'called me a derelict' (241). Where the episodic pull of Winnie's memories is surpassed by more direct moments of narrative prolepsis, expiation reorients towards expectation: 'We would go back, if we were allowed'. Yet she also admits by the next clause that 'back is confused; back is just a story, and sometimes it causes pain' (237). The weight of the past compels her to depart on a new route.

Complementing the felt effects of that compulsion, she capitalizes nouns so as to personify states of being: 'Memories are not Approved subjects; there must be no Before' (237). Sentient yet spurious, memories step into the novel like deceitful guardians of past experience conspiring against those in their custody for whom personal history is so painful. Winnie deems it better to rescind memory's ambivalent donations. Not that denial is condemned by her boarding house Sister, who 'discourages us from going back' (237). Instead, we shadow our narrator's mission to 'learn a different language' for remembrance (237) by claiming a private space in which to practice recollection on her own terms. Predicting her later insistence that '[a] name won't own me' (241), Winnie considers that the hostel enclosing her cannot own its occupants forever. In refusing to be 'taken out into the city' on day-trips into the glaring present (237), she turns to accept memory's entreaty, knowing full well the damaging consequences of stifling its haunting demands. By purposefully 'choos[ing] not to go on these walks' (237), she roams mental contours instead, tracing back all those cumulative events that have ensured '[n]o one remembers me' (238). Reaching for the past because the present is itself insecure, she practises in secret forbidden resurrections that carefully repeal the consolations of repression. The novel thus dramatizes the vulnerability involved when returning to interrogate experiences and the places one associates with them; for by our returning, we encourage personal history to repeat with a force that denies its originary context any kind of emotional closure, while presaging voyages yet to be done.

These consequences are telling. And it is this driving imperative of revisiting as recuperating in *Remember Me* which assumes linguistic form, too. For just as Azzopardi's recapitulations of a verbal kind proffer a twin function to the novel's heroine – at once mnemonic and portentous – then so does the discursive influence of rhyme. Rhyme, of course, functions powerfully as a memory cue: it aurally performs and figuratively transforms the subject of recollection. As Gillian Beer points out: 'Rhyme not only makes things memorable; it seems to vouch for them. It confirms; it persuades; it is part of the rhetoric of belief. But it includes its own improbability, its semantic vagrancy'.[33] In *Remember Me*, Azzopardi becomes fascinated with the presaging effect of rhyme. She focuses our attention on the narrator's ability to perceive everyday routines in terms of what they might foretell; her ability, that is, to 'see ordinary things', while having cause to 'wonder' at people 'for whom the ordinary wasn't enough' (212).

This is perhaps the most tragic yet immersing aspect of *Remember Me* as it explores the intersection of memory and everyday space. Azzopardi involves the reader in the futility of her narrator's perpetual quest to rewrite her history of relentless desertion by roaming the urban present for traces of attachment. Wide circumnavigations are entertained on foot in the hope of activating

predictions of that reparative terrain, as yet unseen, still to be deciphered out
of the ordinary:

> I think I can walk a straight line, but then the road will turn to water under my
> feet. There's nothing to be done but to go back, join another road, and hope it
> will last. The wind becomes unexpectedly brisk, metallic on the tongue. I imagine
> it blowing off the sea, mineral blue. I follow the scent, turning round on myself,
> breathing the air through my mouth, as if taste alone will find it. It feels like
> I won't ever get there, so when I come up over a field, find a road, see the tower
> of St Giles in the distance, I have to bite the tears away: it's then I know I never
> will. (212–13)

The accreted nouns here chime with verbs to gather over the passage into a
collection of dislocated half-rhymes. They impact as choric chimes to a hetero-
topia made not only inaccessible but illusory. Azzopardi emphasizes their
sonority by allowing each to resound on the stressed syllable of an iamb, with
verbs at the head of the sequence where most of the drama of Winnie's sense of
anticipation happens, and nouns concluding the subordinated description of
her devastating disappointment. Pealing forth as a striated series of feminine
rhymes, they work connotatively in many directions. Their delicate euphony
tolls across the passage, with each second rhyming word qualifying retroactively
the semantic implications of its previous partner. This causes that network of
phonetic affinities to assume a pathetic aspect by the end of the paragraph
(which also closes the chapter). For we realize, on a second reading, how the
'sea' will be a place she may never 'see', those 'tears' welling up from her
inability to find what she can so pungently 'taste'. And a second reading
intensifies, too, how cruelly the topography itself behaves. For that obstructing
'field' initially teases and finally taunts her, delaying the visual prospect
that might confirm or disprove the visceral proximity of a new frontier she so
expectantly 'feels'. Correlating with each other, then, across successive clauses,
these slant rhymes enhance the immediacy of presented perception by furnishing an accelerating grammar of anticipation. It is a grammar conveying our
narrator's path towards St Giles as a site that confirms her distance still from the
coast of sanctuary. Azzopardi uses physical space here proleptically rather than
mnemonically: as a destination, the sea forecloses a journey our narrator
'never will' conclude. Offering a miniature parable of memory and perception,
the episode marks a Proustian manoeuvre in which an attempt at forgetting
becomes one of foretelling. Vivid prophecies appear bound up with what
emotionally preceded them. Azzopardi rehearses this conundrum throughout
Remember Me to considerable effect. Her novel reveals how memories provoke us
to anticipate the promise that places can hold yet in such a way that simultaneously compromises our attempt to seek refuge from the past in all-consuming
acts of wishful prediction.

Rhyme thus operates within *Remember Me* to lure its readers in from the outside, proposing a radical means of relating to the text's grammatical production. Rhyme achieves this by turning the novel's thematization of memory into a way of combining interpretation and aesthetic representation, readerly immersion and the rhetoric of remembrance. This is what I would call a process of *participatory recollection*, one that also stimulates the colour of narrative language. For by allowing memory to figure at literal and linguistic levels across the text, Azzopardi's rhyming thereby reveals how the lightest of syllabic inflections can be exploited for their signifying potential, even on the scale of a novel. The passage above, then, epitomizes the presaging, curiously proleptic effects of remembrance; it also proves that in narrative fiction, as forcefully as in poetry, '[r]hyme revivifies words', as Beer reminds us: 'A word, even at line ending, does not impress itself deeply on the auditory memory, but when coupled to another in rhyme it is taken forward and becomes part of a skein of recollection' ('Rhyming as Resurrection', 196). Something comparable happens in that episode of Winnie's approach to St Giles. Ordinary words, drawn from adjacent clauses, yet belonging to different grammatical categories, rhyme together all but tenuously, indecisively – they verify the vulnerability of the narrator who communicates them. The phonetic correlation between 'feel' and 'field', 'taste' and 'tears', across syntactic space seems fragile indeed: they chime too far apart to be held comfortably within the reader's auditory memory span. Yet the effect of Azzopardi's understated use of rhyme here is remarkable for the way it induces that reader to enact a kind of self-implication, involving us in rhyme's textual industry. That is, our task of inferring the subtle harmony between adverb and noun becomes implicitly a matter of retrospection, of second-readings like the one I performed above, in which we return to the scene of the rhyme. Just as Swift's narrator did in *The Light of Day* in making that anniversary visit back to Beecham Close, likewise is the reader compelled in *Remember Me* by the phonology of reiteration as remembrance. What occurs literally in Swift's novel thus occurs extratextually for Azzopardi's, where interpretation itself initiates a 'search in our memory for a forgotten idea', to use William James's own wonderful anecdote, 'just as we rummage our house for a lost object. In both cases we visit what seems to us the probable *neighbourhood* of that which we miss'.[34] For it's as though Azzopardi's vowel-rhymes in that passage above – fugitively placed, rhetorically reticent – actively encourage the reader to enact the very psychological performance of delayed retrieval that this novel has been enunciating throughout.

Remember Me gives privileged access, then, to its narrator's understanding of how everyday spaces come to differ so markedly in memory and in reality. Azzopardi turns our process of comprehension into one that reciprocates Winnie's mental journey throughout the novel, a journey in which recollections are retrieved piecemeal, belatedly, without warning. It is a prime example of what Beer describes as our being compelled, as readers, to assume an active part 'in rhyme's performances of resurrection' (207). There is a further, ethical dimension to this kind of involvement, of course, a dimension that Azzopardi, Swift and Kennedy have all capitalized upon in their work. By each inviting a level of participatory recollection between reader and speaker, they ask us to assume a self-conscious degree of imaginative empathy with their characters' voyages through everyday space. In compelling us to pursue interpretation as a model of strategic and intuitive retrievals across their work, these writers coerce us to consider the penalties of involuntary recollection. Their fictions vigorously test the reader's own capacity to empathize with the isolating consequences of resurrecting experiences from the locations to which memories refer, while revealing the way personal history can work salaciously upon our ability to navigate our immediate surroundings.

These parables of remembrance reveal much about the way memories arise spontaneously from everyday environments. As Azzopardi's narrator shrewdly warns, we risk self-delusion in assuming we can return to places vividly memorized, however confident we feel in recounting every trace of our previous experiences there:

> There's not a lot of wisdom in old age, despite what they say. Truth is, as you get older, things get further away. Objects, I mean, like telephones boxes and the shops and that. Places you have to imagine walking to, or in the case of traffic, getting out of the way of. And near up, everything's such a mist – you're practically blind. Well I am [. . .] Then there's other stuff, memories for instance: now they really should be far away. But just one nudge and they're right under your nose. (169)

Azzopardi's description of 'things' carefully moves towards the promise of restoration – though not unconditionally. Her tactile documentation of known objects dispels estrangement and prospects the hope of attachment. But Azzopardi also holds that process of remembering childhood experiences in a delicate tension for Winnie: holding it between the enduring legibility of a memorialized state of being, and the disembodying consequences of recovering infant memories merely as sensory abstractions into which she can permanently recede. Objects and places alike are thus given ontological value, but at a price. Azzopardi's dispossessed narrator treasures the skills gained in being 'taught to believe in artefacts: to balance them, store the person in an object' (112). Reminiscence here is quashed by the ambiguity of what it meant to be forcefully 'taught'; this verb itself flares up performatively for Winnie, denoting the support she no longer receives. In recalling the value of being 'taught', she seems to claim a paradoxical form of consolation: salvaging 'other stuff' from the past to a present environment where her only teacher is brute survival. Azzopardi implies that while objects often seem endowed with presence, they also verify the corporeal absence of the very 'person' to whom the object clings by association.

To contemplate the dynamics of dwelling through conundrums of this kind, of course, has been a motivation at the heart of Ishiguro's concern with memory and belonging. Most recently in *Never Let Me Go*, a treasured cassette-recording of the eponymous ballad conjures similar associations for the narrator Kathy. After losing it and rediscovering it by chance in an old record shop, Kathy 'really appreciated having the tape – and that song – back again'.[35] Despite her occasional efforts to see herself in no need of such things, her dependence on them as souvenirs is affirmed by the longing that such items inaugurate, recursively, often without warning. 'Even then, it was mainly a nostalgia thing, and today, if I happen to get the tape out and look at it, it brings back memories of that afternoon in Norfolk every bit as much as it does our Hailsham days' (159). Ishiguro suggests that although the most ordinary of objects are often backlit by the pleasures and ravages of the past, they need not always be solicited as stale artefacts to what might have been. As pocket-sized memorials, alternately handled and hidden, they can encapsulate without altogether yielding to melancholia's anterior beckoning. In *Remember Me*, similar kinds of ordinary items also temporarily relieve the insecurities Winnie has long associated with the dehumanizing nature of public space; yet by no means do they guarantee her lasting asylum from the exigencies of age. What does happen, though, in relation to all these accoutrements drawn from memory, is altogether subtler. Aura becomes odour: when objects cue sensorial memories of an individual's singularity, the penumbra of unspecified loss is eclipsed by the pungency of precise associations. And indeed, 'it is *all* in the nose', continues Winnie,

> That innocent scent wafting out of the chemist? That's my father's hands after he danced with my mother; and that particular, early morning winter air with a tang of spring in it? Joseph Dodd, waiting in the church plantation, twirling a feather between finger and thumb. It all means something. Like the rusty railing you've touched, which in a second is the iron chain of a swing you gripped so tight when you were five: fear and bliss, mixed. (169)

The novel's recurrent motif of 'nothing' is here superseded, even redeemed, by a new insistence on 'something'. Azzopardi emphasizes the substantiality of memories recalled when enduring current demands: even in the most inhospitable public place, every intimate connection 'means something'. Vapid as this notion may sound, Azzopardi detects the nemesis of remembering as an interpersonal phenomenon. She permits her narrator to decline regret's invitation to prolonged despair in the aftermath of a life spent displaced; but this permission is only granted by Winnie's renewed vigilance towards the communal possibilities of everyday space itself. In offering this prospect of resistance, however, Azzopardi also allows several incongruous, even irresolvable, propositions to emerge. To the very level of attachment to object-matter that facilitates Winnie's *private* homage, the novel poses the question of whether such attachments can work socially, too, whether our bonds to the past can lend coherence to the self who appears before *public* eyes. For Azzopardi warns that there is a certain futility about the way Winnie confers meaning on objects that emanate 'fear and bliss, mixed', a certain desperation in using them as comforting mnemonics to allay her obliterative daily existence, a certain reliance on their surviving associations to persons no longer alive. *Remember Me* queries these connections between memory and the material world, querying what they foster within us, what they allow us to endure. The novel invites us to wonder whether the urban spaces we daily move through are so inimical to human engagements of an intimate, fugitive kind that one is often compelled to seek solace in gossamer relics.

Azzopardi joins Kennedy and Swift in attempting to reveal how the most familiar objects from ordinary environments are far from culturally opaque or devoid of historical provenance. Everyday places and their material objects are never unreflective in the work of these writers, caught as they are in cycles of extinction and perpetuity. Ordinary accessories bear the personal resonance that characters attach to them; concrete things sustain connections between past and present, consolation and contemporary need. As novelist and cultural critic Marina Warner remarks, '[t]oday, during this era of mechanical reproduction, the body's imprint and presence in the artefact through direct marks of touch and action have become increasingly sought after, and cherished'.[36] By carrying with them smells, tastes and handled textures, such familiar objects emit auratic references to a social world whose events in memory they emblematize as souvenirs. In fact, it is the memorial distinction of object-matter in the fictions discussed above which enfolds a broader issue. For whether they survive primarily 'as ethnographic artefacts or works of art', as Antoinette Barton asserts, 'these "things" serve as witnesses to history, and their material presence testifies to the persistence, durability and commodification of empire in the contemporary present'.[37] This sense of empire as a transitional phenomenon, unresolved as an aspect of our modernity and traceable into Britain's current constitution, will occupy the following chapter, where postcolonial writers show that Will Self is surely right to highlight the way geography informs the link between personal genealogy and adult creativity:

> It matters where you are born. Not just the country or the city, the burg or the hamlet – but the precise location, its height above terra firma, its positioning in the welter of the world; for this is the still point at the exact centre of the ever-expanding shock wave of your life.[38]

Self refuses to understate here the implications of impermanence and detachment for writers who allow experiences of migrancy and memory to reshape and extend their craft. By the same stroke, contemporary postcolonial novelists have insisted that the personal dilemmas of dwelling manifest themselves on a global scale. The public memory of world-historical events shows that British writers can scarcely address issues of subjectivity divorced from those of nation-space. For novelists today cannot solely dramatize the individual's experience of belonging without also recognizing how radically the space of personhood has evolved alongside the international forces of the present.

Chapter 5

Island Encounters

Isolated spaces can be as enthralling as they are foreboding. So it is with the figure of the island. For eighteenth-century Britain, the patriotic conflation of cartographic autonomy with geopolitical sovereignty had become talismanic. The image of Britannia as a severed-off haven, its indigenous population safe from foreign influences like the most inaccessible of islands, belied a nationalistic equation of geophysical actuality with the nation's hallowed independence. Such a connection relied in turn upon the paradox of England's very non-existence as an island: its existence, indeed, as a formative part of the British Isles in its entirety, just one 'land' in an amalgamated (and by no means harmonious) 'kingdom' surrounded by overlapping currents, both commercial and ideological. A compound realm encircled by several intersecting seas, Great Britain has of course been diversely repopulated in ways that fundamentally redefine our understandings of nationhood, settlement and belonging. For postwar urban communities, the so-called *Windrush* generation would famously revitalize that picture of Britain as an island with porous bounds, an island today in which the meanings of *isle*, *landscape* and *home* are vigorously contested rather than conflated in our global, post-national era.

Insignias of nationhood, however, scarcely devolve without gesturing to the past. If the Conservative government often rehearsed through the 1980s a patriotic idea of England's pastoral heritage, it merely epitomized how the purposeful restitution of the nation's mythic past can shadow otherwise progressive debates over the status of post-imperial Englishness. This Anglocentric recourse to self-authenticity bears more than the mark of nostalgia. The political privileging of insular nativism highlights the complex histories that have shaped Britain's ethnic multiplicity. As Hanif Kureishi has asserted, acculturation alone can perpetuate alienation in personal and cartographical respects, particularly when one self-identifies, as he does, as English-born while at the same time a subject of racial prejudice. Reflecting on his attempt 'to deny my Pakistani self', Kureishi sees that this process of self-conscious dislocation may itself be a tactic for reforming national identity.[1] If 'the white British . . . have to learn that being British isn't what it was', then ethnicity after empire is itself 'a more complex thing, involving new elements' (204). Without presuming the scars of decolonization have healed or that the chimera of native purity no longer aggravates discrimination, Kureishi sets forth a clear objective for belonging. It is an entreaty, levelled at the spaces in which new subjectivities might take place, whose challenge seems all the more urgent for sounding so rhetorically forthright: 'there must be a fresh way of seeing Britain and the choices it faces . . . Much thought, discussion and self-examination must go into seeing the necessity for this, what this "new way of being British" involves and how difficult it might be to attain' (204).

Responding to this request for 'a fresh way of seeing', contemporary writers have turned the postcolonial novel into a generic category defined by impermanence and transition. This state of incompletion evidences the formal directions pursued by contemporary novelists who publish in Britain even as they write from abroad: descendants of postwar immigrant families, whose work continues to trace the ramifications of Western imperialism alongside the residual presence of Anglocentrism. We can discern a divide in Kureishi's generation, between writers such as David Dabydeen and Salman Rushdie who historicize the diasporic experience, and those including Sunetra Gupta and Timothy Mo, who complement V. S. Naipaul's fascination with outsiderness by addressing questions of individual settlement in a shared conversation with local traditions. Taken together, we can appreciate how these practitioners have diversified the priorities of stylistic experiment itself, opening out postcolonial fiction through the 1980s and 1990s to new geopolitical concerns. Such writers have exploited a range of formal strategies while reappropriating modes of narration and characterization hitherto regarded as traditionalist or inflexible. Coinciding with the displacement of nationhood as a disposition, postwar Black and Asian novelists have thus appealed by analogy to the very geophysical flux of islands. For as they move from chronicling enforced migration to scrutinizing the sustainability of multiracial communities, postcolonial writers have capitalized on the sense in which Britain's cultural landscape can no longer be thought of as pre-existent, timeless or foundational, but as continually remade in imperialism's wake.

From a contemporary postcolonial standpoint, it is hard to gauge the ideological force with which Britain's image of island autonomy was lauded. As Markman Ellis explains, in the eighteenth century the nation's self-image was that of 'coastal insularity and discreteness', an image that eulogized the 'notion that island geography was essential to British political independence'.[2] Yet as Ellis points out, '[i]n the period of the first British Empire, the island was formulated as a paradox: the independence implied by a geography of land surrounded by water was surmounted by an archipelagic sense of co-dependence and imperial purpose, mediated through culture and commerce' (61). Rapidly expanding imperialist trade in the nineteenth century linked Britain with distant nations who were hitherto considered remote, eccentric, if not uncivilized. This served to established migration routes in and out of native shores. It was across this 'era of commercial capitalism', notes John R. Gillis, that 'coasts and islands

were the core and the continents the periphery of geographical transfers of
capital, people and knowledge'.[3] But people, as much as produce, trammelled
these networks of foreign exchange. This human flow prevailed, and despite
the fact that the nation entered an expansive period of industrialization, 'Great
Britain came to think of itself in insular rather than continental terms', observes
Gillis, 'creating for itself an archipelagic empire beginning with nearby
Ireland and eventually extending throughout the Atlantic' (29). Present-day
Britain is a vivid example of the futility of this self-insulating project, as it
gradually facilitated the hybridization of its own socio-cultural fabric from
within. Indeed, it was as though the privation of other islands accelerated
the demise of racial and ethnic uniformity within the mainland population.
Few other European nations have evolved out of the idolatries of imperialism
in this recapitulatory sense, as the aftershocks of Britain's colonial emigrations
now resonate back, returning to transform the country's provinces. Maritime
expeditions echo from the past as transoceanic routes for immigration enduring into the present, thus establishing the nation's status today as a locus of
intercultural circulation and settlement. Heightening our awareness of its
multicultural constitution, postcolonial writers have shown how Britain cannot
now avoid the ethical and geopolitical repercussions of its foreign policies, past
and present. This has become all the more apparent since globalization at once
facilitates economic profit, while attracting nationalistic predictions of Britain's
waning sovereignty that blend with warnings against unrestricted immigration.
It would seem that the imperious idealization of English exclusivity, of a bucolic
landscape under protection from the sea, has once again piqued the nation's
awareness of colonialism's legacy.

Picturing distant shores

A nation's image of itself as a bounded island thus fosters a series of ambiguous
associations between geography and physiognomy, ancient landform and body
politic, the escalation of foreign passage and the stability of native personhood.
Such an image also makes the incoming encounter by those foreign to its
shores all the more perilous, igniting ferocious resistance and instituting
policies of exclusion. Correlations such as these between space and soma, island
self-sufficiency and political resilience, both pervaded and unnerved the
nineteenth-century imperialist imaginary. Cartographic distinction bore the
promise of ideological autonomy, even though 'in empire and in commerce',
as Ellis reminds us, 'islands are brought into relations of trust and dependence,
connection and association' (44). Britain could entertain the idea of its political body operating from island-based headquarters – the nerve centre of a
patriotic global command. English civility might then continue to be regarded
as both separate from and superior to empire's supposedly uncivilized colonies,

colonies so geographically distant from English soil as to confer upon imperial policies a kind of symbolic immunity. Once again, we see how nation-space could acquire a superficial degree of invulnerability. Transcontinental allegiances were not in themselves inconceivable, so long as they were ideologically or economically advantageous.

A century on, of course, the ambivalent charm of topographical independence persisted in quite different ways for postwar generations appealing to Britain for asylum. Arriving from Zanzibar in 1968, novelist and literary scholar Abdulrazak Gurnah sensed that Britain's story as an island made it such a 'strange land'. A destination for increasing numbers of immigrants, burgeoning new forms of community life typified the kind of accelerating multiculturalism that Thatcherite nationalists would later prefer to disavow.[4] Registering this dispossessing climate for achieving settlement in the face of discrimination, Gurnah's own fiction has refreshed for the contemporary scene that same image of England as part of a composite island, whose sovereignty is as permeated by neighbouring provinces as its shoreline is by the sea. Driven by episodes of literal revisiting or mnemonic recall, novels such as *Memory of Departure* (1987) and the Booker-shortlisted *Paradise* (1994) have figured the East-African island of Zanzibar as a region haunting the mind of narrators pinioned in the jaws of regret. They speak to us as frustrated individuals who, having emigrated in fear, now mourn the political and social upheavals of a native country to whose scarred landscape they partially long to return. Here, the redemption of place and personhood goes hand in hand; it is a reciprocal task of atonement, implicating one's present conscience in the actions of former selves. Gurnah often pursues as his thematic premise the rapidly shifting demography of Britain's provinces. This extends the impulse of major figures such as Rushdie, Ishiguro and Okri who have attended the diverse contexts of migration, while also connecting with those from a new generation addressed earlier in this book, such as Amit Chaudhuri and Monica Ali, who portray a Millennial Britain struggling to keep tradition and difference, preservation and acculturation in balance.

Gurnah attests from his own experience that Britain's socio-geographic fabric has become altogether complex and ethnically multilayered, making the campaigns of assimilationist lobbies seem archaic and imperious. He implies that metropolitan experience alone has long discredited the currency of English purity – again, a purity emblematized cartographically, whenever the nation is eulogized as an island immune from influence, home to an authentic population now consigned to the past. Yet Gurnah's work, in tune with the novels I consider later in this chapter, insists that hybridity can always breed unease among communities who leave intolerance unquestioned. While mid-nineteenth-century Britain may well have been a 'site of pleasure and advancement', as Michael Fisher has documented, with the English aristocracy fostering an unlikely climate of 'personal gratification and elevation' for upper-middle-class immigrant Indian men,[5] within a century a less convivial British society emerged in the melancholic shadow of waning imperialism. Whereas British foreign policies, after nurturing import markets, had benefited the settlement experience of certain Indian diplomats and merchants, the successive waves of West Indians arriving among the visible remnants of the Blitz received an altogether adverse welcome. Bigotry and suspicion mixed with the nation's sense of unprecedented opportunity at the prospect of utilizing Caribbean labour. As Caryl Phillips remarks when revisiting E. R. Braithwaite's debut, *To Sir With Love* (1959):

> Reading it reminds us that in the early 50s, as tens of thousands of easily identifiable 'others' were beginning to enter the country in an attempt to rebuild Britain after the ravages of the second world war, this deep-seated problem of unquestioned hereditary prejudice was waiting to greet them in the streets, in the work place and in institutions of learning.[6]

Yet as Gurnah points out, despite the hostility of interracial relations in industry and social life, today urban communities are exhibiting signs of progression. Diverse accounts of displacement as a common experience have been woven together between neighbourhoods, turning local communities into sites of shared recollection. Individual accounts of coming to Britain strike up mutual affinities, says Gurnah: circumstance can befit change, whereby the close proximity of races and backgrounds makes apparent improbable affinities. This is particularly the case when immigrant communities find they are living alongside other 'people who are in every respect part of a place', as Gurnah put it to Susheila Nasta, 'but who neither feel part of a place, nor are regarded as being part of a place' (352). With the achievement of dwelling comes indeterminacy, rendering provisional one's sensation of belonging. Only by capitalizing upon this sense of rootlessness, recalls Gurnah, was he able to develop a critical and aesthetic sensibility with which he could identify himself as a 'world writer':

> In the past, there was always a kind of hierarchy, so what was meant by 'world' was 'Europe'. Now we know that this is not the case. The 'world' that Walcott is talking about, or the 'world' that I'm thinking of, or even people like Salman Rushdie or Caryl Phillips and others are thinking about, is not that 'world'. T. S. Eliot's world of 'tradition' as Eliot meant it at the time [. . .] was a world of European tradition. Now we have writers who come from a wider world. I am part of that. (362)

While defining himself as a chronicler of migration on an international scale, Gurnah also stresses the need to specify how immigration differs between discrete times and places. And it is the writer he most associates with this bifocal perspective on empire's global and local legacies whose own approach to aesthetic 'tradition' will occupy my focus below. For it is this question of how to historicize migrancy – as an imperial reality and ontological disposition – from the Caribbean archipelago onward, which has returned time and again for Caryl Phillips to influence his formal technique. Moving between fiction and travel-documentary, Phillips is mindful of the manifold succession of diasporic movements, along with the restless progression of those literary modes through which writers have conveyed the emotional consequences of displacement.

Caryl Phillips and the restlessness of form

'We are all born into the world with a sense of place', asserted Alan Sillitoe in 1974, 'simply because a certain part of our senses is rooted forever to the locality in which . . . we first saw light' (*Mountains and Caverns*, 59). However, what if that sensation of origins has been radically diffused, particularly in the cultural afterlife of migration and reacclimatization? What happens to that fragile equation of beginning and belonging under the duress of displacement, whether enforced or willed? On considering his own capacity as a novelist to express the 'anchor-like attachment to the locality he was born in' (59), Caryl Phillips has been compelled to look again at his own formal influences and motivations:

> Britain in 1984 was not a place I cared to spend much time in. There was considerable racial and cultural confusion in the air, which continued to manifest itself in an upsurge of far right-wing activity, and a concomitant backlash from young black people that was principally directed against the police force. As the society reluctantly began to make the transition from 'West Indian' to 'Black British' as the acceptable, and more accurate, term with which to describe non-white citizens, things only seemed to get worse.[7]

Phillips found that this decline impacted upon what publicists required of him when documenting the West Indian immigration. He felt coerced, constrained into privileging autobiographical associations in his fictional writing – using it merely as a vehicle for a wider polemic that only generalized his own experience of travel:

> All too often I found myself being called upon by the media to explain my generation of black people to Britons – meaning white Britons – a predicament that can quickly reduce a writer to the position of being little more than a social commentator.
>
> In such a situation, what is in danger of being lost is the narrative of self. My ability to focus on the interior personal journey was being undermined by

a media-driven pressure that required little of me beyond my agreeing to talk back to the society. I soon understood that in this Britain I would find it difficult to take time out and look inwards and explore a personal identity that is rooted both in and beyond Britain. I was to be given an image; or rather, the choice of an image. ('Necessary Journeys', 5)

Phillips vividly exemplifies this commitment to personalized, inward journeys in his fiction, favouring first-person narrative strategies to convey the subjective experience of migrancy. In reconsidering how best to equip himself technically in order to evoke the racial alienation he felt firsthand, Phillips looked to his near ancestors. He turned to Caribbean fiction-writers who were among the first to tackle what Shamit Saggar has called the '"adjustment-settlement" question' of whether nationhood is something one freely assumes or is ethnically prescribed. To Phillips, these novelists anticipated the widespread impact of acculturation upon second- and third-generation black communities in Britain, and whose narratives delineated that 'causal determinism' which today, in Saggar's analysis, 'makes national identity hard or unlikely to be shared by many first generation immigrants'.[8] Phillips recalls how in exploring the literary treatment of belonging as topic and as form, he moved away from North American experimentalist writing towards predecessors in Britain whose affinities were ostensibly realist. Both the Trinidadian writer Sam Selvon and his Barbadian contemporary George Lamming loomed large. What Phillips admired in Selvon was an

ability to paint a portrait of the gritty inner city, make it attractive, and at the same time people it with characters who were migrating from office to home, from desk to tube, from country to country, people on the move, in between, ambivalent, and lonely, eventually had a larger impact on me than the African-American literature that I had been reading. And then I happened upon the work of his fellow emigrant George Lamming [. . . whose] literature was drawing me in, teasing me with its deeply historical sensibility, challenging me with its structural gamesmanship. (*A New World Order*, 235)

Though shrewd and sympathetic whenever he critiques the prioritization of experiment in other authors, Phillips himself has never subscribed to avid innovation. Of such 'gamesmanship', he notes, it is often assumed that prosaic ruptures are in concert with politically radical aims – what he describes in the case of Edouard Glissant as that confusion of 'intense subjectivity and rampant discursivity' with 'revolutionary action' (*A New World Order*, 185). Nevertheless, in its representation of place and in particular, as we shall see, in its preoccupation with the figure of the island, Phillips's work celebrates a certain 'restlessness of form' as an impulse peculiar to Caribbean literature (130). He sees that this impulse is about exploiting 'linguistic dualities'; as a literary style and native sensibility, it evinces an 'unwillingness to collapse into easy narrative closure'. Such highly poetic features corroborate for Phillips the idea that a 'migratory condition, and the subsequent sense of displacement, can be a gift to the creative mind' (131).

Yet Phillips scarcely epitomizes the postmodernist émigré: to be sure, as his novels and travel documentaries shift between islands and continents, never does he flaunt the poetics of migration to become little more than a sightseer of global space. Indeed, when reviewing Jamaica Kincaid's semi-autobiographical *A Small Place* (1988), he points out how

> It is only when the author steps beyond her preoccupation with the 'tourist' that the essay begins to develop a flavour which marks it out as not only original but historically important as a document that throws light on Caribbean history past and present. (*A New World Order*, 145)

In an openly personalized statement that repels the critical dismissal of Phillips as an intellectual tourist, he here pours scorn on the tendency to romanticize away the diasporic condition into little more than a conceptual commonplace:

> I fear the prolonged wandering of the displaced, who inevitably become the victims of handy theories, particularly if the host country is in trouble. The resultant cultural dislocation they suffer has a longer and deeper effect than mere physical displacement. There is a danger that clichés, symbols or metaphors will be reached for, to substitute for being 'rooted'.[9]

Phillips's use of first-person narration in *Cambridge* (1991), contrasting visions of a Caribbean island treasured by its colonial management, can be read as a corrective at the level of style to the aestheticization of dislocation. As we'll see, the intimacy of the novel's first-person account focuses the reader's attention on the island as a scene of lived experience rather than simply a spatial metaphor. Naipaul himself would no doubt applaud this focus, pointing out the dangers of obscuring social actualities from public consciousness with the rhetoric of resistance. As Naipaul maintained in the mid-1970s: 'Where jargon turns living issues into abstractions [. . .] and where jargon ends by competing with jargon, people don't have causes. They only have enemies; only the enemies are real'.[10] Phillips elaborates on precisely Naipaul's warning. His own 'fear' of the theoretical hijacking of 'prolonged wandering' hints at the propensity of postmodernist cultural critique to valorize that figure of the global migrant only to foster a purely discursive, politically wishful model of postcolonial subjectivity – reducing human experience to 'handy' generalization.

Episodes in *Cambridge* exemplify the cool, reserved voice that Phillips deploys in his documentary prose. The novel exhibits a quietist approach to formal innovation, epitomizing how mindful Phillips is of Michael Awkward's assertion that, for 'minority discourses more generally', expressive 'self-referentiality is not necessarily a sign of the intense self-investigation that minimizes or eliminates the dangers of hegemonic self-interest'.[11] Phillips's original review of Zadie Smith's *White Teeth* (2000) is telling, as it canvasses the successes and limitations of the formal experimentalism taken forward by a new generation of Black and Asian writers. Concluding that Smith's plot is 'rich, at times dizzyingly so', Phillips finds that *White Teeth*'s rhetorical embellishment has consequences for inclusion, excluding as it does 'a more "substantial" white family' of characters from the carnival of domestic scenarios. This leads him to conclude with the caution that '[t]here is, of course, nothing farcical about the pain of wanting to belong' (*A New World Order*, 286). It is precisely this question of how to do justice to the shifting definitions of belonging which Phillips addresses head on. Those writers born outside the United Kingdom will, in his eyes, 'continue to feel a personal ambivalence towards Britain'. And in searching for an aesthetic through which 'to explore their ambivalence, they will discover new formal strategies which will expand our understanding of what is possible in literary form' (296). Phillips is more reticent. Endless acts of formal invention are not necessarily reparative; neither, he implies, can literary [experiment] alone make significant interventions in any given social imaginary. On this point, Phillips the pragmatist suddenly uncloaks:

> Personally, I would rather have a less vigorous literature, and a healthier nation in which the process of moving along the road from the 'outside' to the 'inside' was not burdened with so many psychological obstacles. Writers are generally able to negotiate these obstacles and even flourish while hurdling them. But, in case we forget, most of us are not writers. (296–7)

Syntactically abrupt, spontaneous, resolute – Phillips offers us an assertive yet candid self-examination here. While acknowledging his separation from the majority of readers (who unlike him 'are not writers'), he turns to inspect how an awareness of this privileged state, so unavailable to 'most of us', remains the kernel of his aesthetic concerns. Stylistically daring inventions, implies Phillips, cannot by themselves bring the public consciousness any closer to a radical self-awareness of the challenges of embracing multiculturalism.

We are presented here with an important counter to the tendency to celebrate postcolonial writers simply for their capacity to complement the postmodern precepts of free-play. In Phillips's case, while literal forms of travel seem to endorse a more metaphorical use of migrancy in his work, they also form part of a robust exploration of selfhood and space. 'There has been a long tradition', he asserts, 'of writers from Britain, such as myself, who have found it necessary to travel' ('Necessary Journeys', 4). This interrogation of displacement as an individual condition and a wider historical continuum provides a basis from which his fiction inspects the legacies of colonialism.

For imperialism in Phillips's world has an extant resonance: its afterlife seems so evident, as Paul Gilroy has recently warned, in the fact that an 'imperial and colonial past continues to shape political life in the overdeveloped-but-no-longer-imperial countries'.[12] And by gesturing allegorically beyond the immediate colonial settings he evokes, Phillips extends his political inquiry into our constitutional present. This enables him to span past and present visions of the triangulation of Africa and Britain with the Caribbean. As in *The Nature of Blood* (1997), which links the misery of European Jews to the descendents of African slavery, Phillips allows specific examples of imperial and fascistic imaginaries to resonate for the experience of diasporic persecution across epochs, resonating into our contemporary midst where racial discrimination still flourishes.

It is that same 'tradition of departure', as Phillips calls it, 'and sometimes return [. . .] at its most furious during the period of empire and colonisation' ('Necessary Journeys', 4) that makes his fiction seem more nomadic in matter than in mode. For Anthony Ilona, this peripatetic focus permits Phillips to develop 'a chronicle of the black diasporic experience', forging a disjunctive and occasionally impersonal poetics in which 'crucial information is introduced in oblique fashion'.[13] Ilona also suggests that Lamming's *Natives of My Person* (1972) is a 'literary antecedent' to Phillips's strategy in *Crossing the River* (1993) of 'historical intervention' (3). If indeed Phillips's style often feels sheer and unadorned, then it is for specific purposes, and one can substantiate this assertion by pinpointing the heritage upon which he draws when refashioning historical realism.

Phillips's lucid reserve, his adjectival spareness and concision, when depicting worlds under the grip of colonial rule, draws on the legacies of a several stylistic precedents. What his landscape-writing has inherited, it seems to me, is a type of first-person narration attuned to the complexities of human perception, and often for self-reflexive and deliberately confessional purposes. It was 'during the 1950s and 1960s', notes Robert Fraser, that alongside the likes of Lamming and Selvon 'a number of autobiographical novels had appeared in India, Africa and the Caribbean exploring the representative use of the first person singular in more tentative ways, usually as a means of conveying the inner tensions of marginalized childhoods'.[14] Yet in what follows, I am less concerned with speculating on the biographical composition of Phillips's island imaginary in his fiction, than with how the figure of the colonized island informs and is transformed by his use of narrative testimony. Rather than offer a speculative conflation of prose and place, I want to demonstrate that Phillips's work reveals a signal aspect of testimony's development. It has offered a supple and accommodating mode to recent postcolonial writers for mapping firsthand the effects of imperialism, either in its direct contexts or by charting its proliferating legacies. Such novelists point to a distinctive relationship between their revival of retrospective testimony and their fables of immigration and departure, where the island emerges as a critical metaphor and brute reality. No less distinguished is the role this register plays in Phillips's portrait of island-terrains under imperial governance. As a discursive form it richly articulates the instinctual confessions of his characters, while revealing his own self-consciousness as a vigilant and unsentimental stylist, for whom brevity is always the chosen medium amid the scenery of atrocities.

After Naipaul: Testimonies to arrival

The issue of Phillips's own evolving formal influences and impulses helps us to contextualize some of the wider aesthetic concerns of postcolonial fiction as it intervenes in Britain's historical narrative as an island. That Phillips has come to favour the introspective manner of first-person testimony across his *oeuvre* discloses something of his sensibility as a writer, one 'still engaged in a struggle to recognise and protect my own identity, in all its intricacy'. Narrative testimony is primed for this kind of self-scrutiny; in hindsight, for Phillips, testimony was in many respects a personal imperative: 'for I knew that I had to view it [selfhood] as unique, complicated, open to inspection and re-examination, and binding me not just to a particular tribe, clan, or race, but to the human race'. The impetus behind 'recognising this', he continues, 'would be a prerequisite of writing well, for the more vigorously one resists a narrow view of self, the more one sees' ('Necessary Journeys', 4). Strategies of self-inspection are abundant in his fictional worlds too, dramatized by the way his characters relate to their communal and natural environments. While documenting the vicissitudes of the self as a forever-altering state, testimony also angles outward to the social: it has allowed Phillips to combine introspection with geographical expositions of the kind intensified by the allure and seduction of island realms.

In *Cambridge* testimony takes the form of a discursive yet tensile register. Episodically arranged, the novel's declarative format organizes its chronology. Phillips retains the island's historical specificity while utilizing it as a more abstract, allegorically suggestive space. At once located and liminal, it offers a world in which the contrary forces of colonial entrapment and imaginative self-transformation become coeval. As in J. M. Coetzee's *Foe* (1986) and Marina Warner's *Indigo* (1992), Phillips depicts the island not as an inert, naturalistic exhibition of dazzlingly exotic flora and fauna – although he allows elements of this exoticism to feed into the verbose wonderment of his imperialist narrator, Emily. Rather, with its notional Caribbean setting, the island intrudes as another persona within the text: a figural presence, it engages as fellow interlocutors those who intrude viciously upon its territory to preside over strict hierarchies there. As an isolated landform at the mercy of the sea, it looms before English newcomers as a condemned and condemning domain – presaging the dissolution of the imperialistic ego, an ego whose self-secured boundaries seem to become as duplicitous as the dissolute boundaries of the mapped island. Insufficiently charted places cause the erasure of individual self-sufficiency, again focalized through Emily's expectations. Her instability as a participant-observer results from a self-defeating claim precisely to that illusion of '[b]oundedness' which, as Rod Edmond and Vanessa Smith put it, superficially 'makes islands graspable, able to be held in the mind's eye and imagined as places of possibility and promise'.[15]

Certainly, Phillips's island is presented as a monument to the pretensions of colonial powers able to maintain control over its internal landscapes solely by force and totalizing dominance. But the 'promise' of which Edmond and Smith speak is evident in Phillips descriptions of ambient island surroundings as restorative realms, protective and embalming. It's hard for us to read *Cambridge* without being struck by the novel's investment in the savage sublimity of the places it depicts. Indeed, while returning time and again to the embodied experience of displacement, there is an insistence borne out by Phillips's use of landscapes upon the potential for human and ecological recuperation. 'I perceive a healing force that comes out of fracture', he asserted in 1993: 'I wouldn't say I've always wanted to be an explorer of the fissures and crevices of migration.'[16] The experience of the personal turmoil and the 'fissures' of enforced migration are premises from which he envisions the possibilities of transformation. Phillips has consistently attended to the consequences of displacement in this double-edged manner, consequences whose 'healing force' for the person being involuntarily displaced requires poise and patience from the novelist rather than mere polemic. For Phillips, migrancy is a state neither to be romanticized nor condemned: 'in 1984, I was not thinking in such a clinical manner of travel in terms of fulfilling an obligation to follow in a particular tradition. I was thinking of it as an absolute, and very personal, necessity. I had to leave Britain. Pure and simple' ('Necessary Journeys', 4). Narrative fiction became an apposite medium for Phillips to elaborate the emotional complexities of enforced migration, for transporting his readers to distant shores pictured with a sensuous immediacy devoid of artistic vanity.

Cambridge mirrors within its plot this uncompromising process of authorial self-inspection. Phillips's characters alternately compete and comply with an island zone in transition, the interaction between visited landform and colonial visitor serving to initiate acts of self-analysis. *Cambridge* elaborates upon a vocabulary of rootedness denied and withdrawn, a condition again manifested topographically by the liminal island setting around which the tripartite narrative revolves. Testimony seems honed, as a mode, to the essence of that location: fractures in narration mirror the fractious and invasive presence of the setting upon the perceiver. *Cambridge* conveys the sensation of encountering a region that, for the incoming colonizer and colonized alike, encroaches indelibly upon those who willingly or enforcedly approach its bounds. Emily is the first to be stunned by this dynamic, encountering an island enmeshing those who draw within its vicinity. Hesitant in assuming as credulous her perceptions of the nearing landform, her tentative assertions only emerge when her detached, documentarian travelogue falters. A measure of this uncertainty in pinpointing her position in relation to the nearing island is also expressed by the suddenly declarative yet transitory grammar: 'It would appear that we have finally crawled into the Caribbean sea'.[17] This sentence pivots on its lascivious verb. No longer the dissociated pioneer, Emily realizes she has 'crawled' towards a spectacle of an island whose anticipated image, now literalized in the present, exceeds all her prior speculations. Emily's previous assurance to us that she is 'neither anxious nor full of trepidation' at the journey's end is rapidly dispelled (16). That her journey here has been a *crawling* one suggests that her imperial rite of passage has been achieved belatedly, 'finally', evidently with some relief. Few comforts exist for either colonizer or colonized aboard the ship; however, the fact that this voyage has indeed been so enduring – that she has had *to crawl* – intensifies her anticipation of an island realm with whose strangeness she is impatient to make contact. Cool and composed, Phillips's depiction of that island still yet to be glimpsed in any kind of detail complements Emily's tense expectancy. Its exoticism, its looming vision of menace and magnificence, seems primed for her coming – an enclave poised to *crawl* back upon and enthral her as an outsider in a process of enraptured inquiry:

> And then in the distance, where the horizon invited and detained the eye, I beheld our destination; a mountainous island heavily clothed in vegetation, wooded on the upper slopes, the highest peaks swaddled in clouds, an island held in the blue palm of the sea like a precious green gem. (16–17)

Phillips invokes the trope of the *island-approach* to heighten the tone of Emily's narrative, as she opts for effusive, lyrical projections. The angle from which she views the island from the ship deck provokes her less to objectify it as an aesthetically pleasing 'destination', than to hunger for a treasure that is being 'detained' from her physical encounter, just as it occupies her to the point of distraction. And yet, as much as it is beautiful solely unto itself, that inimitable 'gem' remains an encapsulation of the necessary duty that, for Emily, is non-negotiable: the carrying forth of her father's entreaty to secure the imperial governance of the island. Phillips gradually unveils the island from the perspective of the approaching ship; it is the elevation of the deck which indeed allows that exotic place to be observed in a proleptic fashion, as though forewarning visiting observers of the demands that will beset them upon reaching shore. As the platform from which to inspect and expect an inscrutable landform, the idyll of the ship as vehicle for conquest is overthrown by the place it approaches and the obligations it elicits among the crew. The island quashes the sense of protection and autonomy idealized aboard the vessels that approach it. As an inimitable spectacle, teetering on the verge of indecipherability for those who glimpse it from afar, the island challenges the ideal 'that ships', in Bernhard Klein's analysis, 'can be read as spaces that enable an inversion or contestation of the world they would claim not only to re-create in fact and spirit but even to export wholesale to distant shores'.[18] In Emily's case, the approaching land remains a summons to a quest that becomes less a colonial adventure than an obligation to the efficient organization of a colony in whose fiscal management she can never as a woman participate. This realization impacts stylistically upon the novel, modulating from objective reportage into a more candid form of testimony. Ultimately the island leaves Emily unable to prevent herself from digressing from impartial reportage into impressionistic rhapsody. Arrested, enraptured, her objectivity annulled, that imperialist desire for totalizing knowledge over a 'gem' observed from afar is contradicted and deferred by her affective responses to the island as a spectator.

These formal dynamics ally Phillips with other contemporary writers who often entreat landforms as living presences, embellishing their settings in unnerving, anthropomorphic terms. Just as the new or unexplored house in Pat Barker's *Union Street* and *Another World* (1998) is often assigned the agency of determination over those who reside within it, so in *Cambridge* the island is rendered animate by the way Phillips confers upon its looming spectacle the status of a grammatical subject. Shimmering yet besetting, it subordinates all human volition when enticing the incoming traveller who, like Emily, is soon enthralled and detained by its paradisal beauty, concentrated against the backdrop of an ocean void. While serving as an organizing motif for events, episodically the island-approach motif elevates physical place to the prominence of a syntactic subject, one influencing and governing the very actions of the observers nearing it. This grammatical elevation thus impacts upon narrative duration. Between reported events, the chronology extends when the lyric intensity of scenic description increases; the island's enigmatic approach not only provokes anticipation in the perceiving narrator, but also a deceleration in the narrative itself as the landform is relayed stage by stage rather than all at once. It invites piecemeal statements, rather than sweeping declarations. We can find another example of such rhetorical transitions in Jane Rogers's *Island* (1999). Here the novel's orphaned narrator, Nikki Black, tracks down her mother on whom she seeks revenge to a remote Scottish outcrop:

> It turned out that my mother lived on an island. An island in the Hebrides, a small tear-shaped island called Aysaar just off another bigger island. She had certainly distanced herself. You wouldn't drop in causally, on the off-chance. Perhaps she thought distance would be enough to keep me away.[19]

A region so seemingly isolated as to affirm the isolation she felt as an abandoned child, the experience of first-sighting that island suddenly quells the tone of Nikky's commentary, hitherto so glacial:

> From the ferry the island looks dark and steep, half forested rising to a naked mountain. It's wild and uninhabited. Primitive, a place for primeval actions, perfect for a matricide.
>
> Then when the ferry brings you in, spluttering black exhaust, you come to this neat wooden jetty. Which turns into a road, which trundles off across grassy wasteland towards a village. (52)

That Rogers uses no paragraphical indentations enhances the immediacy with which the motif of the island-approach unfurls; as in *Cambridge*, frontage and foliage materialize gradually – one step at a time. With her snapshot details building the scene little by little, Nikki's voiceover is less remote when brought into physical proximity with the dock in its actuality. There is an impersonal brevity about the way Rogers pictures the dockside through the narrator's mounting insurgency – a shoreline surveyed and then discarded as the perspectival description moves insatiably ashore, as though hungering after new geographies.

Rogers tilts here the concision of first-person introspection over into a coldly mimetic, outward taxonomy of the scenery, its surfaces inspected piecemeal. The perceiver's eye is distracted in anticipation, her expectancy piqued; apprehensiveness prevails on arrival at an island zone, unbounded and unknown. Place stirs mixed feelings of seduction and dispossession, a strategy that V. S. Naipaul has utilized for his narratives of racial exile. In *The Enigma of Arrival* (1987), Naipaul conveys the perilous experience of entering ashore as igniting the process of acculturation itself:

> A classical scene, Mediterranean, ancient-Roman—or so I saw it. A wharf; in the background, beyond walls and gateways (like cut-outs), there is the top of the mast of an antique vessel; on an otherwise deserted street in the foreground there are two figures, both muffled, one perhaps the person who has arrived, the other perhaps a native of the port. The scene is one of desolation and mystery: it speaks of the mystery of arrival.[20]

In this 'The Journey' section of *Enigma*, the exterior narrator has intervened explicitly, speculatively, in thrall of a surrealist seaport painting by Giorgio de Chirico. Conjuring the painting's action for the purposes of initiating his own historical tale, its scenic detail becomes mediated by the narrator's memory and refracted by 'a free ride of the imagination' (92). The mediation is also evident in the Naipaul's limping enunciations. Descriptions across the harbour region unfold paratactically, as the speaker shadows moment by moment an imagined exilic figure across the haven wall and into an exotic city, where shortly 'the feeling of adventure would give way to panic' (92). For the 'quayside of arrival' offers a threshold that beckons towards a deceptive sense of permanence. 'Belonging' here, as Phillips himself puts it, becomes 'a contested state. Home is a place riddled with vexing questions' (*A New World Order*, 5). A triadic sense of futurity, opportunity and solace flashes up for Naipaul's newly arrived figure, helpless and hapless among 'the noise of a crowded city'. But after his immigration, this place only affirms for him the absence of a home country to which he can never return: 'The antique ship has gone. The traveller has lived out his life' (92).

It is precisely that haunting trope of returning to a ship that facilitated one's immigration, only to find it has already disembarked, with the porthole across continents closing off in its wake, which Abdulrazak Gurnah employs in *By the Sea* (2001). Latif has arrived in Plymouth, fleeing persecution in a Zanzibar gripped by post-independence uprising, and 'feeling as if I had circumnavigated the world's oceans'.[21] He also feels initially that his peripatetic passage north across Europe has suddenly been translated onto land: 'I walked for hours in the town, grateful at the luck beyond belief which had attended my wanderings so far. No one, it seemed, was that worried about me' (137–8). But Latif hovers ashore, unsure as to whether he should return to the austerity of East Germany, and, beyond that, to a Zanzibar whose image in memory is as inaccessible as only an island can be – its macabre isolation as an abandoned homeland provoking in him the interminable twin-pain of guilt and regret. Gurnah's pathetic fallacy complements Latif's irresolution, when 'a chilly summer rain began to fall, and I turned back towards the port, not sure what to do' (138). As a scene of arrival it confers foreboding associations on the vessel it no longer harbours, and the dockside's vacancy bears upon the narrator as an anthropomorphic reflection of his desolated state. Latif can no longer resign himself to chance, to the fortunes of consequence, despite the fact that he has so often relied up until now on fleeting encounters with the benevolence of others to secure his safe passage through the former Eastern Block. Such happenstance gestures of charity seem improbable here. It's as if his own encounter with the harbour has concluded the journey irrevocably now, following his decision to disembark in England. For while he entertains the freedoms of Plymouth's townscape, his indecision over whether to stay and persevere in Britain has already and irreversibly been resolved for him by the very function of the port – a site for which impermanence and finality coexist in the course of its daily service:

Perhaps I should just get back on the boat and keep going, and see where I would end up. Live my life like that until I bumped into my fate. It was fear and shrivelling will that made me think like that. Leave my life to someone else, to events. But when I got back to the harbour, the ship had gone and my journey was over. (138)

Dockside here partially prescribes destiny; it mediates immediate decisions. Again, this recurring personification seems portentous. Behaving like a sentinel to a barracked zone, the shoreline dictates a one-way threshold: it delineates that cultural line our narrator has crossed in anticipation of a new homeland, only to become severed irreversibly from his origin. Eliminating any option of native return, the dock exhibits the absence of the opportunity it once afforded when facilitating this migrant's safe entry. Thus the ship's disappearance suggests to Gurnah's new arrival that he cannot assume as permanent the freedom he has just tasted, moments before, amid the hustle and bustle of urban Plymouth. A place, then, ostensibly of transition and exchange, the harbour's workaday operations offer the uncertain prediction that Latif's fortunes as a refugee will never remain anchored. Each opportunity to depart once more and relent to his native shore will never merely remain at his command.

How islands are encountered within the dramatic world of these texts can thus condition their affect upon narrative form. Whereas Naipaul's defenceless narrator in *The Enigma of Arrival* 'would lose his sense of mission' (92) after crossing ashore into a subsuming colony, in Jane Rogers's first-person account, the event of arriving accelerates a quest for a character who relishes the degree of anonymity only a remote island could afford. Coming into visceral contact with the island's enigmatic fringe renews Nikki's sense of imperative, an imperative that overtakes the hitherto interiorized mode of recollection in *Island*. As we telescope in, beyond the quayside a 'blindingly ordinary' village is mapped out factually, ominously so, its desolate aspect relayed with documentary precision. And in so doing, Rogers offers the reader a kind of rapid preview of her narrator's chosen route in. Confessional heroine turned calculating hunter, 'I went up the road into the grim little village. A few cars from the ferry drove past me. I felt OK, as if I knew what to do' (52). Oblique yet poised, it's as though the territory awaits Nikki's pursuit – a setting that portentously waits to receive from the coast her demanding quest for answers inland.

This same trope of the *island-approach*, as I have called it, evokes a scene again of personal desolation, but of a more horrific order in *Cambridge*. When Phillips turns to Cambridge's testimony in the novel's second part, the narrative becomes suddenly more granitic and austere. Paul Sharrad notes how Cambridge's 'slave-narrative/gallows-confession story is a dramatic rupture in the fabric of the novel, made potent by its conciseness and emotional restraint. It succinctly contradicts or undermines almost every confident observation Emily has made'.[22] And indeed the reader is lent a perspective, angled from aboard the ship on its final leg towards land, which affords nothing like the leisurely depiction of an exotic frontier to echo Emily's 'precious green gem'. Instead, the nearing shoreline signals for the captive, Cambridge, both his severance from the English society into which he was indigenized as well as the imminence now of his impending re-enslavement:

> After many weeks of torment, the ship finally came to anchor. Having the advantage of a Christian education, I had no doubt that we were in the region of the Americas. My countrymen, however, were seized with great fear, knowing neither location nor their destiny. We articles of trade, once liberated from the intolerable aroma of the pestilential hold, were directed to remain on deck. From this vantage point we were able to observe the tropical new world that was now, *home*. (156)

Being re-deported as 'a virtual Englishman', and once more 'treated as base African cargo' (156), Cambridge knows the horror that is coming into focus. In this scene, Phillips inverts one of the ship's functions in providing, as Klein suggests, a *heterotopic* space for the colonial voyager. The enclosed ship matched the island's purpose as an image encapsulating the Empire's proficiency when claiming and taming other worlds. For those travelling in authority over the slaves they transport towards incarceration, the provisional community aboard the ship 'create[s] a space of cultural expansion and imaginative possibility' ('Staying Afloat', 93). Cambridge's possibilities, along with his fellow 'articles of trade', are all too easily spied from aboard the raised deck. For there is a harsh irony indeed to his being able to view the island from his relative elevation on deck-level. In affording a panoramic degree of surveillance, this prospect-view offers Cambridge an all-too perfect 'vantage point' on his awaiting fate. The island couches ominously in between 'location' and 'destiny'; as ontological spheres they inform the novel's critique in its entirety. No longer dislocated and inscrutable, suddenly distilled, it is a place devoid of alternatives. That 'new world' is a one-way destination, offering cruel confirmation to Cambridge of the futility of creolization as a transformative ideal, the ideal to which he has surrendered much of his life thus far by ceding to the mechanical policies of racial assimilation.

In a formal sense, the island furnishes Phillips's novel with a highly suggestive yet 'manageable' backdrop. It establishes a scene of expectancy where macabre destinies beckon – a shoreline waiting in anticipation of all that is sanctioned by imperialism as appalling yet inevitable. But in other ways, *Cambridge* exceeds its ostensible context, loading the island with a studied evanescence that springs open within the text a broader web of association. Cambridge himself detects in others about him an intensifying recognition of loss, once docked off the island, sensing that the 'African world of my sad, dark brethren had been truly abandoned across the waters' (157). Cambridge proleptically glances towards later twentieth-century paradigms of migration necessitated by race, prophesying a 'triple heritage of journeying', as Phillips himself has sketched it, triangulating 'British, African diasporan, Caribbean' ('Necessary Journeys', 4). In this capsule episode, *Cambridge* exemplifies a recurrent stratagem for Phillips. The event of Cambridge's encounter with a 'tropical new world' offers a parable, allowing the novel to look ahead to historical epochs closer to our own as a means of 'grappl[ing] with these vexing issues', in Phillips eyes, 'of British identity and belonging' (4). Driven ashore to confront '*home*' (italicized for seeming so alien) Cambridge poses for those issues a substantial precedent, greeting involuntarily a territory that confirms the physical recapture of those already denied a homeland. It reveals Phillips's articulation of the spectacle of the island as an oracular resource: a platform from which to project events whose legacy we inherit in the present. He asserts in his article 'Necessary Journeys' that 'for people of the African diaspora',

> 'home', is a word that is often burdened with a complicated historical and geographical weight. This being the case, travel has been important for it has provided African diasporan people with a means of clarifying their own unique position in the world. (4)

An abstractly 'tropical' figure for Cambridge, nearing inimically out of the ocean, the sight of the *island as imminent home* spells a painful epiphany. Clearly for Phillips, this manner of describing a locale looming sinisterly, proleptically, also becomes his way of ventriloquizing his own character's perspective. Phillips exercises that 'ability to leave and see oneself through another prism', something which 'has long been part of the legacy of being a writer of African origin in the west' ('Necessary Journeys', 4). Distant shores, now closing in, thus have the function not only of siphoning the island's anthropomorphic properties into a wider, allegorical set of associations, but also of enabling Phillips to write about places freighted with such autobiographical resonance in order to perform that act of seeing himself anew. In so doing, Phillips also questions the reader's capacity to access and sympathize with contrasting points of view as they angle towards a single landscape. Given that *Cambridge*, like much of his work since, is devoid of exterior authorial commentaries of the kind that weave in and out of the experiences of those characters he vindicates, Phillips announces the absence of authoritative voice only to pronounce his own recrimination. For *Cambridge* epitomizes how subtle Phillips's self-reflexivity appears alongside his postmodern contemporaries, since it only emerges through a form of muted self-withdrawal. It's as if he is mindful that the tendency to 'announce one's situatedness', in David Simpson's phrase, is a symptom peculiar to contemporary polemicists, caught up in the belief that eternal self-declaration is both necessary and laudable. Using one's prosecuting standpoint as an occasion for demonstrative admission 'appears to pre-empt the accusation that one is not being inadequately self-aware, and at the same time to provide a limited authority to speak from a designated position'.[23] Phillips is altogether less defensive: proficient, if not imperturbable, when overseeing the colonial horrors he documents through the eyes and assumptions of others. This sense of reserve complements the way his readers are left to their own devices; left without the help of interjections, we have to negotiate for ourselves that interpretative triangle whereby narratorial testimony can elicit complicity and estrangement in the reader it addresses. Phillips's ventriloquy allows him to evoke an island whose internal atrocities are revealed all but gradually, relayed through the observations of those landing on its shores. Rhetorically disciplined yet sustained – such is the composure with which Phillips operates as a curator of a world under imperial dominance, while stimulating the reader's 'ability to leave and see oneself through another prism'.

Andrea Levy's parables of discovery and disenchantment

Cambridge reveals how the contours of the island become talismanic: encapsulating and inimitable, they equate with the singularity of nationhood, while complementing the expansionist aspirations of the state at large. Shores represent a threshold for the nation-state; but they also offer a protective fringe as much as they present frontiers for maritime exploration. As the deserted-dock trope reveals, a trope uniting Naipaul's and Gurnah's parables of immigrant arrival, island-encounters entail decisions and persecute indecision. The choice to cross between islands also carries with it the responsibility of departing a place in circumstances that may affect whether one can ever associate that place with *home* again – if, indeed, one ever has the freedom to return. Gurnah and Naipaul also show how the migrant's enforced egression from her homeland affirms that ultimately she must alone bear the responsibility for what she anticipates (or has been told to anticipate) of her destination, particularly if she expects the host country to offer a safer place than the one from which she has departed. In conversation with Susheila Nasta, Gurnah diagnoses this dual sense of arrival and self-realization as integral to 'the condition of the migrant'. Throughout refugee history, notes Gurnah, Britain has been encountered as a place of opportunity only to become the scene of disillusionment. Devoid of the comfort it promised, the nation 'becomes', in Gurnah's account, 'an interior landscape where it doesn't matter quite as much where you are', for it's often the case that 'the negotiations go on inside'. External places wilt in comparison to those interior spaces of longing and regret which spring from being disenchanted with the present. Painfully the migrant soon discovers for herself that 'The outside world is not irrelevant, but it is not quite so central'. And for Gurnah, 'it's that sense of people carrying their worlds *within* them that I became interested in'. Disenchantment occupies a mental space whose condition can decline despite any improvement in living space; it feeds a form of introspection immune from the benevolence of the host country. As Gurnah sees it, this interiorizing phenomenon is only exacerbated for those in transit between the ill-fortunes of one island and the anticipated welcome of the next, epitomized by 'characters who are constantly shuttling back and forth in terms of the ways in which their stories travel' (*Writing Across Worlds*, 357).

What Gurnah is diagnosing here is the affliction of 'disappointed love'. This results from the impact upon the immigrant subject of matching up expectation with the unfolding experience of cosmopolitanism. And for Gurnah, the primary 'feeling at the base of this sense of dislocation is disappointment' (357). Disappointment springs from the disparity between cherished predictions and the everyday present; it is a side-effect of confronting the improbability of ever achieving the quality of life one had hoped to find in Britain as an accommodating host. Gurnah also seems to suggest that the effect of this bewildering disenchantment is ultimately more visceral and less about material possessions. Discovering Britain as an island thwarting previous hopes is 'not simply a question of a disillusionment with England'; it also afflicts the newcomer as a mocking mnemonic, a cruel reminder of expectations that can't now be substantiated: 'It's also disappointment with the self, disappointment with how the displaced person has been able to cope with the experience' (357).

In her Orange Prize winner *Small Island* (2004), Andrea Levy traces how this cycle of enchantment and disenchantment became endemic for Caribbean immigrants in the 1940s. Her twin-island story affords an insight into the effects of racial alienation in the context of radically different nation-states. Feelings of disillusionment were sparked when the 'illusion' of a welcoming motherland, as Donald Hinds recorded it, was altogether betrayed, all too late for those migrants who so forcefully cherished the promise of British hospitality.[24] In *Small Island*, Levy charts the onset of this realization. She makes structural and geographical transitions, alternating between settings to analyse disenchantment comparatively between different places as a symptom of anticipating new homelands against the memory of those left behind. The novel alternates between London '1948' and contexts entitled 'Before', in years preceding the Blitz. First-person encounters throughout the narrative with different aspects of Britain's interior quickly contradict the imaginary anticipation of the country's landscape as one of provincial safety and futurity. Wartime southern England scarcely fulfils the predictions of Levy's newly arrived Jamaican recruits, each longing to have confirmed the wonder they feel towards it as 'Mother Country'. As Phillips did for the contemporary African refugee Gabriel in *A Distant Shore* (2003), in Levy's novel island-encounters ignite a sequence of surprise and disbelief ending in disenchantment:

> Some of the boys shook their heads, sucking their teeth with their first look at England. Not disappointment – it was the squalid shambles that made them frown so. There was a pained gasp at every broken-down scene they encountered.

The wreckage of this bombed and ruined place stumbles along streets like a devil's windfall. Other boys looking to the gloomy, sunless sky, their teeth chattering uncontrolled, gooseflesh rising on their naked arms, questioned if this was the only warmth to be felt from an English summer. Small islanders gaped like simpletons at white women who worked hard on the railway swinging their hammers and picks like the strongest man.[25]

England emerges as a disappointingly meagre, exhausted zone. Its tired terrain provokes Gilbert to reinspect his own relationship to Jamaica as a home, now vividly present in memories leading back to early childhood. Jamaica returns as an imposing, tangible environment in the mind of his adult self who has taken a route out to what seems like the most inhospitable of developed foreign cities. And in light of his search for England's originary essence as 'Mother Country', Gilbert has a further request. Angling away from the context of immediate events he recalls, his query is not for the reader, but for the land itself: 'for me I had just one question – let me ask the Mother Country just this one simple question: how come England did not know me?' (117). What does provoke Gilbert to face his readers once more is a shift across geography itself. His concerns as a narrator soon change for a landscape outlying the metropolis. Outside their training barracks, his RAF contingent is met with wide-eyed curiosity by villagers in Hunmanby. Residents there are alarmed to hear that these Caribbean troops have volunteered to defend a nation they have never encountered, and where they are considered as exotic – surviving exhibits from imperial history. Gilbert turns towards us as readers now with an anecdote to explain the compulsion driving his fellow Caribbean troops. It's as though the reader too were in danger of imbibing the same bewilderment of those English villagers. 'Let me ask you to imagine this', says Gilbert: 'Living far from you is a beloved relation whom you have never met' (116). He returns to his own bewilderment, gesturing in disbelief at the ignorance of the English, living contentedly in a landscape self-insulated from the concerns of Caribbean territories with whom Britain has been tied for centuries: 'It was inconceivable that we Jamaicans, we West Indians, we members of the British Empire would not fly to the Mother Country's defence when there was a threat. But, tell me, if Jamaica was in trouble, is there any major, any general, any sergeant who would have been able to find that dear island?' (118).

Offered a map, and even senior British officers would be hard-pushed to pinpoint Jamaica's place among other islands in the Caribbean. Levy insinuates that it presents a shore all too distant to defend, a 'region [. . .] lost on the back' of any military map (118), and whose need, however expressed to British eyes, would immediately seem irrelevant and obscure. But for Gilbert it is evidently the reverse. He is drawn ineluctably back to Britain: greeted by an island that betrays its imperial ancestry in showing only a grudging willingness to know him or embrace his beneficent actions now, at a time of war, as he himself embraces a public duty. This ability to navigate 'back' to defend England is seen as visceral, immanent, predetermining: 'But give me that map', he asserts, 'blindfold me, spin me round three times and I, dizzy and dazed, would still place my finger squarely on the Mother Country' (119).

Something of that impulse of necessary return was apparent for Gilbert back in Jamaica before conscription. Somewhat more and idealistic then, he awaited departure itching and impatient – dissatisfied with the scale of his home island: 'I was a giant living on land no bigger than the soles of my shoes. Everywhere I turn I gazed on sea. The palm trees that tourists thought rested so beautiful on every shore were my prison bars'. Levy concludes that chapter with the image of visible 'horizons' remaining his 'tormenting borders' (173). Yet this playfully exposes Gilbert's sense of incarceration as exaggerated, hyperbolic, if not tempting fate in lieu of the journey to come – a journey ending in his chilly encounter with English shores. For moments later, Levy ironizes Gilbert's exasperation with that tropical 'prison', but without losing the pathos it generates as an anticipation of the austere scenery awaiting him in Britain. In a stark scenic contrast, Levy juxtaposes his complaint against sultry confinement in the Caribbean by switching across the Atlantic to open the following chapter with an altogether greyer episode. Here Gilbert recollects the way his fellow contingent, fresh from the dockside, approached the capital confounded. Stunned, muted, their disappointment is momentarily allayed by confusion:

> You see, most of the boys were looking upwards. Their feet might have been step-ping on London soil for the first time – their shaking sea legs wobbling them on the steadfast land – but it was wonder that lifted their eyes. They finally arrive in London Town. And, let me tell you, the Mother Country – this thought-I-knew-you place – was bewildering these Jamaican boys. See them pointing at the train that rumbles across a bridge. They looked shocked when billowing black smoke puffed its way round the white washing hung on drying lines – the sheets, the pants, the babies' bonnets. Come, they had never seen houses so tall, all the same. And what is that? A chimney? They have a fire in their house in England? No! And why everything look so dowdy? Even the sunshine can find no colour but grey. Staring on people who were staring on them. (175)

Phillips himself echoes the subtle testimony played out in *Small Island* in a candid memoir 'Northern Soul' from 2005. There he details the way his solidarity with Leeds (as his hometown) increased a certain alertness in his youth to 'occasional glamorous sightings', spectacles that thwarted expectations of its industrial density and expanse:

> From my doorstep I surveyed the bell-shaped towers of the gasworks, and the grey sky that was spiked with chimneys that never seemed to tire of belching smoke, and the dramatically shaped spires of the many churches, which were, in their

own way, as darkly ominous as the factories. To my young eyes, Leeds never appeared to be truly glum or depressing.[26]

Phillips's parents were less spirited when arriving in the city that would become their home. Informed only by 'Technicolor Caribbean', recalls Phillips, they 'had sternly refused to believe that English people were crazy enough actually to light fires inside their houses. Strange new world to their immigrant eyes, but their son was clearly seeing something else' (22). Industrial Leeds, viewed firsthand, would conflict with their anticipations, precisely as 'London soil' did for Levy's bewildered recruits.

'It's disappointed desires', Gurnah assures us, 'as much as a sense of disappointed realities' (*Writing Across Worlds*, 357). And in *Small Island*, Levy enables this shift from material to mental zones by shifting the geographical emplacement of her first-person narrative. She delineates a journey with Jamaican RAF recruits towards the shores of a stern 'Mother Country' where they are frequently, sometimes ferociously, unaccepted. Cutting across landscapes while retaining the intimacy of a retrospective narrative inflected by contrasting idiolects, *Small Island* maps a set of diverging attitudes to racial difference in order to enhance our understanding of the complexities of mid-twentieth-century immigration and its ramifications for contemporary British nationhood.

Prospects and panoramas: Envisioning historical landscapes

Small Island is the latest of Andrea Levy's attempts to historicize the gradual reconstitution of islands by foreign cultural influences, picturing the British landscape as imminently though begrudgingly yielding to patterns of repopulation. Moreover, *Small Island* epitomizes Levy's compulsion to revisit Jamaican emigration in its historical moment, extending her earlier endeavour in *Every Light in the House Burnin'* (1994) and *Fruit of the Lemon* (1999) to detail period-specific habits, idiolects and perspectives. In a similar commitment to historical idiom, Caryl Phillips has also allowed autobiographical elements to resonate with the colonial geographies in his fiction. And his own personal sensibility is nowhere more self-disclosing than when depicting the figure of the island, calling into question the imperial reflections of the person who perceives it. Through the disjuncture between Emily's startling mental impressions and her reportorial clichés, Phillips evokes the tensions between perception and knowledge that inform the depiction of space in *Cambridge*. In so doing, he questions the imperialistic presumption that merely by achieving a prospect-view over a physical environment the viewer can claim authority over people enslaved within it. Not only are polemic and perception inextricable in Phillips's narrative poetics; *Cambridge* also reveals how the prospect-view affords a self-referential device. For it is a device directed at Phillips's own authorial self as well as his characters, whereby the representation of perception dramatizes that very process of 'inspection and re-examination' which, in his view, is so crucial as 'a prerequisite to writing well'.

As Chapter 2 explored in the context of regional landscapes, acts of surveying rural prospects carried with them the aim of synthesizing detachment and possession, distance and understanding. In eighteenth-century landscape portraiture, the pastoral prospect invited what John Barrell describes as a contradictory pursuit of 'unerring judgement and a generous benevolence'. [27] Based on an assumption that a viewpoint over the conditions of a landscape in their totality might precipitate forms of munificent knowledge, the achievement of a 'pure and wide prospect' was a crucial part of this aesthetic recreation: standing back to survey rustic places and their native inhabitants (64). What follows here seeks to explore how Phillips deliberately invokes, if only to test and complicate, those 'traditional political virtues of detachment and disinterestedness'. He probes the historical dynamics of a viewpoint that is at once exclusive and self-implicating. For as Barrell explains

> if the ability of the gentleman to judge impartially how to exercise his virtues depends on his vision of the whole, and if that vision depends in turn on his retirement, or at least on a detachment from immediate interests represented by the metaphor of a space between his viewpoint and the field of political conflict, then to descend into that field to pacify and regulate the contestants was surely to resign the detachment which enables him to know how they should be regulated. (64)

The attractions of the rustic prospect for its witness are thus twofold: that 'ability' to look and then 'judge' is conveniently accompanied by the pleasure of self-distantiation, conferred upon the observer after assuming a suitable vantage-point. Achieving the prospect entails a combined effort between intuitive response and exacting reconnaissance. The outcome is sublime for the paradox it seems to resolve, whereby the viewer's sensuous attention to the scenery as spectacle enriches the scientific vocabulary with which he must describe its topography.

In *Cambridge*, Phillips not only leaves that paradox unresolved; he uses it to spotlight a whole series of ethical dilemmas. The prospect-view invites the aestheticization of the island by those who observe it through a bifocal lens of racial dominance and romantic appreciation. Assuming such a viewpoint is equated with the way those in colonial authority presume they govern with virtue, conflating overseeing with protecting. Phillips reveals that the manner in which one chooses to *survey* natural space necessitates a reconsideration of how one should *act* socially. Recurring throughout the *Bildungsroman* of Emily's account as her father's troubleshooter, a landscape outwardly observed ignites her awareness of her complicity with colonial atrocity. It's as though the very event of observing the magnificence of the Caribbean island in a prospect containing its scenic totality provokes, initially, a disinterested defence of the slavery being instituted there. But eventually, and in a way too late to be self-redeeming for Emily, that same wide prospect prompts a more introspective viewpoint on her gradual corruption by an institution that can only be condemned.

In *Cambridge* Emily is only able to explore the island's perimeter by using its colony's acting supervisor, Brown, as her authoritative if chauvinistic guide. This excludes her from debating 'ethical and moral questions' relating to the British occupation, questions with which, as a woman, she is deemed 'not yet qualified to engage' (85). The seduction of island boundaries – tidal, diffuse, outlying the principal sector of the colony – dispels her potential resistance. She tolerates gendered segregations more or less normalized within this realm, as colonial governance remains, in her world-view, an inherently masculinist enterprise. After all, her father has sent her into a settlement whose previous governor was deposed for dealing too delicately with slaves. And so long as Brown doesn't 'again abandon me', as she puts it, 'unchaperoned, to the caprices of plantation life', Emily can shadow him into open landscape, finding new material there to supplement her written travelogue. Indeed, her being restricted from freely accessing the terrain only piques her appetite; more and more possible worlds are beckoning despite the island's confined scale:

> Our plantation occupies only one small part of this realm, albeit an enchanting and delectable part, but I dearly wish to taste fully each hidden corner of the land. So it was with a light heart and eager anticipation that I accepted Mr Brown's unexpected and generous offer to spend a day touring with him. (100)

Phillips equates the broad prospect with a colonialist indulgence in topographic exoticism: in taking pleasurable opportunities to appraise the island's flora and fauna. By elevating from time to time the narrative perspective, Phillips subjects the description of the island to a more exteriorly angled mode than immediate, first-person scene sketching has allowed in the novel thus far. For this effect, and accompanied this time by Emily's more companionable guide, Arnold, we travel gradually by incline above the canopy on a 'skyward journey, in silence, which gave me the opportunity to survey the beauty of the abundant flora all around' (109). The resulting prospect-view provides an expansive documentary, surveying 'all around', with scars everywhere present of conquest and subsequent rule. This opens up the introspection of Emily's narration to outward impressions of the island as a manifold zone, possessing multiple overlapping regions and personal realities, rather than as a tropical enclosure contained by colonial powers, uniform and impervious. With the surrounding view broadening out now, she 'wandered some twenty yards to the west and discovered a picturesque, shaded, though now deserted cottage, which had the great advantage of a magnificent prospect over the ocean' (110). The fact that it is 'deserted' is significant – something of a relief for the imperialist observer, realizing they are alone, without natives threatening what they observe. Gurnah has noted that, in instances such as these, both exotic wilderness and vacant slaves are figures rendered intelligible solely through comparison. Natural space and native subject can only be comprehended when conflated. By offering Emily the prospect of unoccupied wilderness, Phillips betrays her propensity to make the male African (as in the case of Cambridge himself) 'both part of the landscape', as Gurnah records, 'one and the same time with it, eternally signifying that which Western discourse has banished through progress', but simultaneously 'dangerous and disturbing, preferably represented as absent'.[28] By rendering the landscape vacant of slaves in a way that pleases and appeases this visitor who he ventriloquizes, Phillips reminds us of the metonymic relationship between colonial landscape and colonized African in which both are condemned to aestheticization.

By negotiating between reflection and perception from one setting to the next, *Cambridge* elaborates on the idea of first-person narration as a politically and ethically charged mode for relaying the realities of colonial oppression. When recording perceptions of the island from afar, Phillips highlights the tendency for islands to being perceived as social worlds in miniature. Phillips courted this tendency himself when visiting Gibraltar. 'Nothing could escape my gaze', he recalls, 'Gibraltar's existence denies Spain a decent look-out point'. He remedies this obscured line of sight, shifting into a stance of self-isolating detachment to dramatize how, as Peter Hulme points out, that 'trope of the castaway is very closely linked to the trope of the island'.[29] Posing as a surveyor at once elevated and engrossed at the summit, choicely positioned on an outcrop under blue skies, Phillips assumes a position that awards him a curiously possessive view over the coastline:

> Looking across the straits of Gibraltar on a clear day, Africa appears to be a small symmetrical island rising in the centre to a high summit. Europeans could have imagined it as just that, an island. A thin circle of cirrus cloud makes a halo just below the peaks of the Rif mountains to the east of Tangier. (*The European Tribe*, 24–5)

Physical elevation gives way here to the dissemination of a legacy, prefacing concerns running throughout *The European Tribe*. While 'looking across' Phillips's panoramic prospect also looks back. His view of Africa provokes a historical retracing of its spectacle from afar. Its coastal topography becomes geometrically legible as the 'small symmetrical island' that may have once compelled the imperialist gaze to look upon this uncharted neighbour as strange and yet – in the scale of an island – conceivably disposable to foreign rule. 'Much of the exploration of the Pacific' too, as Edmond and Smith point out, 'involved replacing a dream of continents with a reality of islands, mapping the slow erosion of a desired haven' (*Islands in History and Representation*, 1). From his elevated stance, Phillips retrieves a vision of miniaturized continent before the lapse of that dream. Replicated here is an indelible image of Africa seducing the colonizer into misperception, replacing continent with island. To recall Susan George's analysis, 'Africa is on its own'.[30] And Phillips himself notes how peculiar though significant it is that

> Lloyds of London maintain a monitoring post here. From their look-out station at Europa Point, it is possible to see Africa lying to the front, Spain behind, the Mediterranean to the east, and the Atlantic to the west. There is no better place to watch the world's business go floating by. (*The European Tribe*, 24)

This bank-branch has situated itself like an exemplary Nissen hut, impassive on its 'watch' over the frontier where need meets neglect. In the imperious eyes of the world economy, Africa is severed off as an island; and this, despite the fact, as George pointed out nearly two decades ago now, that the continent 'is transferring more capital abroad in debt-service and other payments than it is receiving in aid and new loans' (*A Fate Worse than Debt*, 86). Phillips pursues the many ramifications of this peculiar, geographically disproportioning perspective, beginning with the way it seduced the colonial gaze – a gaze for which the prospect of distant otherness can be graspable so long as it falls within immediate reach or *as far as the eye can see*, reducing Africa's magnitude as a continent into the manageable coordinates of an island.

Conjuring the illusion it may have once emitted, Phillips thus shows how Africa is vulnerable to being at once romanticized and reviled: how, when it is dissociated from empirical geography in the intoxicated mind of the colonizer, the continent serves as a diabolic emblem to fathomless worlds beyond the horizon. In his reflexive adoption of a prospect-view in the present, Phillips rehearses from the imperial imaginary of Europe's past an impression of an isolated Africa, still crowned today by that 'circle of cirrus cloud'. For it is a continuing testament to the continent's present-day isolation, too, testament to Africa's neglect by the multinational control of global capital. Hence that 'halo' conjures a sinister parallel between epochs. The lasting image confirms Africa's emblematic status as a remote place to be brought under the aegis of a more advanced, if ideological, set of development policies – the crowning achievement for the West's ability to conceal the often insidious nature of its own financial benevolence. Representing the 'high summit' of political and economic self-interest, Africa remains a jewel-island here, vulnerable to any beneficent government able to assume tacit control of it as a colony mediated by debt-servicing trade.

This small though suggestive episode from Phillips's travelogue is worth unpacking in detail, as the rhetorical set-piece it performs is so pertinent for the poetics of place this chapter has been tracing. If only implicitly, Phillips's use of the island simile in his own documentary reveals a highly reflexive dimension to his authorial persona that recurs elsewhere in his writing. He certainly resists what Gurnah calls 'the pressures of the travel-narrative form', which tempt the writer, when recording a journey in retrospect, 'to appear more ignorant than he could possibly be, so that he can arrive at his epiphanic moment'.[31] No such epiphanies, amenable to abstraction, spring from Phillips's perceptual documentation of place. Moreover, when he invokes the island phenomenon, it is notable how Phillips calls into question his own physical perspective as a voluntary castaway when historicizing a spectacle from the present. Therefore what seems like an impressionistic inscription of metaphor actually invites a kind of authorial self-conscription. Curiously enough, it appears as though we are left with an image of Phillips himself feeling detached, cast away: a spectator as solitary as the island he analogically evokes, caught in freeze-frame upon the shore of Gibraltar, and communicating to us at the interface of place and perspective, the real and the rhetorical. As Thorpe's nineteenth-century photographer revealed in *Ulverton*, immediately observed settings serve to implicate and comment upon the observer's implied omniscience. Phillips dramatizes his own implication in the way that 'hilltop situation of the observing eye does more than create a prospect', as J. M. Coetzee warns. Phillips courts the kind of topophilia to which imperial pioneers were so prone: the simultaneous effect of elevation and panorama 'puts the kind of phenomenological distance between viewer and painting, creating a predisposition to see landscape as art' (*White Writing*, 46). Phillips's panoramic view moreover contradicts the tacitly privileged viewpoint associated so eminently with the leisure of savouring a natural panorama when bearing witness to the geologically spectacular. He relinquishes that sense of gaining an imperious vantage-point over the wide prospect of land and sea, but without forgoing the very device his elevated position narratively enables: a documentary episode that blurs into allegorical projection. Via this interanimation, Phillips critiques his own interpretative stance before the prospect he deciphers, while remaining 'capable of *calling forth*', in Barrell's phrase, 'the ability to abstract substance from accident, the general from the particular'.[32] These are indeed the very narrative facets which proliferate in Phillips's fiction, facets that he calls into question when confronting his own documentarian repose in *The European Tribe*. The interpenetration of sight and insight intensifies in *Cambridge*, when Phillips presents perception in such a way that critiques Emily's ability to pose as an eyewitness to the unfolding history of colonial space.

Late in Emily's testimony, her visual exploration of the island modulates into a self-inquest. Just as it would do for Cambridge deported back to the

West Indies in briars, the extensive view of a landscape's indeterminate bounds becomes oracular, prophesying Emily's destiny. In this respect, Phillips conjures various etymological derivations of the word *prospect*, particularly the Latin *prospicere* – to 'look forward'. Emily is given a sensuous perspective over her surroundings, which at the same time given her a sense of the fate awaiting her, as a woman, back in England. Her confiscation there into domestic constraint and intellectual confinement is made to seem all the more imminent as a result of beholding this Caribbean scenery to which she has become attached. Her bedroom offers an alluring twilight outlook, yielding spectacular surprises, every evening different. But that same outlook increasingly focuses inward upon Emily's repressed aspirations, no longer the occasion for enthralment:

> I have still not accustomed myself to the alarming speed with which the tropical day gives way to night, ignoring the lingering deepening of the blue to which those of England are familiar. I stood by the window to my bed-chamber and watched the last embers of daylight die out in dusky red streaks along the horizon, and marvelled as the red ball of the sun buried herself in the heart of the ocean. After the great heat of the day the delightful occasion was to be enjoyed. The possession of an expansive view of the ocean adds greatly to the attractions of the scene, but this theatre seems never truly complete until I descry the image of the mist-bedimmed moon atop the watery world. Only then am I ready to drag my weary bones into my cot, and for many an hour surrender to the feverish caprices of an ill-ventilated dreamworld. (*Cambridge*, 113)

The spectacle of the ocean prompts and predicts regression with equal measure. It shimmers as object of mournful acknowledgement of that which she stands to lose on returning to England. Dusk too is a spectacle through which Emily claims reparation – but ultimately, all for whom, we ask, and at what price? 'England of course. And a life sacrificed to the prejudices which despise my sex. Of loneliness. Of romance and adventure. Of freedom' (113). This is Phillips at his most stylistically stark: probing and relentless he uncovers layer upon layer of anxious private thought. But it also epitomizes the novel's subjectivism operating at its most tender and humane. The very 'possession of an expansive view' refuses her ability to encode and translate it, becoming a 'theatre' in which her stock imperialist vocabulary is put under the spotlight. As a region, it provokes a kind of 'non-logocentric discursive spatiality', in Avtar Brah's phrase: a space resistant to imperial articulation and possession through the colonizer's language, a space which, for Emily, 'produces such electric moments of "recognition"'.[33] No longer has she a discourse adequate to her role of participant-observer; no longer can she write about her affinity with this place with the measured words of a pragmatic and detached anthropologist, while serving her father's mission. For the figure of the island itself resists its figuration by way of sentimental recollection over the course of her travel diary. She can only contemplate this scenery fractiously, rather than recount it factually; her rhapsodic impressionism overtakes the imperialist desire for undisputable naturalism.

The isle protrudes as an object of conscious reference in the mind of *Cambridge*'s heroine. Wide prospects facilitate sinister prospectuses for our narrator, no longer disinterested, indelibly implicated. Phillips invites us to reassociate here the sense of what it is to attain a *prospect* with its sixteenth-century meaning: as the *OED* tells us, it implies the achievement of a 'mental picture' and, as a corollary, an 'anticipated event'. The seemingly incalculable seascape expanse predicts the divestment of Emily's agency back on her native island, anticipating her journey back into the aridity of an English society which in the past she has found disabling as a woman. The episode echoes a typically personal avowal from Orhan Pamuk, who notes that '[t]he closer people live to the water, the scarier their dreams.'[34] Animating his setting in this portentous respect, Phillips traces Emily's attempted self-exposé to show how her superficial privacy in this colony offers little solace; it merely exacerbates a fevered kind of temporary contentment in isolation amidst an exotic expanse that coerces as insistently as it enthrals her. In *By the Sea*, Gurnah's Saleh Omar indeed records how the oceans can be duplicitous in this respect. Lawless, untamed, 'the sea and all its unruly emptiness had a way of turning minds, making people intense and eccentric, or even strangely violent' (*By the Sea*, 182). Similarly, in *Cambridge*, the seascape offers an anthropomorphic double to the narrator's tempestuous mind. Assailed forebodingly by her surroundings, Emily's candid delight in the 'attractions of the scene' outside impels a process of fraught self-admission soon awaiting her, imminently, in a 'dreamworld' within.

By interpolating experiences of historical space from captive and colonist alike, Phillips reveals a dynamic aspect to the island genre. Here the 'writer's native tongue', as Gillian Beer notes, 'is freighted on to the island with the first-person speaker and then is borne away again with the speaker from the island'.[35] As in Emily's case, the novel's pronominal voice is increasingly haunted, its authority faltering before events to come. Phillips shadows her recollection of being altered irrevocably by the Caribbean – altered by her encounter there with an island poised as a uterine zone of possibility, as well as by the anticipation of leaving it for a delimiting English society. With Emily as our principal guide to life in the colony, *Cambridge* exemplifies precisely the collusive effect of this shared-witnessing, whereby literary comprehension parallels the process of self-implication played out in her journey from ignorance to partial insight. 'Reader and narrator explore the island bounds of the book', notes Beer, 'but can never be its permanent inhabitants or establish there a foundation population. That sense of exile corrects the reader's hope of possession' ('Island Bounds', 42). In fact, in that twilight passage I quoted above, Phillips predicts the dispossession that will recapitulate in terms of Emily's emerging psychosis, fragmenting at the novel's climax. And Phillips has been quite self-revealing about his motivations here. 'I had no understanding', he admits, 'of why I narrated the last part of the novel through Emily's eyes till about a year afterwards'. It would appear her island story conjured unavoidable parallels to his own:

> Emily made a self-defining journey to the Caribbean, and so did I. She made it but the journeys changed her life dramatically, and mine. And the supreme irony in *Cambridge* is that the black man becomes the character you're supposed to like the least, because she grows, he shrinks.[36]

Authorial testimony here reciprocates the confessional tenor pursued throughout the novel, whereby we discover how racial self-definition for writer and character alike is contradictory and demanding. Similar to the way Barker and Thorpe used perception in their work to revivify the critical textures of regional fiction, Phillips and Levy have taken the relatively conventional idiom of first-person recollections as a mode for historicizing the contexts of racial displacement, while at the same time advancing those interconnections between setting and perception which have so richly informed the postcolonial novel. They utilize the restrictive perspective of the first-person to evoke strange sensations within island settings, from initial approach to native encounter, while refusing to exploit their metaphoricity for its own sake. In these island fictions, the identical pronoun is scarcely possessive; instead, the 'I' acquires a certain elasticity before the locations which it focalizes. Single voices assume our acquaintance as readers, initiating a shared language, a shared medium of attention. Individual reflections connect us to the complex realities of landscapes drawn from history via immediate perceptions – places whose legacies are transposed across time to animate our reading experience in the present.

Epilogue

'Because Time Is Not Like Space'

'The island is not a story in itself', said Foe gently, laying a hand on my knee. 'We can bring it to life only by setting it within a larger story.'

J. M. Coetzee, *Foe* (1986)[1]

Drawing our attention to the intersection of 'story' and 'setting', the novels we've encountered throughout this book reveal the ways in which a landscape doesn't simply offer the writer an ambient backdrop, but also the opportunity for her to 'bring it to life' in relation to 'larger' concerns. Working on the frontiers between topography and parable, between discrete geographies and deeper histories of belonging, contemporary novelists have sought to do justice to the particularity of local places while observing the far-ranging associations that such places often evoke. Drawing here on her firsthand memories as a castaway in *Foe*, Susan Barton feels justified to declare that the sense of Britain as '"a great island"' appears '"a mere geographer's notion"' (26). Yet she has seen enough of the Empire at work to know that the 'earth under our feet is firm in Britain' in comparison to the islands it has governed and exploited (26). In a post-imperial age, Britain's historical self-awareness as a landmass distinct but far from immune from other continents holds implications that indeed exceed 'a mere geographer's' abstractions. While ultimately our sense of belonging is irreducible to any map, Hilary Mantel also warns that we shouldn't underestimate the tensions between landforms and affiliations, seeing that 'the English are literal-minded about borders' ('No Passports or Documents Are Needed', 99). As a novelist and a citizen, Mantel divulges an ambivalent compulsion to 'draw an imaginary line around ourselves' in an effort to 'say, this is my space, my territory, this is where I belong' (94). Much of this compulsion is linked to Britain's cartographic appearance on the globe. 'For obvious reasons', continues Mantel, the English

do not make a territorial identification with the continent of Europe. A stretch of water cuts them off. If you are in England, you can easily dismay your fellow citizens of Europe by a chance remark: by speaking of 'Crossing to Europe'. You are speaking geographically, of course. You do not mean to imply that you are not 'in' Europe. Nevertheless, the unfortunate turn of phrase has some significance. It is difficult, from the point of view of a small offshore island, to develop a sense of the integrity of Europe. (99)

The 'integrity' of a collective state viewed from a distant shore; the 'crossing' that makes the thought of convivial climate with 'your fellow citizens' seem so inconceivable; the sense that deceptive outcomes of discourse itself, from the political stage down to an 'unfortunate turn of phrase', can thwart hopes of 'territorial identification' ever transcending territorial distance – all these aspects highlight the interrelating forces of spatial perception and perceived cultural difference so active in the way nation-states understand one another. Such are the intersections of vision, comprehension and voice that can be traced throughout this book as it cuts across boundaries of geography and genre. By allowing the way places are perceived to stimulate new formal and thematic ambitions, contemporary writers show that the spatialization of literary form is integral to their description of the material world. Their work allows us to appreciate the role that narrative aesthetics play in our attempts to map the politics and poetics of space in British fiction today.

Evaluating the representation of place can transform the way we read the intersection of structure and symbolism in narrative discourse. As we have seen, recent British novelists have endorsed this kind of reciprocal engagement, emphasizing the multifaceted nature of perception as a visual and visceral aperture for conveying the experience of physical environments. Both in fiction and reportage alike, spatial formations affect myriad aspects of language and form, while eliciting from the reader new processes of aesthetic reception. Rhyme-schemes, for instance, in Azzopardi's latest work pose cognitive implications for the way we relate to printed space when retracing verbal patterns across narrative time. Similarly, Phillips's postcolonial travelogue and Thorpe's pastoral allegory both reveal through their use of visual prospects the way perceptual space punctuates structure itself. Such writers show how spatial phenomena can be symbolically cued, grammatically encoded as well as literally complemented by a plot's scenic sweep between locations.

It may seem obvious to assert that place and perception provide more than a thematic function for the novel today. Scene-setting is forever susceptible to such critical platitudes; yet as we have seen, complex distinctions mediate this apparent unity between depicted places and the spatial features of their description. Writers are extending the long-standing power of the novel to initiate forms of intersubjective knowledge. Whether reviving or declining, landscapes in fiction serve to exercise the reader's capacities for sensory intellection, compelling us to cherish our reactions to fictional landscapes and relate them to situations of universal significance. Measuring how successful contemporary writers are at negotiating this tension between particularity and abstraction has only been one of a range of objectives for this study. For my concern has also been with how landscapes intensify the reader's *participative* role in the creation and evaluation of novelistic space. Contemporary writers freely capitalize, of course, upon the sense in which seemingly inanimate surroundings disrupt our view of what temporally unfolds there. Mark Haddon's celebrated narrator of *The Curious Incident of the Dog in the Night-Time* (2003) offers a cautionary note on the difference between sensing time as a tangible quantity and the possibility of conjuring sensations of a place using a map of its resident objects. For Christopher, suffering from Asperger syndrome, school holidays offer little relaxation. The cessation of familiar schedules evacuates his sense of daily contact with the physical environment outside:

> Because time is not like space. And when you put something down somewhere, like a protractor or a biscuit, you can have a map in your head to tell you where you have left it, but even if you don't have a map it will still be there because a map is a *representation* of things that actually exist so you can find the protractor or the biscuit again. And a timetable is a map of time, except if you don't have a timetable time is not there like the landing and the garden and the route to school.[2]

As he recalls from a previous vacation in France with his parents, without a 'routine' destination to reach every morning he feels stranded between days that pass without set timescales. With the freedom of not having to be anywhere in particular, the time it takes to visit new places seems all the more immeasurable in comparison to objects 'that actually exist' within the places themselves. Christopher knows that to 'map' our understanding of time as a set of routines entails a quite different perceptual system of categorization to the one used in retracing an object to 'where you have left it' in space. Where public places are concerned – areas stretching beyond his own 'landing and the garden' – the terms of perception and expectation are formidably unpredictable. A whole new sensibility is summoned for navigating the local community and its bustling anonymity, leaving Christopher 'unaware', as psychologist Lorna Wing has noted, 'of the boundaries between objects that to others seem so obvious'.[3] For it's not that he lacks an understanding of how other people define their sensation of time and place, so much as any conception that fellow pedestrians *could* be so mentally receptive to begin with. 'I see everything', he admits, but '[t]hat is why I don't like new places' (174). This resistance to stepping into the unknown makes him not only defensive but clinically protective of set-arrangements, like the school-run routine, that help him to systematize space into a sequence of destinations. Christopher is by no means used as a mere case-study by the novel; yet by revealing, firsthand, the compulsiveness with which his narrator upholds strict distinctions between time and space, Haddon highlights how the agility of human perception when fully functional is something we readily take for granted. As our guide to the strictures that Asperger sufferers involuntarily exercise as they shift between unfamiliar locations,

Haddon draws attention to our fortunate ability to make sense of our physical surroundings in ways sensitive to others whom we perceive there.

Not that Haddon is asking us to confuse the processes of reading and writing. His point is also a reflexively metafictional one, bringing into focus his own efforts as an innovator to envision the built environment from such a concentrated, and occasionally debilitating, point of view. Christopher's intrusion there is itself an exemplary instance, echoing Joseph Frank, of how a temporary halt in sequential narrative can create spatial form: plunged into this protracted moment of introspection by a narrator uniting memory and anecdote, Haddon's second-person narration seems to stretch-out sideways from the novel's prevailing path of events. Cutting away from the text's overarching, temporal sense of succession between present-day episodes, Christopher digresses down a route of remembrance scarcely navigable in linear terms. But *The Curious Incident* also dramatizes issues of space at a plot-level as well, namely, by addressing topology as an inadequate source of reference-points in comparison to the sensory maps we make of the world. By following Henry James's instruction against relying too heavily on 'existing names' for the places he evokes, Haddon offers a more textured account of spatial perceptions, as though obliging himself as a technician to present more than a mere 'handful of impressions' (The Art of the Novel, 8). Evoking the idiom of passing time, implies Haddon – either by transposing it into scheduled departures and destinations, or by encoding it as an incremental journey – is quite different from evoking the experience of those spaces through which observing narrators pass. Because time indeed feels distinct from space, even while seeming incomprehensible without it; because our engagement with *where* events take place can have a different effect to measuring the timescale along which those events unfold; because a narrative's duration and location elicit discrete responses from the cognitive intellect – such are the contentions behind this study's appeal to a more processual manner of envisioning literary space.

Haddon echoes formal concerns recurring for many writers today who render the experience of their settings so palpable. Far from aspiring to refer consistently to precise landmarks, they invite us to read kinetically as though moving through the spaces they describe. Versed in myriad grammars of perspective, these fictions have revealed that material locations are inseparable from their perceptual articulation. We therefore can't evaluate the pertinence or resonance of where a novel is set without fully understanding how its settings influence the composition of narrative form. Remember that, despite her emphasizing the primacy of plot for analyzing fictional worlds, Eudora Welty conceded that, as a 'lowlier angel', place 'has been rather neglected of late', and that 'maybe she could do with a little petitioning' (*The Eye of the Story*, 116). Inasmuch as the present study has sought to prioritize an attention to technique in order to carry out that 'petitioning', it has also attempted to highlight the formal legacies that contemporary writers extend by retracing their poetics of place back to its distinctive antecedents. Rather than survey a multitude of writers who are representative of the diverse local, natural and global contexts of our time, I have tried to restore critical attention to issues of aesthetic value and distinction – neglected issues crucial to our understanding of how parables of place continue to inform the contemporary enterprise of literary experiment.

Hence, although this study has somewhat compressed its discussion of narrative space in order to scrutinize these aesthetic implications, it has argued that this 'continuous dialogue with form', as B. S. Johnson once celebrated it,[4] can persist in a richly metacritical respect. Particularizing something as ephemeral and abstract as literary space provokes us to reflect on current critical pursuits. By no means has this been a tacit attempt to think through such issues theoretically without resorting to the language of theory. On the contrary, the argument for a fresh focus on the distinctive rhetorical properties of the writing of place provides a basis for reflecting on the priorities that direct our attention to contemporary prose, the theoretical predispositions with which we frame and evaluate fiction today, as well as the ethical implications of proposing an alternative canon of ecologically engaged novelists attuned to endangered geographies. While demanding that we distinguish our attentiveness to form from any reverence to formalism, writers today also reanimate our sense of the value and vulnerability of our surroundings. If landforms in fiction always threaten to dissolve the dividing line between figurative and historical space, they also disrupt the self-certainties of many theoretical agendas by which place has previously been analysed in fiction. Spatial formations and typographic style, physical location and tonal pitch – interlacements of this kind, as we have seen, ramify diversely for writers who represent place via the rhetoric of spatial perceptions. Provoking the reader's cognitive and emotional response, perception offers writers a catalyst for innovation as well as a thematic subject, expanding the tenets of comprehension itself. An emerging body of novelists are taking responsibility for creating a *poiesis* of space that can re-envision the landscape of everyday life, receptive to the social and historical forces under which new habitats are forged. Forever drawing attention to that ambiguous yet vital point at which metaphor becomes the thing itself, they commit to illuminating spatial possibilities even from within places that appear so unique unto themselves.

Notes

Introduction: The Spatial Imaginary of Contemporary British Fiction

1 Graham Swift quoted in Sophie Harrison, 'Voice from the Street', *The Guardian, Review*, 14 April 2007, 11.
2 Henri Lefebvre, *The Production of Space*, trans. Donald Nicholson-Smith (1974; Oxford: Blackwell, 1991).
3 Caren Kaplan, *Questions of Travel: Postmodern Discourses of Displacement* (Durham and London: Duke University Press, 1996), 144.
4 Fredric Jameson, *Postmodernism: Or, the Cultural Logic of Late Capitalism* (Durham: Duke University Press, 1991); Edward W. Soja, *Postmetropolis: Critical Studies of Cities and Regions* (Oxford: WhileyBlackwell, 2000); and David Harvey, *Spaces of Hope* (Edinburgh: Edinburgh University Press, 2000).
5 Janet Wolff, for instance, has drawn attention to the development of 'travelling theory' as symptomatic of the post-structuralist fetishization of *the liminal*: 'notions of mobility, fluidity, provisionality and process', are claimed as supposedly radical, derived from a material world to which they can be re-ascribed as model spatial practices wholly 'preferable to alternative notions of stasis and fixity'. ('On the Road Again: Metaphors of Travel in Cultural Criticism', *Cultural Studies* 7, no. 1 [1993], 228.)
6 Andrew Thacker, 'The Idea of a Critical Literary Geography', *New Formations* 57 (Winter 2005/6), 57–8.
7 Edward W. Said, *Culture and Imperialism* (London: Chatto & Windus, 1993), 100–1.
8 David Lodge, 'Consciousness and the Novel', *Consciousness and the Novel: Connected Essays* (London: Penguin, 2002), 10.
9 This imbalance is being corrected, though, and new understandings of space and the novel are now emerging. The idea of spatialization as a structural and linguistic property of narrative fiction has become a valuable focus for recent narratologists. See, for instance, Marie-Laure Ryan, 'Cognitive Maps and the Construction of Narrative Space', in *Narrative Theory and the Cognitive Sciences*, ed. David Herman (Stanford, CA: Centre for the Study of Language and Information, 2003), 214–42. Herman himself substantially discusses this 'cognitive turn' among theories of literary space in *Story Logic* (Lincoln: University of Nebraska Press, 2002).

[10] William Empson, *The Structure of Complex Words* (1951; Harmmondsworth: Penguin, 1995), 434.

[11] Richard Cavell, 'Geographical Immediations: Locating *The English Patient*', *New Formations* 57 (Winter 2005/6), 95.

[12] See Gaston Bachelard, *The Poetics of Space*, trans. Maria Jolas (1958; Boston: Beacon Press, 1994), ch. 7.

[13] Eudora Welty, 'Place in Fiction', *The Eye of the Story* (New York: Random House, 1977), 116.

[14] The phrase borrows Georges Perec's title to his shrewd meditation on human dwelling, 'Species of Spaces' (1977), repr. in the volume *Species of Spaces and Other Pieces* (London: Penguin, 1999).

[15] Lorna Sage, 'Living on Writing', in *Grub Street and the Ivory Tower: Literary Journalism and Literary Scholarship from Fielding to the Internet*, ed. Jeremy Treglown and Bridget Bennett (Oxford: Clarendon Press, 1998), 268–9.

[16] Robert Macfarlane, 'Where the Wild Things Were', *The Guardian, Review*, Saturday 30 July 2005, 4.

[17] Susan Sontag, 'The Aesthetics of Silence', *Styles of Radical Will* (London: Vintage, 2001), 10.

[18] Rose Tremain, *The Colour* (London: Chatto & Windus, 2003), 178.

[19] Thomas Hardy, *The Life and Work of Thomas Hardy*, ed. Michael Millgate (Basingstoke: Macmillan, 1984), 192.

[20] Thomas Hardy, *Tess of the D'Urbervilles*, ed. Juliet Grindle and Simon Gatrell (1891; Oxford: Oxford University Press, 2005), 118.

[21] Ian McEwan, *The Child in Time* (London: Jonathan Cape, 1987), 93.

[22] Elizabeth Bowen, 'Notes on Writing a Novel', *The Mulberry Tree: Writings of Elizabeth Bowen*, ed. Hermione Lee (1946; London: Vintage, 1999), 39.

[23] Ian McEwan, Interview by Zadie Smith, *The Believer* 26 (August 2005), 50.

[24] Ian McEwan, *On Chesil Beach* (London: Jonathan Cape, 2007), 120.

[25] Zadie Smith, 'Read Better', *The Guardian, Review*, 20 January 2007, 21.

[26] Amit Chaudhuri, 'On Belonging and Not Belonging: A Conversation with Amit Chaudhuri', by Fernando Galvá, *Wasafiri* 30 (Autumn 1999), 47.

[27] Amit Chaudhuri, *Afternoon Raag* (London: Heinemann, 1993), 73.

[28] Amit Chaudhuri, 'Colonized and Classicist', *TLS*, no. 5340, 5 August 2005, 7.

[29] Jonathan Crary, *Suspensions of Perception: Attention, Spectacle, and Modern Culture* (Cambridge, MA: MIT Press, 2001), 3.

[30] J. Hillis Miller, *Topographies* (Stanford, CA: Stanford University Press, 1995), 4.

[31] Milan Kundera, *The Curtain: An Essay in Seven Parts*, trans. Linda Asher (London: Faber and Faber, 2007), 13.

[32] Rob Shields, 'A Guide to Urban Representation and What to Do about It: Alternative Traditions of Urban Theory', in *Re-Presenting the City: Ethnicity, Capital and Culture in the Twenty-First Century Metropolis*, ed. Anthony D. King (London: Macmillan, 1996), 229. Likewise, Silvia Mergenthal has pointed out that 'Literary representations of cities in postmodern novels can be described as exercises in spatiality because they insist that there are no straightforward spatial references with correspondent "true" meanings.' But on an admittedly 'less optimistic note', she insists that 'one needs to inquire whether, in those novels some spatialities are privileged over others, and which patterns of power and domination, or

inclusion and exclusion, are cloaked in the language of spatial distribution'. ('"Whose City?" Contested Spaces and Contesting Spatialities in Contemporary London Fiction', in *London in Literature: Visionary Mappings of the Metropolis*, ed. Susana Onega and John A. Stotesbury [Heidelberg: University of Heidelberg Press, 2002], 133.)

33 Richard Todd, *Consuming Fictions: The Booker Prize and Fiction in Britain Today* (London: Bloomsbury, 1996), 132.

34 Jeremy Seabrook, 'The End of the Provinces', *Granta* 90 (Summer 2005), 241.

35 Doris Lessing, 'Writing Autobiography', *Time Bites: Views and Reviews* (London and New York: Fourth Estate, 2004), 103.

36 Peter Ackroyd, 'The Englishness of English Literature', *The Collection: Journalism, Reviews, Essays, Short Stories, Lectures* (London: Vintage, 2001), 340.

37 Michel Foucault, 'The Eye of Power', *Power/Knowledge: Selected Interviews and Other Writings, 1972–1977* (Brighton: Harvester Wheatsheaf, 1980), 149.

38 Ben Okri, 'The Joys of Storytelling II', *A Way of Being Free* (London: Phoenix, 1997), 63.

39 Robert Macfarlane, 'Call of the Wild', *The Guardian, Review*, Saturday 6 December 2003, 38.

40 Raymond Williams, *Resources of Hope: Culture, Democracy, Socialism* (New York: Verso, 1989), 87.

41 Iain Sinclair, *The Verbals: Kevin Jackson in Conversation with Iain Sinclair* (Kent: Worple, 2003), 76.

Chapter 1: Landscape and Narrative Aesthetics

1 Edward W. Said, 'Invention, Memory, and Place', *Critical Inquiry* 26, no. 2 (Winter 2000), 180.

2 Simon Schama, *Landscape and Memory* (New York: Vintage, 1995), 9.

3 See Karla Armbruster and Kathleen R. Wallace, *Beyond Nature Writing: Expanding the Boundaries of Ecocriticism* (Charlottesville: University Press of Virginia, 2001); and Glen A. Love, *Practical Ecocriticism: Literature, Biology and the Environment* (Charlottesville: University Press of Virginia, 2003).

4 Richard Strier, 'How Formalism Became a Dirty Word, and Why We Can't Do Without It?', in *Renaissance Literature and Its Formal Engagements*, ed. Mark David Rasmussen (New York: Palgrave, 2002), 211.

5 Edward Soja, *Postmodern Geographies: The Reassertion of Space in Critical Social Theory* (New York: Verso, 1989), 23.

6 Georg Lukács, 'The Moment and Form', *Soul and Form* (London: Merlin, 1974), 113–14.

7 Henry James, *The Wings of the Dove* (1902; London: Penguin, 2003), 174.

8 Maria Balshaw and Liam Kennedy 'Introduction', in *Urban Space and Representation*, ed. Maria Balshaw and Liam Kennedy (London: Pluto, 2000), 6.

9 Said, 'Invention, Memory, and Place', 182.

10 Ken Warpole, 'Mother to Legend (or Going Underground): The London Novel', in *Peripheral Visions: Images of Nationhood in Contemporary British Fiction*, ed. Ian A. Bell (Cardiff: University of Wales Press, 1995), 183.

[11] Andrew Gibson, *Towards a Postmodern Theory of Narrative* (Edinburgh: Edinburgh University Press, 1996), 278.

[12] Minrose Gwin, *The Woman in the Red Dress: Gender, Space and Reading* (Urbana: University of Illinois Press, 2002), 52.

[13] Michel de Certeau, *The Practice of Everyday Life* (Berkley: University of California Press, 1984), 117.

[14] Paul Smethurst, 'There Is No Place Like Home: Belonging and Placelessness in the Postmodern Novel', in *Space and Place: The Geographies of Literature*, ed. Glenda Norquay and Gerry Smyth (Liverpool: Liverpool John Moores University Press, 1997), 374.

[15] Jeanette Winterson, *Art Objects: Essays on Ecstasy and Effrontery* (London: Jonathan Cape, 1995), 165.

[16] Mieke Bal, *Narratology: Introduction to the Theory of Narrative* (Toronto: University of Toronto Press, 1999), 132.

[17] For Joseph Frank's original proposals, see 'Spatial Form in Modern Literature', repr. in *The Widening Gyre: Crisis and Mastery in Modern Literature* (New Brunswick: Rutgers University Press, 1963), 3–62; reprinted again, as a kind of career retrospective, in his *The Idea of Spatial Form* (New Brunswick: Rutgers University Press, 1991), 5–66.

[18] Christine Brooke-Rose, *Stories, Theories, Things* (Cambridge: Cambridge University Press, 1991), 27.

[19] Observe, for instance, the evolving sympathies towards the relevancy of 'spatial form' between William Holtz, 'A Reconsideration of Spatial Form', *Critical Inquiry* 4, no. 2 (Winter 1977), 231–52; Frank Kermode, 'A Reply to Joseph Frank', *Critical Inquiry* 4, no. 3 (Spring 1978), 579–88; and Joseph Frank's own earlier defence, 'Spatial Form: An Answer to Critics', *Critical Inquiry* 4, no. 2 (Winter 1977), 231–52. As Frank would remember it, Kermode exhibited a 'puzzling "space-shyness"' that appeared to have 'accepted everything about spatial form except the terminology'. 'Spatial Form: Thirty Years After', in *Spatial Form in Narrative*, ed. Jeffrey R. Smitten and Ann Daghistany (Ithaca: Cornell University Press, 1981), 215.

[20] W. J. T. Mitchell, 'Spatial Form in Literature: Toward a General Theory', *Critical Inquiry* 6, no. 3 (Spring 1980), 550.

[21] See, for instance, Peter Stockwell's taxonomy of 'mental spaces' in a discussing the way readers infer varying levels of semantic reference within possible text-worlds, in *Cognitive Poetics: An Introduction* (London and New York: Routledge, 2002), 96–103.

[22] Lynda D. McNeil, 'Toward a Rhetoric of Spatial Form: Some Implications of Frank's Theory', *Comparative Literature Studies* 17, Special Issue (December 1980), 356.

[23] Martin Amis, 'The American Eagle', *The War Against Cliché: Essays and Reviews, 1971–2000* (London: Jonathan Cape, 2001), 467.

[24] Ronald Faust, 'The Aporia of Recent Criticism and the Contemporary Significance of Spatial Form', *Spatial Form in Narrative*, 185.

[25] Peter Middleton and Tim Woods, *Literatures of Memory: History, Time and Space in Postwar Writing* (Manchester: Manchester University Press, 2000), 280.

[26] Michèle Roberts, 'Michèle Roberts', interview by Jenny Newman, in *Contemporary British and Irish Fiction: An Introduction through Interviews* (London: Arnold, 2004), 126.

27 Margaret Ann Doody, *The True Story of the Novel* (London: HarperCollins, 1997), 304.

28 Maggie Gee, 'Politics at Play', *TLS*, no. 5322, 1 April 2005, 19.

29 Bruce King, *The Oxford English Literary History, Volume 13. 1948–2000: The Internationalization of English Literature* (Oxford: Oxford University Press, 2004), 8. For Richard Todd, the annual Booker Prize itself has aided in this deterritorialization of contemporary British fiction. Gradually over the years the award has punctuated 'the history of the replacement of "the English novel" by "the novel [published] in Britain" since about 1980. This realization necessitates discussion of what "Englishness" and "Britishness" now mean in terms of the production and consumption of fiction in Britain' (*Consuming Fictions: The Booker Prize and Fiction in Britain Today* [London: Bloomsbury, 1996], 78). This chimes with Philip Tew's justification for delimiting 'the contemporary scene' as a literary-critical frame, in terms of 'what themes and issues, events or activities can be taken as ongoing, relevant to current practice'. In answering the eternally open-ended question of 'Who, What, Why and When?', Tew thus suggests that 'the phase from the mid-1970s offers a sufficiently discrete mode of new writing and response to historical conditions to be regarded as relevant to the present. To engage with this period requires situating fiction in a larger and changing conception of Britishness, about which opinions abound' (*The Contemporary British Novel* [London: Continuum, 2004], 185).

30 See for instance Aijaz Ahmad's 'Jameson's Rhetoric of Otherness and the "National Allegory"', *Social Text* 17 (Autumn 1987), 11. For Jameson's original prolegomena, see 'Third-World Literature in the Era of Multinational Capitalism', *Social Text* 15 (Autumn 1986), 65–88.

31 Caryl Phillips, 'Extravagant Strangers', *A New World Order: Selected Essays* (London: Vintage, 2002), 294.

32 Salman Rushdie, 'The Best of Young British Novelists', *Step Across This Line: Collected Non-Fiction 1992–2002* (London: Vintage, 2003), 38.

33 Hilary Mantel has reflected in comparable terms, pausing to consider her own compound status, descending from a family of Irish immigrants brought up in the Peak District:

When we travel abroad, our hosts ask us to account for ourselves, define ourselves. When I speak or read abroad I am sometimes described as a British writer, sometimes as an English writer. To me, the first description is meaningless. 'Britain' can be used as a geographicalterm, but it has no definable cultural meaning. As for calling me 'an English writer' — it is simply what I am not.

('No Passes or Documents Are Needed: The Writer at Home in Europe', in *On Modern British Fiction*, ed. Zachary Leader [Oxford: Oxford University Press, 2002], 94.)

34 D. J. Taylor, 'Gone to Seed', rev. of *Six*, by Jim Crace, *The Guardian, Review*, 6 September 2003, 26.

35 Caryl Phillips, 'Preface', *Extravagant Strangers: A Literature of Belonging* (London: Faber and Faber, 1997), xiii.

36 Cairns Craig, 'Scotland and the Regional Novel', in *The Regional Novel in Britain and Ireland, 1800–1990*, ed. K. D. M. Snell (Cambridge: Cambridge University Press, 1998), 255.

37 See Benedict Anderson, *Imagined Communities: Reflections on the Origin and Spread of Nationalism* (London: Verso, 1983).

38 Mantel, 'No Passes or Documents Are Needed, 94.

39 Salman Rushdie, 'Imaginary Homelands', *Imaginary Homelands: Essays and Criticism 1981–1991* (London: Granta, 1992), 10.

40 Orhan Pamuk, *Istanbul: Memories of a City* (London: Faber and Faber, 2005), 6.

Chapter 2: New Horizons for the Regional Novel

1 Phyllis Bentley, *The English Regional Novel* (London: George Allen and Unwin, 1941), 13.

2 Interestingly, Bentley herself discovers in C. A. Dawson Scott, founder of her series publishers P. E. N., a corrective to that nineteenth-century mythologization of travelling westward. For Bentley, Scott's own 'Cornish novels, *They Green Stones* (1925) and others, do not lose sight of sociological implications in their depiction of the landscape and dialect of that picturesque county' (*The English Regional Novel*, 35).

3 D. J. Taylor, 'When the North Invaded Hampstead', *The Guardian, Review*, 30 November 2002, 26.

4 K. D. M. Snell, 'The Regional Novel: Themes for Interdisciplinary Research', in *The Regional Novel in Britain and Ireland*, 1.

5 Edward W. Said, *Humanism and Democratic Criticism* (New York: Columbia University Press, 2003), 91.

6 See, for example, Storey's most recent *Thin-Ice Skater* (London: Jonathan Cape, 2004); and Jim Crace's interrogative return to the pastoral idyll of the 'garden city' in *Arcadia* (London: Jonathan Cape, 1992).

7 Richard Mabey, 'Ground Force', interview by Ed Douglas. *The Guardian, Review*, 10 December 2005, 11.

8 Peter Brooks, *Realist Vision* (New Haven: Yale University Press, 2005), 3.

9 Brooke-Rose, *Stories, Theories, Things*, 210.

10 Pat Barker, 'An Interview with Pat Barker', by John Brannigan, *Contemporary Literature* 46, no. 3 (Fall 2005), 377.

11 Dominic Head, *The Cambridge Companion to Modern British Fiction* (Cambridge: Cambridge University Press, 2002), 44.

12 Andrzej Gasiorek's important survey questioned the dichotomy between realisms and avant-garde radicalism, arguing that 'there is no necessary link either between particular narrative strategies and the goal of accurate representation or between realism, however it is conceived, and any given political position' (*Post-War British Fiction: Realism and After* [London: Edward Arnold, 1995], vi).

13 Jean Baudrillard, *Simulations*, trans. Paul Foss, Paul Patton and Philip Beitchman (New York: Semiotexte, 1983), 12.

14 Ian Baucom, *Out of Place: Englishness, Empire and the Locations of Identity* (Princeton: Princeton University Press, 1999), 167.

15 Alan Sillitoe, *Saturday Night and Sunday Morning* (1958; London: Flamingo, 1994), 113.

16 See Raymond Williams, 'Pleasing Prospects', *The Country and the City* (Oxford: Oxford University Press, 1973), 120–6.

17 Stephen Daniels and Simon Rycroft, 'Mapping the Modern City: Alan Sillitoe's Nottingham Novels', in *The Regional Novel in Britain and Ireland*, 260.

18 Alan Sillitoe, *Mountains and Caverns* (London: W. H. Allen, 1975), 71.

19 Adam Thorpe, 'Waiting and Leaping', *The Guardian, Review*, 15 May 2004, 31.

20 Adam Thorpe, *Ulverton* (London: Secker & Warburg, 1992), 42.

21 Storm Jameson, 'Documents', *Fact* 4 (July 1937), 15.

22 Margaret Drabble, *A Writer's Britain: Landscape in Literature* (London: Thames and Hudson, 1984), 59.

23 J. M. Coetzee, *White Writing: On the Culture of Letters in South Africa* (New Haven and London: Yale University Press, 1988), 40.

24 Robert Macfarlane, 'Where the Wild Things Were', *The Guardian, Review*, 30 July 2005, 5.

25 Roland Barthes, *Writing Degree Zero*, repr. with *Elements of Semiology* (London: Jonathan Cape, 1984), 48.

26 Sharon Monteith, *Pat Barker* (Travistock: Northcote House, 2002), 5.

27 Robert Macfarlane, 'Where the Wild Things Are', *The Guardian, Review*, 30 October 2004, 37.

28 Raymond Williams, 'Social Environment and Theatrical Environment: The Case of English Naturalism', *Problems in Materialism and Culture* (London: Verso, 1988), 127.

29 Paul de Man, 'Symbolic Landscape in Wordsworth and Yeats', *The Rhetoric of Temporality* (New York: Columbia University Press, 1984), 126.

30 Pat Barker, *Blow Your House Down* (1984; London: Virago, 1990), 163.

31 Gérard Genette, *Essays in Aesthetics* (Lincoln and London: University of Nebraska Press, 1999), 162.

32 Joseph Rykwert, *The Seduction of Place: The History and Future of the City* (Oxford: Oxford University Press, 2000), 246.

33 Ernst Bloch, *The Utopian Function of Art and Literature* (Cambridge, MA: MIT Press, 1988), 148.

34 Williams, *Border Country* (1960; Cardigan: Parthian, 2005), 89.

35 Pat Barker, 'Pat Barker', interview by Sharon Monteith, in *Contemporary British and Irish Fiction*, 31.

36 Salman Rushdie, 'The Power of Love', *The Guardian, Review*, 23 April 2005, 7.

Chapter 3: Urban Visionaries

1 Ford Madox Ford, *The Soul of London: A Survey of a Modern City* (1905; London: Everyman, 1955), 16.

2 Peter Ackroyd, *London: The Biography* (London: Chatto & Windus, 2000), 77.

3 Steve Pile, 'The Un(known) City . . . or, an Urban Geography of What Lies Buried below the Surface', in *The Unknown City: Contesting Architecture and Social Space*, ed. Iain Borden, Joe Kerr and Jane Rendell (Massachusetts: MIT Press, 2002), 265.

[4] Jack London, *The People of the Abyss* (1902; London: Arco, 1963), 11.

[5] Theodor W. Adorno, *Prisms* (Cambridge, MA: MIT Press, 1983), 240.

[6] Sinclair quoted in Robert Bond, *Iain Sinclair* (London: Salt, 2005), 134–5.

[7] Nicholas Shakespeare, *Londoners* (London: Sidgwick and Jackson, 1986), 18.

[8] See, for instance, Shklovsky's 1917 commentary on strategies of literary defamiliarization in 'Art as Technique', repr. in *Russian Formalist Criticism: Four Essays*,
ed. Lee T. Lemon and Marion J. Reis (Nebraska: University of Nebraska Press,
1965).

[9] Marc Atkins and Iain Sinclair, *Liquid City* (London: Reaktion, 1999), 40.

[10] Roger Luckhurst, 'The Contemporary London Gothic and the Limits of the
"Spectral Turn"', *Textual Practice* 16, no. 3 (Winter 2002), 541.

[11] Sukhdev Sandhu, 'Come Hungry, Leave Edgy', rev. of *Brick Lane*, by Monica Ali,
London Review of Books 25, no. 19, 9 October 2003, 12.

[12] Monica Ali, 'Signs of the Times', *The Guardian, Review*, 4 November 2006, 22.

[13] Monica Ali, *Brick Lane* (London: Doubleday, 2003), 208.

[14] Raymond Williams, 'Commitment', *What I Came Here to Say* (London: Hutchinson
Radius, 1989), 260.

[15] Andrzej Gasiorek, *J. G. Ballard* (Manchester: Manchester University Press,
2005), 5.

[16] Iain Sinclair, 'Paint Me a River', *The Guardian, Review*, 5 February 2005, 16.

[17] Iain Sinclair, *Downriver* (1991; London: Granta, 2002), 371.

[18] Tim Adams, 'Singing his prose', rev. of *Landor's Tower*, by Iain Sinclair, *The
Guardian, Review*, Saturday 8 April 2001, 15.

[19] Bond, *Iain Sinclair*, 132.

[20] Hilda Kean, 'The Transformation of Political and Cultural Space', in *London:
From Punk to Blair*, ed. Joe Kerr and Andrew Gibson (London: Reaktion,
2003), 155.

[21] Iain Sinclair, 'Woking at War', *The Guardian, Review*, 26 June 2004, 37.

[22] James Donald, *Imagining the Modern City* (London: Athlone, 1999), 27.

[23] Patrick Wright, 'The Last Days of London: A Conversation with Joe Kerr', in *The
Unknown City*, 484.

[24] W. G. Sebald, *On the Natural History of Destruction* (London: Penguin, 2004), 53.

[25] Ballard, *Super-Cannes* (2000; London: Flamingo, 2001), 140.

[26] Michael Wood, 'Consulting the Oracle', *Essays in Criticism* 43, no. 2 (April 1993),
93, 101.

[27] J. G. Ballard, 'Conversations: J. G. Ballard', interview by Will Self, *Junk Mail* (London: Penguin, 1996), 332.

[28] Will Self, 'The Seer of Shepperton', *Sore Sites* (London: Ellipsis, 2000), 14.

[29] J. G. Ballard, *Millennium People* (London: Flamingo, 2003), 25.

[30] J. G. Ballard, 'Up With the Celestial Helmsmen', rev. of *The Spectacle of Flight: Aviation and the Western Imagination, 1920–1950*, by Robert Wohl, *The Guardian, Review*,
7 May 2005, 9.

[31] Theodor W. Adorno, 'Functionalism Today', trans. Jane Newman and John
Smith, *Oppositions* 17 (1979), 31–41, repr. in *Rethinking Architecture: A Reader in
Cultural Theory*, ed. Neil Leach (London: Routledge, 1997), 12.

[32] Roger Luckhurst, *'The Angle Between Two Walls': The Fiction of J. G. Ballard*
(Liverpool: Liverpool University Press, 1997), 137.

33 Iain Sinclair, 'Museums of Melancholy', *London Review of Books* 27, no. 16, 18 August 2005, 14.

34 J. G. Ballard, 'Interview with J. G. Ballard', by Andrea Juno and Vivian Vale, *J. G. Ballard* (San Francisco: V/Search, 1998), 8.

35 Michael Moorcock, *Mother London* (1988; London: Scribner, 2004).

Chapter 4: Cartographers of Memory

1 Kazuo Ishiguro, *The Remains of the Day* (1989; London: Faber and Faber, 1990), 128.

2 Suzanne Nalbantian, *Memory in Literature: From Rousseau to Neuroscience* (Basingstoke: Palgrave Macmillan, 2003), 7.

3 Lodge, *Thinks . . .* (London: Secker & Warburg, 2001), 148.

4 Paul W. Burgess and Tim Shallice, 'Confabulation and the Control of Recollection', *Memory* 4, no. 4 (1996), 367.

5 A. S. Byatt, 'Memory and Making of Fiction', in *Memory: The Darwin College Lectures*, ed. Patricia Fura and Karolyn Patterson (Cambridge: Cambridge University Press, 1998), 47.

6 Nicola King, *Memory, Narrative, Identity: Remembering the Self* (Edinburgh: Edinburgh University Press, 2000), 180.

7 Swift, 'Triumph of the Common Man', Profile of Graham Swift, by John O'Mahony, *The Guardian, Review*, 1 March 2003, http://books.guardian.co.uk/departments/generalfiction/story/0,,904963,00.html [last accessed 10 June 2008].

8 Paul Ricoeur, *Memory, History, Forgetting* (Chicago and London: University of Chicago Press, 2004), 149.

9 Graham Swift, 'Making an Elephant', *Granta* 87 (Autumn 2004), 301.

10 Graham Swift, *Waterland* (1983; London: Picador, 2002), 129.

11 Sarah M. Dunnigan, 'A. L. Kennedy's Longer Fiction', in *Contemporary Scottish Women Writers*, ed. Aileen Christianson and Alison Lumsden (Edinburgh: Edinburgh University Press, 2000), 154.

12 Candida Clark, *The Mariner's Star* (London: Review, 2002), 74.

13 Hermione Lee, 'Someone to Watch Over You', rev. of *The Light of Day*, by Graham Swift, *The Guardian, Review*, 8 March 2003, 9.

14 James Wood, 'How's the Empress?', rev. of *The Light of Day*, by Graham Swift, *London Review of Books* 25, no. 8, 17 April 2003, 29.

15 Lynne Hapgood, *Margins of Desire: The Suburbs in Fiction and Culture, 1880–1925* (Manchester: Manchester University Press, 2005), 36.

16 B. S. Johnson, *Trawl* (1966), repr. in *Omnibus: Trawl, Albert Angelo, House Mother Normal* (London: Picador, 2004), 9.

17 Edward S. Reed, 'Perception Is to Self as Memory Is to Selves', in *The Remembering Self: Construction and Accuracy in the Self-Narrative*, ed. Ulric Neisser and Robyn Fivush (Cambridge: Cambridge University Press, 1994), 278.

18 James Olney, *Memory and Narrative: The Weave of Life-Writing* (London and Chicago: University of Chicago Press, 1998), 11.

19 Graham Swift, *The Light of Day* (London: Hamish Hamilton, 2004), 19.

[20] Richard Hoggart, *Everyday Language and Everyday Life* (New Brunswick: Transaction, 2003), 156–7.

[21] Susan Stewart, *On Longing: Narratives of the Miniature, the Gigantic, the Souvenir, the Collection* (Durham: Duke University Press, 1993), 31.

[22] Matthew Campbell, Jacqueline M. Labbe and Sally Shuttleworth, 'Introduction', in *Memory and Memorials, 1789–1914* (London: Routledge, 2000), 8.

[23] A. L. Kennedy, *Looking for the Possible Dance* (1993; London: Minerva, 1994), 7.

[24] A. L. Kennedy, *Day* (London: Jonathan Cape, 2007), 4.

[25] James Wood, *The Irresponsible Self: On Laughter and the Novel* (London: Jonathan Cape, 2004), 208.

[26] A. L. Kennedy, *Paradise* (London: Jonathan Cape, 2004), 7.

[27] John A. Dussinger, *The Discourse of the Mind in Eighteenth-Century Fiction* (The Hague and Paris: Mouton, 1974), 21–2.

[28] Anthony Vilder, *The Architectural Uncanny: Essays in Modern Unhomely* (Cambridge, MA: MIT Press, 1996), 180.

[29] Trezza Azzopardi, *Remember Me* (London: Picador, 2004), 4–5.

[30] Elizabeth Bowen, *The Heat of the Day* (1949; London: Penguin, 1986), 21.

[31] Scott McQuire, *Visions of Modernity: Representation, Memory, Time and Space in the Age of the Camera* (London: Sage, 1998), 152.

[32] Marc Augé, *Oblivion* (Minneapolis: University of Minnesota Press, 2004), 39.

[33] Gillian Beer, 'Rhyming as Resurrection', in *Memory and Memorials*, ed. Campbell, Labbe and Shuttleworth, 192.

[34] William James, *Principles of Psychology*, vol. 1 (1890; New York: Dover, 1950), 654. Quoted in Nalbantian, *Memory and Literature*, 21.

[35] Kazuo Ishiguro, *Never Let Me Go* (London: Faber and Faber, 2005), 159.

[36] Mariner Warner, 'Game On', *The Guardian, Review*, 19 March 2005, 16.

[37] Antoinette Barton, 'India, Inc.? Nostalgia, Memory and the Empire of Things', in *British Culture and the End of Empire*, ed. Stuart Ward (Manchester: Manchester University Press, 2001), 219.

[38] Will Self, 'Charing Cross Hospital', in *London: City of Disappearances*, ed. Iain Sinclair (London: Hamish Hamilton, 2006), 59.

Chapter 5: Island Encounters

[1] Hanif Kureishi, 'London and Karachi', in *Patriotism: The Making and Unmaking of British National Identity*, vol. 2: *Minorities and Outsiders*, ed. Raphael Samuel (London: Routledge, 1989), 272.

[2] Markman Ellis, '"The Cane-Land Isles": Commerce and Empire in Late Eighteenth-Century Georgic and Pastoral Poetry', in *Islands in History and Representation*, ed. Rod Edmond and Vanessa Smith (London: Routledge, 2003), 58; 44.

[3] John R. Gillis, 'Taking History Offshore: Atlantic Islands in European Minds, 1400–1800', in *Islands in History and Representation*, 29.

[4] Abdulrazak Gurnah, 'Abdulrazak Gurnah with Susheila Nasta', in *Writing Across Worlds: Contemporary Writers Talk*, ed. Susheila Nasta (London: Routledge, 2004), 352.

[5] See Michael H. Fisher, *Counterflows to Colonialism: Indian Travellers and Settlers in Britain, 1600–1857* (New Delhi: Permanent Black, 2004), 298–9.

[6] Caryl Phillips, 'To Ricky with Love', *The Guardian, Review*, 23 July 2005, 28–9.

[7] Caryl Phillips, 'Necessary Journeys', *The Guardian, Review*, 11 December 2004, 5.

[8] Shamit Saggar, 'Immigration and Minority Policy Debate in Britain: Multicultural Political Narratives Contested', in *The Politics of Belonging: Migrants and Minorities in Contemporary Europe*, ed. Andrew Geddes and Adrian Favell (Aldershot: Ashgate, 1999), 52.

[9] Caryl Phillips, *The European Tribe* (New York: Vintage, 2000), 126.

[10] V. S. Naipaul, 'The Return of Eva Peron', repr. in *The Return of Eva Peron, with The Killings in Trinidad* (London: Andre Deutsch, 1980), 112.

[11] Michael Awkward, *Negotiating Difference: Race, Gender, and the Politics of Positionality* (Chicago: University of Chicago Press, 1995), 84.

[12] Paul Gilroy, *After Empire: Melancholia or Convivial Culture* (London: Routledge, 2004), 2.

[13] Anthony Ilona, 'Crossing the River: A Chronicle of the Black Diaspora', *Wasafiri* 22 (Autumn 1995), 7.

[14] Robert Fraser, *Lifting the Sentence: A Poetics of Postcolonial Fiction* (Manchester: Manchester University Press, 2000), 75.

[15] Rod Edmond and Vanessa Smith, 'Introduction', in *Islands in History and Representation*, 2.

[16] Caryl Phillips, 'Caryl Phillips with Maya Jaggi', in *Writing Across Worlds*, 121.

[17] Caryl Phillips, *Cambridge* (1991; London: Faber and Faber, 2000), 16.

[18] Bernhard Klein, 'Staying Afloat: Literary Shipboard Encounters from Columbus to Equiano', in *Sea Changes: Historicizing the Ocean*, ed. Bernhard Klein and Gesa Mackenthun (London: Routledge 2004), 93.

[19] Jane Rogers, *Island* (1999; London: Abacus, 2000), 49.

[20] V. S. Naipaul, *The Enigma of Arrival* (Harmondsworth: Viking, 1987), 91–2.

[21] Abdulrazak Gurnah, *By the Sea* (London: Bloomsbury, 2001), 137.

[22] Paul Sharrad, 'Speaking the Unspeakable: London, Cambridge and the Caribbean', in *De-scribing Empire: Post-Colonialism and Textuality*, ed. Chris Tiffin and Alan Lawson (London: Routledge, 1994), 203.

[23] David Simpson, *Situatedness, or, Why We Keep Saying Where We're Coming From* (Durham: Duke University Press, 2002), 195.

[24] See Donald Hinds, *Journey to an Illusion: A Study of West Indians in Britain* (London: Heinemann, 1966).

[25] Andrea Levy, *Small Island* (London: Review, 2004), 116–17.

[26] Caryl Phillips, 'Northern Soul', *The Guardian, Weekend*, 22 October 2005, 19.

[27] John Barrell, *English Literature in History: An Equal, Wide Survey* (London: Hutchinson, 1983), 63.

[28] Abdulrazak Gurnah, 'Settler Writing in Kenya: "Nomenclature Is an Uncertain Science in These Wild Parts"', in *Modernism and Empire*, ed. Howard T. Booth and Nigel Rigby (Manchester: Manchester University Press, 2000), 284–5.

[29] Peter Hulme, 'Cast Away: The Uttermost Parts of the Earth', in *Sea Changes*, 188.

[30] Susan George, *A Fate Worse Than Debt* (London: Penguin, 1988), 86.

[31] Gurnah, 'Ghana Times', *TLS*, no. 5340, 5 August 2005, 11.

[32] John Barrell, 'The Public Prospect and the Private View: The Politics of Taste in Eighteenth-Century Britain', in *Projecting the Landscape*, ed. J. C. Eade (Australia: Humanities Research Centre, Australian National University, 1987), 21.

[33] Avtar Brah, 'The Scent of Memory: Strangers, Our Own and Others', in *Hybridity and Its Discontents: Politics, Science, Culture*, ed. Avtar Brah and Annie E. Coombes (London: Routledge, 2000), 275.

[34] Orhan Pamuk, 'The Boy Who Watched the Ships Go By', *Granta* 61 (Spring 1998), 78.

[35] Gillian Beer, 'Island Bounds', in *Islands in History and Representation*, 42.

[36] Caryl Phillips, 'Caryl Phillips with Maya Jaggi', in *Writing Across Worlds*, 117.

Epilogue: 'Because Time Is Not Like Space'

[1] J. M. Coetzee, *Foe* (1986; London: Penguin, 1987), 117.

[2] Mark Haddon, *The Curious Incident of the Dog in the Night-Time* (London: Jonathan Cape, 2003), 193.

[3] Lorna Wing, *The Autistic Spectrum: A Guide for Parents and Professionals* (London: Constable, 1996), 90.

[4] B. S. Johnson, *Christie Malry's Own Double-Entry* (1973; London: Picador, 2001), 166.

Bibliography

Ackroyd, Peter. *The Collection: Journalism, Reviews, Essays, Short Stories, Lectures.* London: Chatto & Windus, 2001.

—. *London: The Biography.* London: Chatto & Windus, 2000.

Adams, Tim. 'Singing His Prose'. Rev. of *Landor's Tower*, by Iain Sinclair, *The Guardian, Review*, 8 April 2001, 15.

Adorno, Theodor W. 'Functionalism Today'. Trans. Jane Newman and John Smith, *Oppositions* 17 (1979): 31–41, repr. in *Rethinking Architecture: A Reader in Cultural Theory*, ed. Neil Leach (London: Routledge, 1997).

—. *Prisms.* Trans. Samuel and Shierry Weber. 1967; Cambridge, MA: MIT Press, 1983.

Ahmad, Aijaz. 'Jameson's Rhetoric of Otherness and the "National Allegory"'. *Social Text* 17 (Autumn 1987): 3–25.

Ali, Monica. *Brick Lane.* London: Doubleday, 2003.

—. 'Signs of the Times'. *The Guardian, Review*, 4 November 2006, 22.

Amis, Martin. *The War against Cliché: Essays and Reviews, 1971–2000.* London: Jonathan Cape, 2001.

Anderson, Benedict. *Imagined Communities: Reflections on the Origin and Spread of Nationalism.* London: Verso, 1983.

Armbruster, Karla, and Kathleen R. Wallace. *Beyond Nature Writing: Expanding the Boundaries of Ecocriticism.* Charlottesville: University Press of Virginia, 2001.

Atkins, Marc, and Iain Sinclair. *Liquid City.* London: Reaktion, 1999.

Augé, Marc. *Oblivion.* Minneapolis: University of Minnesota Press, 2004.

Awkward, Michael. *Negotiating Difference: Race, Gender, and the Politics of Positionality.* Chicago: University of Chicago Press, 1995.

Azzopardi, Trezza. *The Hiding Place.* 2000; London: Picador, 2001.

—. *Remember Me.* London: Picador, 2004.

Bachelard, Gaston. *The Poetics of Space.* Trans. Maria Jolas. 1958; Boston: Beacon Press, 1994.

Bal, Mieke. *Narratology: Introduction to the Theory of Narrative.* 2nd edn. Toronto: University of Toronto Press, 1999.

Ballard, J. G. *Concrete Island.* 1973; London: Vintage, 1994.

—. *High-Rise.* 1975; London: Flamingo, 2003.

—. *Millennium People.* London: Flamingo, 2003.

—. *Super-Cannes.* 2000; London: Flamingo, 2001.

—. 'Up With the Celestial Helmsmen'. Rev. of *The Spectacle of Flight: Aviation and the Western Imagination, 1920–1950*, by Robert Wohl. *The Guardian, Review*, 7 May 2005, 9.

Balshaw, Maria, and Liam Kennedy, eds. *Urban Space and Representation*. London: Pluto, 2000.

Barker, Pat. *Blow Your House Down*. 1984; London: Virago, 1990.

—. *Double Vision*. London: Hamish Hamilton, 2003.

—. *Union Street*. 1982; London: Virago, 1999.

Barrell, John. *English Literature in History: An Equal, Wide Survey*. London: Hutchinson, 1983.

Barthes, Roland. *Writing Degree Zero*, reissued with *Elements of Semiology*. London: Jonathan Cape, 1984.

Baucom, Ian. *Out of Place: Englishness, Empire and the Locations of Identity*. Princeton: Princeton University Press, 1999.

Baudrillard, Jean. *Simulations*. Trans. Paul Foss, Paul Patton and Philip Beitchma. New York: Semiotexte, 1983.

Bell, Ian A., ed. *Peripheral Visions: Images of Nationhood in Contemporary British Fiction*. Cardiff: University of Wales Press, 1995.

Benjamin, Walter. *The Arcades Project*. Ed. Rolf Tiedemann, trans. Howard Eiland and Kevin Mclaughlin. Cambridge, MA: Harvard University Press, 2002.

—. *Selected Writings, Vol. 1: 1913–1926*. Cambridge, MA: Harvard University Press, 2004.

Bentley, Phyllis. *The English Regional Novel*. London: George Allen & Unwin, 1941.

Bloch, Ernst. *The Utopian Function of Art and Literature*. Cambridge, MA: MIT Press, 1988.

Bond, Robert. *Iain Sinclair*. London: Salt, 2005.

Booth, Howard T., and Nigel Rigby, eds. *Modernism and Empire*. Manchester: Manchester University Press, 2000.

Borden, Iain, Joe Kerr and Jane Rendell, eds. *The Unknown City: Contesting Architecture and Social Space*. Massachusetts: MIT Press, 2002.

Bowen, Elizabeth. *The Heat of the Day*. 1999; London: Penguin, 1966.

—. *The Mulberry Tree: Writings of Elizabeth Bowen*. Ed. Hermione Lee. London: Vintage, 1999.

Brah, Avtar, and Annie E. Coombes, eds. *Hybridity and Its Discontents: Politics, Science, Culture*. London: Routledge, 2000.

Brannigan, John. 'An Interview with Pat Barker'. *Contemporary Literature* 46, no. 3 (Fall 2005): 366–92.

Brooker, Peter. *Modernity and Metropolis: Writing, Film and Urban Formations*. Basingstoke: Palgrave Macmillan, 2001.

Brooke-Rose, Christine. *Stories, Theories, Things*. Cambridge: Cambridge University Press, 1991.

Brooks, Peter. *Realist Vision*. New Haven: Yale University Press, 2005.

Burgess, Paul W., and Tim Shallice. 'Confabulation and the Control of Recollection'. *Memory* 4, no. 4 (1996): 359–411.

Caines, Michael. 'Out of the Esoteric Metropolis'. Rev. of *Dining on Stones*, by Iain Sinclair. *TLS*, no. 5273, 23 April 2004, 19–20.

Campbell, James. 'Conflict Zones'. *The Guardian*, *Review*, 3 April 2004, 20–4.

Campbell, Matthew, Jacqueline M. Labbe and Sally Shuttleworth, eds. *Memory and Memorials, 1789–1914*. London: Routledge, 2000.

Cavell, Richard. 'Geographical Immediations: Locating *The English Patient*'. *New Formations* 57 (Winter 2005/6): 95–106.

Chakrabarty, Dipesh. *Provincializing Europe: Postcolonial Thought and Historical Difference*. Princeton: Princeton University Press, 2000.

Chaudhuri, Amit. *Afternoon Raag*. London: Heinemann, 1993.

—. 'Colonized and Classicist'. *TLS*, no. 5340, 5 August 2005, 6–7.

—. 'On Belonging and Not Belonging: A Conversation with Amit Chaudhuri'. By Fernando Galvá. *Wasafiri* 30 (Autumn 1999): 42–50.

Christianson, Aileen, and Alison Lumsden, eds. *Contemporary Scottish Women Writers*. Edinburgh: Edinburgh University Press, 2000.

Clark, Candida. *The Mariner's Star*. London: Review, 2002.

Coetzee, J. M. *Foe*. 1986; London: Penguin, 1987.

—. *White Writing: On the Culture of Letters in South Africa*. New Haven: Yale University Press, 1988.

Crary, Jonathan. *Suspensions of Perception: Attention, Spectacle, and Modern Culture*. Cambridge, MA: MIT Press, 2001.

de Certeau, Michel. *The Practice of Everyday Life*. Trans. Steven Rendall. 1980; Berkley: University of California Press, 1984.

de Man, Paul. *The Rhetoric of Temporality*. New York: Columbia University Press, 1984.

Dennis, Ferdinand, and Naseem Khan, eds. *Voices of the Crossing: The Impact of Britain on Writers from Asia, the Caribbean and Africa*. London: Serpent's Tail, 2000.

Donald, James. *Imagining the Modern City*. London: Athlone, 1999.

Doody, Margaret Ann. *The True Story of the Novel*. London: HarperCollins, 1997.

Douglas, Ed. 'Ground Force'. Interview with Richard Mabey. *The Guardian, Review*, 10 December 2005, 11.

Drabble, Margaret. *A Writer's Britain: Landscape in Literature*. London: Thames & Hudson, 1984.

Dussinger, John A. *The Discourse of the Mind in Eighteenth-Century Fiction*. Paris: Mouton, 1974.

Eade, J. C., ed. *Projecting the Landscape*. Australia: Humanities Research Centre, Australian National University, 1987.

Edmond, Rod, and Vanessa Smith, eds. *Islands in History and Representation*. London: Routledge, 2003.

Fisher, Michael H. *Counterflows to Colonialism: Indian Travellers and Settlers in Britain, 1600–1857*. New Delhi: Permanent Black, 2004.

Ford, Ford Madox. *The Soul of London: A Survey of a Modern City*. 1905; London: Everyman, 1995.

Foucault, Michel. 'Of Other Spaces'. Trans. Jay Miskowiev. *Diacritics* 16, no. 1 (Spring 1986): 22–7.

—. *Power/Knowledge: Selected Interviews and Other Writings, 1972–1977*. Brighton: Harvester Wheatsheaf, 1980.

Frank, Joseph. *The Idea of Spatial Form*. New Brunswick: Rutgers University Press, 1991.

—. 'Spatial Form: An Answer to Critics'. *Critical Inquiry* 4, no. 2 (Winter 1977): 231–52.

—. *The Widening Gyre: Crisis and Mastery in Modern Literature.* New Brunswick: Rutgers University Press, 1963.

Fraser, Robert. *Lifting the Sentence: A Poetics of Postcolonial Fiction.* Manchester: Manchester University Press, 2000.

Fura, Patricia, and Karolyn Patterson, eds. *Memory: The Darwin College Lectures.* Cambridge: Cambridge University Press, 1998.

Gasiorek, Andrzej. *J. G. Ballard.* Manchester: Manchester University Press, 2005.

—. *Post-War British Fiction: Realism and After.* London: Edward Arnold, 1995.

Geddes, Andrew, and Adrian Favell, eds. *The Politics of Belonging: Migrants and Minorities in Contemporary Europe.* Aldershot: Ashgate, 1999.

Gee, Maggie. *The Flood.* London: Saqi, 2004.

—. 'Politics at Play'. *TLS*, no. 5322, 1 April 2005, 19.

Genette, Gérard. *Essays in Aesthetics.* Trans. Dorrit Cohen. Lincoln: University of Nebraska Press, 1999.

—. *Figures of Literary Discourse.* Trans. Alan Sheridan. Oxford: Blackwell, 1982.

George, Susan. *A Fate Worse Than Debt.* London: Penguin, 1988.

Gibson, Andrew, *Towards a Postmodern Theory of Narrative.* Edinburgh: Edinburgh University Press, 1996.

Gilroy, Paul. *After Empire: Melancholia or Convivial Culture.* London: Routledge, 2004.

Gurnah, Abdulrazak. *By the Sea.* London: Bloomsbury, 2003.

—. 'Ghana Times'. *TLS*, no. 5340, 5 August 2005, 11.

—. *Memory of Departure.* London: Jonathan Cape, 1987.

—. *Paradise.* London: Hamish Hamilton, 1994.

—. 'Welcome to Britain: Fear and Loathing'. *The Guardian, G2*, 22 May 2001, 6.

Gwin, Minrose. *The Woman in the Red Dress: Gender, Space and Reading.* Urbana: University of Illinois Press, 2002.

Haddon, Mark. *The Curious Incident of the Dog in the Night-Time.* London: Jonathan Cape, 2003.

Hapgood, Lynne. *Margins of Desire: The Suburbs in Fiction and Culture, 1880–1925.* Manchester: Manchester University Press, 2005.

Harbison, Robert. *Eccentric Spaces.* Cambridge, MA: MIT Press, 2000.

Hardy, Thomas. *The Life and Work of Thomas Hardy.* Ed. Michael Millgate. Basingstoke: Macmillan, 1984.

—. *Tess of the D'Urbervilles.* Ed. Juliet Grindle and Simon Gatrell. 1891; Oxford: Oxford University Press, 2005.

Harris, Wilson. *Selected Essays of Wilson Harris: The Unfinished Gesture of the Imagination.* London: Routledge, 1999.

Harrison, Sophie. 'Voice from the Street'. *The Guardian, Review*, 14 April 2007, 11.

Harvey, David. *Spaces of Hope.* Edinburgh: Edinburgh University Press, 2000.

Head, Dominic. *The Cambridge Companion to Modern British Fiction, 1950–2000.* Cambridge: Cambridge University Press, 2002.

Herman, David, ed. *Narrative Theory and the Cognitive Sciences.* Stanford, CA: Centre for the Study of Language and Information, 2003.

—. *Story Logic.* Lincoln: University of Nebraska Press, 2002.

Hinds, Donald. *Journey to an Illusion: A Study of West Indians in Britain.* London: Heinemann, 1966.

Hoggart, Richard. *Everyday Language and Everyday Life.* New Brunswick: Transaction, 2003.

Holtz, William. 'A Reconsideration of Spatial Form'. *Critical Inquiry* 4, no. 2 (Winter 1977): 231–52.

Ilona, Anthony. 'Crossing the River: A Chronicle of the Black Diaspora'. *Wasafiri* 22 (Autumn 1995): 3–9.

Ishiguro, Kazuo. 'Interview: Kazuo Ishiguro', by Maya Jaggi. *Wasafiri* 22 (Autumn 1995): 2–4.

—. *Never Let Me Go.* London: Faber and Faber, 2005.

—. *A Pale View of Hills.* 1982; London: Faber and Faber, 1991.

—. *The Remains of the Day.* 1989; London: Faber and Faber, 1990.

—. *The Unconsoled.* London: Faber and Faber, 1995.

James, Henry. *The Art of the Novel: Critical Prefaces.* New York: Scribner's Press, 1934.

—. *The Wings of the Dove.* Ed. John Bayley. 1902; London: Penguin, 2003.

Jameson, Fredric. 'The End of Temporality'. *Critical Inquiry* 29 (2003): 695–718.

—. *Postmodernism: Or, the Cultural Logic of Late Capitalism.* Durham: Duke University Press, 1991.

—. 'Third-World Literature in the Era of Multinational Capitalism'. *Social Text* 15 (Autumn 1986): 65–88.

Jameson, Storm. 'Documents'. *Fact* 4 (July 1937): 9–18.

Johnson, B. S. *Christie Malry's Own Double-Entry.* 1973; London: Picador, 2001.

—. *Omnibus: Trawl, Albert Angelo, House Mother Normal.* London: Picador, 2004.

Juno, Andrea, and Vivian Vale, eds. *J. G. Ballard.* San Francisco: V/Search, 1998.

Kaplan, Caren. *Questions of Travel: Postmodern Discourses of Displacement.* Durham: Duke University Press, 1996.

Kennedy, A. L. *Day.* London: Jonathan Cape, 2007.

—. *Looking for the Possible Dance.* 1993; London: Minerva, 1994.

—. *Now That You're Back.* 1994; London: Vintage, 1995.

—. *Paradise.* London: Jonathan Cape, 2004.

Kermode, Frank. 'A Reply to Joseph Frank'. *Critical Inquiry* 4, no. 3 (Spring 1978): 579–88.

King, Anthony D., ed. *Re-Presenting the City: Ethnicity, Capital and Culture in the Twenty-First Century Metropolis.* London: Macmillan, 1996.

King, Bruce. *The Oxford English Literary History, Volume 13. 1948–2000: The Internationalization of English Literature.* Oxford: Oxford University Press, 2004.

King, Nicola. *Memory, Narrative, Identity: Remembering the Self.* Edinburgh: Edinburgh University Press, 2000.

Klein, Bernhard, and Gesa Mackenthun, eds. *Sea Changes: Historicizing the Ocean.* London: Routledge, 2004.

Kundera, Milan. *The Curtain: An Essay in Seven Parts.* Trans. Linda Asher. London: Faber and Faber, 2007.

Kunzru, Hari. 'Host Not Found'. *The Guardian, Review,* Saturday 31 March 2007, 21.

Kureishi, Hanif. *The Buddha of Suburbia.* London: Faber and Faber, 1990.

—. *Gabriel's Gift.* London: Faber and Faber, 2001.

Leader, Zachary, ed. *On Modern British Fiction.* Oxford: Oxford University Press, 2002.

Ledent, Benedicte. *Caryl Phillips*. Manchester: Manchester University Press, 2002.

Lee, Hermione. 'Reading Beyond the Fridge Magnets'. Rev. of *Collected Stories*, by Carol Shields, *The Guardian, Review*, 3 July 2004, 26.

—. 'Someone to Watch over You'. Rev. of *The Light of Day*, by Graham Swift, *The Guardian, Review*, 8 March 2003, 9.

Lemon, Lee T., and Marion J. Reis, eds. *Russian Formalist Criticism: Four Essays*. Nebraska: University of Nebraska Press, 1965.

Lessing, Doris. *Time Bites: Views and Reviews*. London: Fourth Estate, 2004.

Levy, Andrea. *Every Light in the House Burnin'*. London: Review, 1994.

—. *Fruit of the Lemon*. London: Review, 1999.

—. *Small Island*. London: Review, 2004.

Lodge, David. *Consciousness and the Novel: Connected Essays*. London: Penguin, 2002.

—. *Thinks . . .* London: Secker & Warburg, 2001.

London, Jack. *The People of the Abyss*. 1922; London: Arco, 1963.

Love, Glen A. *Practical Ecocriticism: Literature, Biology and the Environment*. Charlottesville: University Press of Virginia, 2003.

Lubbock, Percy. *The Craft of Fiction*. London: Jonathan Cape, 1921.

Luckhurst, Roger. *'The Angle between Two Walls': The Fiction of J. G. Ballard*. Liverpool: Liverpool University Press, 1997.

—. 'The Contemporary London Gothic and the Limits of the "Spectral Turn"'. *Textual Practice* 16, no. 3 (Winter 2002): 527–46.

Lukács, Georg. *Soul and Form*. London: Merlin, 1974.

Macfarlane, Robert. 'Call of the Wild'. *The Guardian, Review*, 6 December 2003, 38.

—. 'Where the Wild Things Are'. *The Guardian, Review*, 30 October 2004, 37.

—. 'Where the Wild Things Were'. *The Guardian, Review*, 30 July 2005, 4–5.

Massey, Doreen. *For Space*. London: Sage, 2005.

McEwan, Ian. *The Child in Time*. London: Jonathan Cape, 1987.

—. Interview by Zadie Smith. *The Believer* 26 (August 2005): 47–63.

—. *On Chesil Beach*. London: Jonathan Cape, 2007.

McNeil, Lynda D. 'Toward a Rhetoric of Spatial Form: Some Implications of Frank's Theory'. *Comparative Literature Studies* 17 (December 1980): 355–67.

McQuire, Scott. *Visions of Modernity: Representation, Memory, Time and Space in the Age of the Camera*. London: Sage, 1998.

Mezei, Kathy, ed. *Ambiguous Discourse: Feminist Narratology and British Women Writers*. Chapel Hill: University of North Carolina Press, 1996.

Middleton, Peter, and Tim Woods. *Literatures of Memory: History, Time and Space in Postwar Writing*. Manchester: Manchester University Press, 2000.

Miller, J. Hillis. *Topographies*. Stanford, CA: Stanford University Press, 1995.

Mitchell, W. J. T. 'Spatial Form in Literature: Toward a General Theory'. *Critical Inquiry* 6, no. 3 (Spring 1980): 539–67.

Monteith, Sharon. *Pat Barker*. Travistock: Northcote House, 2002.

Monteith, Sharon, Jenny Newman and Pat Wheeler, eds. *Contemporary British and Irish Fiction: An Introduction through Interviews*. London: Arnold, 2004.

Moorcock, Michael. *Mother London*. 1988; London: Scribner, 2004.

Morton, H. V. *In Search of London*. London: Methuen, 1951.

Mukhopadhyay, Bhaskar. 'Writing Home, Writing Travel'. *Comparative Studies in Society and History* 44, no. 2 (April 2002): 293–317.

Naipaul, V. S. *The Enigma of Arrival.* Harmondsworth: Viking, 1987.

—. *The Return of Eva Peron, with the Killings in Trinidad.* London: Andre Deutsch, 1980.

Nalbantian, Suzanne. *Memory in Literature: From Rousseau to Neuroscience.* Basingstoke: Palgrave Macmillan, 2003.

Nasta, Susheila, ed. *Writing Across Worlds: Contemporary Writers Talk.* London and New York: Routledge, 2004.

Neisser, Ulric, and Robyn Fivush, eds. *The Remembering Self: Construction and Accuracy in the Self-Narrative.* Cambridge: Cambridge University Press, 1994.

Norquay, Glenda, and Gerry Smyth, eds. *Space and Place: The Geographies of Literature* Liverpool: Liverpool John Moores University Press, 1997.

Okri, Ben. *A Way of Being Free.* London: Pheonix, 1997.

Olney, James. *Memory and Narrative: The Weave of Life-Writing.* Chicago: University of Chicago Press, 1998.

Onega, Susana, and John A. Stotesbury, eds. *London in Literature: Visionary Mappings of the Metropolis.* Heidelberg: University of Heidelberg Press, 2002.

Pamuk, Orhan. *Istanbul: Memories of a City.* Trans. Maureen Freely. London: Faber and Faber 2005.

Perec, Georges. *Species of Spaces and Other Pieces.* London: Penguin, 1999.

Perril, Simon. 'A Cartography of Absence: The Work of Iain Sinclair'. *Comparative Criticism* 19 (1997): 309–39.

Phillips, Caryl. *Cambridge.* 1991; London: Faber and Faber, 2000.

—. *A Distant Shore.* London: Secker & Warburg, 2003.

—. *The European Tribe.* New York: Vintage, 2000.

—. *Extravagant Strangers: A Literature of Belonging.* London: Faber and Faber, 1997.

—. *The Nature of Blood.* New York: Knopf, 1997.

—. 'Necessary Journeys'. *The Guardian, Review,* 11 December 2004, 4–6.

—. *A New World Order: Selected Essays.* London: Vintage 2002.

—. 'Northern Soul'. *The Guardian, Weekend,* 22 October 2005, 18–27.

—. 'The Silenced Minority'. *The Guardian, Review,* 15 May 2004, 34–5.

—. 'To Ricky with Love'. *The Guardian, Review,* 23 July 2005, 28–9.

Pile, Steve, and Nigel Thrift, eds. *City: A–Z.* London and New York: Routledge, 2000.

Proctor, James. *Dwelling Places: Postwar Black British Writing.* Manchester: Manchester University Press, 2003.

Rasmussen, Mark David. *Renaissance Literature and Its Formal Engagements.* New York: Palgrave, 2002.

Rattansi, Ali. 'Dialogues on Difference: Cosmopolitans, Locals and "Others" in a Post-National Age'. *Sociology* 38, no. 3 (2004): 613–21.

Ricoeur, Paul. *Memory, History, Forgetting.* Chicago: University of Chicago Press, 2004.

Rogers, Jane. *Island.* 1999; London: Abacus, 2000.

Ronen, Ruth. 'Space in Fiction'. *Poetics Today* 7, no. 3 (1986): 421–38.

Rushdie, Salman. *Imaginary Homelands: Essays and Criticism 1981–1991*. London: Granta, 1992.

—. *Midnight's Children*. 1981; London: Vintage, 1995.

—. 'The Power of Love'. *The Guardian, Review*, 23 April 2005, 7.

—. *The Satanic Verses*. 1988; London: Vintage, 1998.

—. *Step across This Line: Collected Non-Fiction 1992–2002*. London: Vintage, 2003.

Rykwert, Joseph. *The Seduction of Place: The History and Future of the City*. Oxford: Oxford University Press, 2000.

Said, Edward W. *Culture and Imperialism*. London: Chatto & Windus, 1993.

—. *Humanism and Democratic Criticism*. New York: Columbia University Press, 2003.

—. 'Invention, Memory, and Place'. *Critical Inquiry* 26, no. 2 (Winter 2000): 175–92.

Samuel, Raphael, ed. *Patriotism: The Making and Unmaking of British National Identity*, vol. 2: *Minorities and Outsiders*. London: Routledge, 1989.

Sandhu, Sukhdev. 'Come Hungry, Leave Edgy'. Review of *Brick Lane*, by Monica Ali, *London Review of Books* 25, no. 19, 9 October 2003. www.lrb.co.uk/v25/n19/sand01_.html [last accessed 10 June 2008]

Schama, Simon. *Landscape and Memory*. New York: Vintage, 1995.

Seabrook, Jeremy. 'The End of the Provinces'. *Granta* 90 (Summer 2005): 225–41.

Sebald, W. G. *On the Natural History of Destruction*. London: Penguin, 2004.

Self, Will. *Junk Mail*. London: Penguin, 1996.

—. *Sore Sites*. London: Ellipsis, 2000.

Shakespeare, Nicolas. *Londoners*. London: Sidgwick & Jackson, 1966.

Sillitoe, Alan. *Mountains and Caverns*. London: W. H. Allen, 1975.

—. *Saturday Night and Sunday Morning*. 1958; London: Flamingo, 1994.

Simpson, David. *Situatedness, or, Why We Keep Saying Where We're Coming From*. Durham: Duke University Press, 2002.

Sinclair, Iain. *Dining on Stones*. London: Hamish Hamilton, 2004.

—. *Downriver*. 1991; London: Granta, 2002.

—. *Landor's Tower*. 2001; London: Granta, 2002.

—. *Lights Out for the Territory*. London: Granta, 1997.

—. *London Orbital*. London: Granta, 2002.

—. 'Museums of Melancholy'. *London Review of Books* 27, no. 16, 18 August 2005, 14–15.

—. 'Paint Me a River'. *The Guardian, Review*, 5 February 2005, 16–17.

—. *Sorry Meniscus*. London: Profile, 1999.

—. 'Wave City: A Bank Holiday Odyssey to the Haven That Is Hastings'. *Independent on Sunday, Features*, 2 May 2004, 1.

—. 'Woking at War'. *The Guardian, Review*, 26 June 2004, 37.

Sinclair, Iain, ed. *London: City of Disappearances*. London: Hamish Hamilton, 2006.

Smith, Zadie. 'Read Better'. *The Guardian, Review*, 21 January 2007, 21–2.

—. *White Teeth*. London: Penguin, 2000.

Smitten, Jeffrey R., and Ann Daghistany, eds. *Spatial Form in Narrative*. Ithaca: Cornell University Press, 1981.

Snell, K. D. M., ed. *The Regional Novel in Britain and Ireland, 1800–1990*. Cambridge: Cambridge University Press, 1998.

Soja, Edward. *Postmetropolis: Critical Studies of Cities and Regions.* Oxford: Wiley Blackwell, 2000.

—. *Postmodern Geographies: The Reassertion of Space in Critical Social Theory.* New York: Verso, 1989.

Sontag, Susan. *Styles of Radical Will.* London: Vintage, 2001.

—. *Where the Stress Falls: Essays.* London: Jonathan Cape, 2002.

Stewart, Susan. *On Longing: Narratives of the Miniature, the Gigantic, the Souvenir, the Collection.* Durham: Duke University Press, 1993.

Stockwell, Peter. *Cognitive Poetics: An Introduction.* London: Routledge, 2002.

Storey, David. *Thin-Ice Skater.* London: Jonathan Cape, 2004.

—. *This Sporting Life.* London: Longmans, 1960.

Svorou, Soteria. *The Grammar of Space.* Amsterdam and Philadelphia: John Benjamins Publishing Co., 1994.

Swift, Graham. *Ever After.* London: Picador, 1992.

—. *Last Orders.* 1996; London: Picador, 1997.

—. *The Light of Day.* London: Hamish Hamilton, 2004.

—. 'Making an Elephant'. *Granta* 87 (Autumn 2004): 299–316.

—. 'Triumph of the Common Man'. Profile of Graham Swift, by John O'Mahony. *The Guardian, Review,* 1 March 2003, 20–4. http://books.guardian.co.uk/departments/generalfiction/story/0,,904963,00.html [last accessed 10 June 2008].

—. *Waterland.* 1983; London, Picador, 2002.

Taylor, D. J. 'The Blacksmith's Progress'. Rev. of *A Man of His Time,* by Alan Sillitoe, *The Guardian, Review,* 17 April 2004, 26.

—. 'Gone to Seed'. Rev. of *Six,* by Jim Crace, *The Guardian, Review,* 6 September 2003, 26.

—. 'When the North Invaded Hampstead'. *The Guardian, Review,* 30 November 2002, 26.

Tew, Philip. *The Contemporary British Novel.* London: Continuum, 2004.

Thacker, Andrew. 'The Idea of a Critical Literary Geography'. *New Formations* 57 (Winter 2005/6): 56–73.

Thorpe Adam. *Pieces of Light.* London: Jonathan Cape, 1998.

—. *Ulverton.* London: Secker & Warburg, 1992.

—. 'Waiting and Leaping'. *The Guardian, Review,* 15 May 2004, 31.

Tiffin, Chris, and Alan Lawson, eds. *De-scribing Empire: Post-Colonialism and Textuality.* London: Routledge, 1994.

Todd, Richard. *Consuming Fictions: The Booker Prize and Fiction in Britain Today.* London: Bloomsbury, 1996.

Tremain, Rose. *The Colour.* London: Chatto & Windus, 2003.

Vilder, Anthony. *The Architectural Uncanny: Essays in Modern Unhomely.* Cambridge, MA: MIT Press, 1996.

Ward, Stuart, ed. *British Culture and the End of Empire.* Manchester: Manchester University Press, 2001.

Warner, Mariner. 'Game On'. *The Guardian, Review,* 19 March 2005, 16–17.

—. *Indigo.* 1992; London: Vintage, 1993.

Welty, Eudora. *The Eye of the Story.* New York: Random House, 1977.

Williams, Raymond. *Border Country.* 1960; Cardigan: Parthian, 2005.

—. *The Country and the City*. Oxford: Oxford University Pres, 1973.

—. *Problems in Materialism and Culture*. London: Verso, 1988.

—. *Resources of Hope: Culture, Democracy, Socialism*. Ed. Robin Gable. London: Verso, 1989.

—. *What I Came Here to Say*. Ed. Neil Belton, Francis Mulhern and Jenny Taylor. London: Hutchinson Radius, 1989.

Wing, Lorna. *The Autistic Spectrum: A Guide for Parents and Professionals*. London: Constable, 1996.

Winterson, Jeanette. *Art Objects: Essays on Ecstasy and Effrontery*. London: Jonathan Cape, 1995.

Wolff, Janet. 'On the Road Again: Metaphors of Travel in Cultural Criticism'. *Cultural Studies* 7, no. 1 (1993): 224–31.

Wood, James. 'How's the Empress?' Rev. of *The Light of Day*, by Graham Swift, *London Review of Books* 25, no. 8, 17 April 2003, 28–9.

—. *The Irresponsible Self: On Laughter and the Novel*. London: Jonathan Cape, 2004.

Wood, Michael. 'Consulting the Oracle'. *Essays in Criticism* 43, no. 2 (April 1993): 93–111.

Index

Lightning Source UK Ltd.
Milton Keynes UK
UKOW050649151112

202205UK00003B/5/P